WALL
STREET
JOURNAL
BOOKS

The 18 Immutable Laws of Corporate Reputation

Creating, Protecting, and Repairing Your Most Valuable Asset

Ronald J. Alsop

A WALL STREET JOURNAL BOOK

PUBLISHED BY FREE PRESS

New York   London   Toronto   Sydney

WALL STREET JOURNAL BOOKS

A WALL STREET JOURNAL BOOK
Published by Free Press
Rockefeller Center
1230 Avenue of the Americas
New York, NY 10020

For information regarding special discounts for bulk purchases,
please contact Simon & Schuster Special Sales at 1-800-456-6798
or business@simonandschuster.com

Manufactured in the United States of America
Designed by Leslie Phillips

6   8   10   9   7   5

Library of Congress Cataloging-in-Publication Data

Alsop, Ronald J.
The 18 immutable laws of corporate reputation : creating, protecting, and
repairing your most valuable asset / Ronald J. Alsop.
    p.   cm. — (A Wall Street journal book)
Includes bibliographical references and index.
1. Corporate image. 2. Brand name products—Manangement.
3. Corporations—Public relations. I. Title: Eighteen immutable laws of corporate reputation.
II. Wall Street journal. III. Title. IV. Series.
HD59.2.A47 2004
659.2—dc22
2003064354

ISBN 0-7432-3670-X

To Marybeth and Matthew

Contents

PART THREE: REPAIRING A DAMAGED REPUTATION

PREFACE

Associate yourself with men of good quality if you esteem your own reputation, for 'tis better to be alone than in bad company.
> —Maxim from George Washington's "Rules of Civility and Decent Behavior in Company and Conversation"

Corporate executives of good repute must feel rather lonely these days.

Scandals have brought down or tarnished company after company, as executives became obsessed with short-term profits and ever-rising stock prices and lost sight of reputation, their most valuable long-term asset. They lived for today and destroyed their corporate reputations.

All of the corporate malfeasance not only showed how precious and fleeting reputation is, but it also demonstrated how one company's misdeeds can taint an entire industry—and even the whole of corporate America. The scandals and increased government oversight have created a corporate environment in which extra vigilance is required to protect reputations. Some businesses with superb reputations have found themselves unfairly lumped with the pack of fraudulent companies. A news report about an investigation into alleged problems at a Johnson & Johnson pharmaceutical plant in Puerto Rico put J&J into the company of the accounting-fraud scoundrels. The company requested a retraction.

Ron Sargent, the CEO of Staples, told me about having visited a high school in suburban Boston to talk with students and being appalled by a couple of their questions. "How much money do you make?" one teen asked, while another wondered, "Do you have a $6,000 shower curtain?" a reference to the extravagant purchases that Dennis Kozlowski, former CEO of Tyco International, allegedly used company funds to pay for. Unfortunately, many corporate officials have been unfairly tarred by the accounting fraud and executive greed.

The business world, ever more global and more competitive, has become even more difficult to navigate. In this new climate of suspicion and scrutiny, a good reputation is more important than ever and provides one of the few safety nets companies can count on.

It is my hope that this book will guide you in creating that good reputation. Toward that end, I have drawn upon my coverage of corporate reputation and branding over the past twenty years, as well as my experience as a marketing columnist and editor at *The Wall Street Journal.* The book is also based on my interviews with dozens of corporate executives, market researchers, communications experts, and academics over the past two years.

Whenever people learned that I was writing a book about managing corporate reputation, they automatically assumed it was a response to the Enron blowup and the corporate scandals that followed. That reaction is understandable, but in fact, I began planning in summer 2001, long before any of the corporate abuses came to light. My project was briefly interrupted by the September 11 attack on the World Trade Center, which forced the *Wall Street Journal* staff to evacuate its offices in the nearby World Financial Center, where all of my reputation files lay amid dust and debris. But my files were recovered, and the book proposal was completed and approved before Enron even filed for bankruptcy protection in December.

Long before the scandals broke, I had sensed that companies were beginning to understand how important—but neglected—their reputations were. Whenever I wrote an article about reputation for *The Wall Street Journal,* I received calls and e-mails from managers hungry to know more about the subject. They asked me questions about how to get their arms around the concept. They didn't understand how to define reputation, how to measure it, or, most important, how to manage it. "Your package of articles today regarding corporate reputations is excellent," the senior vice president and director of corporate communication at PNC Financial Services Group wrote me in an e-mail message. "I'm sharing it with all of my advertising and PR colleagues here as we wrestle with the factors that impact reputation and what to do about it."

Reputation management is more of an art than a science, but there are definite guiding principles that constitute the eighteen immutable laws. Divided into three parts, this book is a road map to maximizing the benefits of your most priceless asset. Through detailed examples, I demonstrate the benefits of a good reputation, the consequences of a bad reputation, and ways to protect good reputations and fix bad ones. I explain that every company must learn to measure its reputation, appoint senior executives to nurture it, and understand who among its many constituencies can do its reputation the most good—or the most harm. I deal at length with some of the hot-button issues, such as ethics, corporate citizenship, and the Internet's impact on reputation. How, for example, can you both use the Internet as a tool to improve perceptions of your company and guard against its many dangers? How can you strike the best compromise between gratuitous publicity and getting the word out about your company's good deeds? These are just a couple of the tough issues that every company should be grappling with.

The book also includes a number of rankings of best and worst reputations, and it examines the companies making the headlines, such as how Merrill Lynch is struggling to mend its image and what lessons can be gleaned from the harm Martha Stewart inflicted on her company. The scandals, of course, offer many cautionary tales about reputation pitfalls. But the majority of the book is devoted to companies that weren't major players in the corporate chicanery. There is much more to learn from companies that have long valued their reputations and work hard every day to preserve them. I believe their stories clearly show the value of reputation management—how Johnson & Johnson inculcates a sense of integrity throughout its global workforce, how DuPont vigilantly monitors its 200-year-old reputation, how IBM projects a consistent corporate image, and how Timberland and Levi Strauss make social responsibility the essence of their corporate cultures.

I do dwell on one company with a negative reputation—Philip Morris—but less because of its troubled image than because it is working so hard to improve it, from changing its name to writing a new ethics code. Whether or not you believe Philip Morris, now known as Altria Group, deserves a better reputation, the company still provides a unique and fascinating case study of a business trying to sell a legal but demonized product in a more responsible manner.

While I focus on corporate reputation in this book, many of the same lessons apply to any organization, whether or not it produces a profit. After all, poisoned reputations aren't restricted to corporate America these days. Just consider the recent damage to the reputations of the Roman Catholic Church, Major League Baseball, and even the Boy

Scouts of America. The Catholic Church, for instance, violated Law 17 by being defensive rather than dealing with the problem of pedophile priests openly and honestly. The Boy Scouts of America could have learned from Law 3 that an organization needs to understand and try to cater to all of its many audiences. It didn't seem to realize how many of its loyal backers would be offended by its antigay membership policy and withdraw financial aid and other support. And Major League Baseball, whose image has suffered from the labor strife between the owners and players, could benefit from Law 10, Make Your Employees Your Reputation Champions, and Law 15, Fix It Right the First Time. The message of Law 15: Three strikes and you're out!

Read on and use these eighteen immutable laws to write your own playbook for managing your most valuable asset.

PART ONE

——

Establishing a Good Reputation

The purest treasure mortal times afford is a spotless reputation.

—WILLIAM SHAKESPEARE

MAXIMIZE YOUR MOST POWERFUL ASSET

As Bill Margaritis drove back to FedEx Corporation's headquarters after lunch, his stomach grew queasy. It wasn't a reaction to the spicy calamari he orders whenever he dines at Memphis's Pacific Rim restaurant. He had just answered his cell phone, and the message on the other end had unnerved him: a FedEx truck was in flames on a highway near Saint Louis. Already pictures of the fiery truck adorned with the brightly colored FedEx logo had shown up on national television. Some news programs were spreading rumors that the driver had fallen asleep—or had been the target of a terrorist attack.

Such news coverage didn't bode well for FedEx's carefully nurtured reputation. There was no time to waste as Margaritis sped to the "war room" back at headquarters to start the reputation damage control. Once there, Margaritis, the corporate vice president for worldwide communications and investor relations, joined a team of lawyers, security officials, and media relations managers in a spacious conference room equipped with an array of telecommunications and computer equipment.

Meanwhile, in Pittsburgh, the base of FedEx's ground delivery business, managers were busy trying to determine the circumstances of the fire and how much damage it had caused. The first order of business was

3

finding out if a bomb had been involved and if there were any dangerous materials in the truck's burning cargo. At the same time, workers arrived at the crash scene to try to conceal the company's logo on the truck with stickers and orange spray paint. The less exposure, of course, the better for the corporate reputation.

Once the crisis team learned it could rule out terrorism, the public relations staff was on the phone pronto to CNN, Fox News, and the news departments of other networks. They relayed the correct version of the accident: a FedEx tractor-trailer had collided with a highway sign near Saint Louis, rupturing its fuel tank and causing the blaze.

FedEx contacted the governor's office in Missouri to enlist credible third parties there to help dispel rumors about hazardous cargo and a sleeping driver. Margaritis and his team also made sure that government regulatory agencies and the company's sales and customer service representatives received updates throughout the day. And e-mails were sent to all of the company's employees, detailing the facts of the accident.

Margaritis was well aware that misinformation is hard to correct once it begins circulating via the news media and the Internet. "We defused the speculation quickly, and coverage immediately waned," he says. "We kept it off the major evening news programs and out of the leading daily papers." Mission accomplished for Margaritis and colleagues.

There's no better example of dedication to corporate reputation than FedEx. Containing the truck-fire crisis in fall 2002 was all in a day's work for Bill Margaritis, who has become an evangelist for reputation management. Beyond nurturing FedEx's reputation, he has written articles about reputation management for an academic journal and become a member of the Reputation Institute, a New York City–based research organization.

He credits FedEx's frequent crisis simulation drills and contingency planning with helping it maneuver through the truck fire. FedEx prepares for virtually every possible emergency situation, from earthquakes and terrorism to snowstorms and Internet attacks, because it's the rare crisis that doesn't touch its shipping service in some way. "The reputation management process is like a mosaic that I help bring together in a cohesive fashion," he says. "I galvanize the investor relations, employee communications, and public relations departments to operate under the same game plan." It's important that all of those groups report to Margaritis to achieve consistency in internal and external messages. What employees see on the internal FXTV network should align with what

FedEx founder and CEO Frederick Smith is telling an interviewer on CNBC.

Margaritis's authority at the company is clear. He reports to an executive vice president but has Smith's ear whenever he needs it. While Margaritis is the day-to-day point man for reputation, Smith is an equally ardent champion of reputation management, another reason for FedEx's image-building success. It's critical that a corporate CEO understand and value reputation, and Fred Smith really does. He sees the global corporate brand and FedEx's sterling reputation for service as its most treasured assets.

Smith and Margaritis have proselytized so well that virtually every FedEx executive and manager speaks about his job in terms of its impact on corporate reputation. It isn't simply an issue for managers, either. FedEx tries to turn all of its employees into corporate ambassadors. FedEx realizes that its reputation is affected by every employee encounter with every stakeholder, from customers to investors to government regulators. "We're not like Coca-Cola, where people buy the product off the shelf or in a vending machine and don't see a Coke employee," says Joan Lollar, manager of corporate public relations. "With FedEx, you always see a face representing the company. Many people see their FedEx guy every day."

Loyal FedEx workers talk about the "purple blood" coursing through their veins, a reference to the purple part of the company logo. And FedEx rewards workers who go above and beyond their job responsibilities and enhance its reputation. For example, it bestows its Golden Falcon awards on employees such as Darren Docherty, a senior manager in Minneapolis who drove three and a half hours to personally deliver a heart catheter that had been lost in the FedEx system, just in time for emergency surgery. Those are the experiences that deepen the emotional connection between the public and the FedEx brand. They also motivate other employees to excel. When 10,000 workers troop into the FedEx facilities at a major airport hub operation at midnight to begin the package-sorting process, they pass television monitors running stories about heroic employees or delivering an inspirational message from Fred Smith. "We must provide superior service, and we can't do that without motivated employees," says Mr. Smith. "If we achieve both of those goals, a good reputation naturally follows."

The company constantly reinforces the importance of well-groomed, smiling employees who cater to customers. If a customer looks nervous about whether a package will arrive on time, FedEx employees are supposed to make copies of his shipping form and call him the next day to let him know the delivery was completed. If customers wait too long in line at a FedEx office or a package arrives late, FedEx has begun giving them inexpensive gifts, such as a pen-and-pencil set. A pristine office reflects well on FedEx, too. "Employees must keep an office professional-looking and make sure it smells good," says Glenn Sessoms, vice president of FedEx Express retail operations and strategies. "We don't want any pizza or chicken smells." Training videos urge employees to "let customers hear you smile" when they call, develop an "energized attitude," and provide "extreme service" so that customers will spread the word about FedEx to friends, family members, and coworkers.

FedEx has developed measurement systems to assess the service quality of its operating teams and rewards them with monetary bonuses based on their scores. For example, a team is penalized fifty points if it loses a package and ten points if a package arrives a day late.

Research is one of the first steps in maximizing corporate reputation, and FedEx keeps a close eye on the perceptions of all of its major stakeholders and the impact of media coverage on reputation. The company measures reputation on a variety of attributes to determine its weak spots. For example, it has earned high marks for the quality of its products and services and for its emotional appeal but received lower scores for such factors as vision, leadership, and social responsibility. On all three counts, the company believes its performance exceeds the public's perceptions. The company redesigned part of the FedEx Web site to include more information about its philanthropic activities and the corporate vision. "Fred Smith created an entire industry when he founded FedEx, so we really should score higher on vision and leadership," says Lollar. "But we're not communicating the message well enough."

Reputation management is a global proposition. Reputation strategies must be tailored to fit different cultures. For example, FedEx has determined that social responsibility drives reputation more in Europe than in the United States. And in Japan, financial performance and leadership count more heavily than social responsibility and emotional appeal.

FedEx's global reputation management is divided into three layers: the Americas, major foreign countries such as Germany and China, and local markets with large operations such as the Philippines and Indianapolis. FedEx also segments its strategy based on whether it considers a market mature or emerging. It gives more attention to competitive differentiation and new services in older markets such as Britain, while emphasizing brand awareness and a positive reputation more in newer markets such as China.

FedEx understands the reputation value of being an upstanding corporate citizen. It knew it was simply the right thing to do when it flew donated clothing and other supplies to earthquake victims in El Salvador and transported pandas from China to the National Zoo in Washington. But FedEx was also well aware of the public relations value of such deeds with the many government officials it must deal with as it seeks to expand its international business.

FedEx tries to manage its media image carefully, too. For example, the internal FXTV operation produces video news releases and stock footage of FedEx planes and trucks for television stations. That way there's less risk that a local station will go out and shoot its own footage of a FedEx driver with his shirt hanging out. There's also "the truth squad" assigned to provide "proof points" to correct inaccurate stories. Corporate executives frequently meet with editorial boards to promote FedEx's strategy of complete transportation services. And during times of crisis the PR staff tries to divert media attention to more positive stories. For example, when FedEx pilots threatened to strike in 1998, Margaritis's department managed to generate national stories about Fed Ex's technology, operational expertise, high employee morale, and confident customers.

FedEx is always on guard for threats to its reputation. A huge danger emerged by the end of 2001 in the form of Arthur Andersen, FedEx's accounting firm. Andersen's involvement in the Enron Corporation scandal set off the company's reputation management radar almost immediately. "We knew early on it was going to be a debacle," Smith says. "It was clear that Andersen would bring into question the integrity of FedEx's financial statements." FedEx began shopping around and announced that it would fire Andersen and replace it with Ernst & Young on March 11, 2002. Three days later, federal prosecutors charged Andersen with obstruction of justice, setting into motion the firm's demise.

Although FedEx has become almost a generic term for fast delivery—people talk about "FedExing" their packages whether or not their mailrooms actually use FedEx—the company believes there is much untapped potential in its corporate brand. To maximize the benefits of its enviable reputation, FedEx constantly tries to increase its corporate brand exposure. That's why the company paid some $200 million to plaster its name throughout the Washington Redskins football stadium and why it teams up with Amazon.com to rush the latest Harry Potter book to hundreds of thousands of eager children. Such corporate brand promotion sparks free media publicity and strengthens FedEx's goodwill with customers.

While FedEx protects its image like a precious jewel, it doesn't always play it safe. Imagine a company agreeing to let a Hollywood studio cast its product or service as the victim of a disaster. Sounds like reputation suicide. But that's exactly the risk FedEx took. The movie: *Cast Away.* The star: crowd-pleasing actor Tom Hanks. The plot: A FedEx plane crashes into the Pacific Ocean, killing all of the crew members aboard except Hanks, who survives for four years as a modern-day Robinson Crusoe on a remote island.

"We discussed the risks, but I was confident that people could separate fiction from the reality of FedEx," says Smith, who felt he could trust the screenwriter, Bill Broyles, a longtime friend. Smith even ended up with a cameo appearance in the film, playing himself. FedEx was nervous about the plane crash, of course, and it also had to give in on other objectionable parts of the script, including a scene of FedEx employees drinking wine from a paper bag on the jump seat of one of its planes and a shot of a filthy FedEx truck driving through the streets of Moscow. Not quite in sync with the squeaky clean FedEx image. The company did manage, however, to persuade the film director to edit out an exterior shot showing the FedEx plane plunging into the ocean. Margaritis didn't want to worry that a disgruntled FedEx customer or ex-employee would lift the scene from the movie and start circulating it on the Internet.

The movie proved to be a box-office hit and earned Tom Hanks an Oscar nomination. All of the attention put FedEx in the limelight, too. In the end, the company considered the movie a boon to its reputation because it depicted Hanks as a FedEx pilot obsessed with delivering customers' packages on time and in perfect condition. He even rescued one waterlogged package after the plane crash and delivered it upon his return to civilization. "The movie showed that FedEx employees treat every package as if it's the golden package," says Margaritis. "We do business in more than two hundred countries, and Tom Hanks' international appeal was a big plus for us." FedEx invited customers throughout the world to parties for preview showings of *Cast Away* and promoted the company's starring role in the movie to employees to instill corporate pride.

Clearly, you must take such chances from time to time to maximize your reputation. But reputation management generally calls for less daring and more due diligence. Every major business decision at FedEx involves an assessment of its impact on the company's reputation. After the air express company expanded into ground, home delivery, and freight transportation to compete more aggressively with United Parcel Service, it weighed carefully whether to put the FedEx name on its new businesses. On the one hand, FedEx's positive image could help the company sell its new delivery options and attract new employees. A robust reputation typically pays big dividends whenever a company expands into new lines of business.

On the other hand, FedEx had to determine how elastic its corporate brand really was. It feared its new ground service might damage its reputation for reliable overnight air delivery and exceptional customer service. What if its network of trucks couldn't meet the same standards for on-time delivery that are expected of its air fleet? FedEx knew it had to be careful not to overpromise and then fail to meet expectations. "White trucks with the bold FedEx logo make for great billboards on the nation's streets and highways," says James Clippard, staff vice president for investor relations. "But they significantly increase the risk to reputation when something negative happens involving a truck."

Before stamping its valuable name on the trucking companies that it acquired for its moves into ground and freight service, FedEx conducted both quantitative and qualitative research with current and prospective customers, asking if such a branding decision made sense to them and what their expectations would be of trucking companies bearing the FedEx name. The company concluded that it could in fact satisfy customers, as well as maintain and perhaps even embellish FedEx's reputation. So the company proceeded to create a new corporate "brand architecture" for the various business units, all connected by the same FedEx logo design but in different color schemes. The company thoroughly trains drivers and keeps its trucks sparkling clean, but it realizes that its ground delivery business is vulnerable to hazards that may be beyond the control of its managers. FedEx's reputation couldn't endure too many incidents like the Missouri fire or pedestrians being struck and killed by its growing fleet of delivery trucks.

Ultimately, the proof of successful reputation management is in the numbers. The bottom line is that FedEx places in the top ten of both *Fortune* magazine's most admired companies list and the consulting firm CoreBrand's ranking of the best corporate reputations. Those surveys reflect the views of corporate executives and financial analysts. But FedEx placed out of the top ten—at number 12—in Harris Interactive's 2002 Reputation Quotient ranking, which reflects the general public's opinion. That's nevertheless a strong performance, but it's also a signal that Margaritis still has work to do to make the most of FedEx's reputation potential with the American public.

REPUTATION 101

Like it or not, every individual, every company, every organization develops a reputation that is based on people's perceptions of it over time. Though reputation takes years to form, it can be ruined in an instant. Just consider how quickly Enron Corporation, the accounting industry, Wall Street, and the Catholic Church fell from grace. As they all stunningly learned, nothing is more priceless or fleeting than a good reputation.

The key question for companies is whether they will passively let others form opinions about them or actively manage and maximize their most valuable asset. Put most simply, a good corporate reputation attracts customers, investors, and talented employees, leading to higher profits and stock prices. And over time, companies that nurture their reputations enjoy a halo effect that makes people trust them and give them the benefit of the doubt during rocky periods.

In tending their reputation, companies must fully understand the large cast of players that influence it and must measure the perceptions of those many stakeholders. And of course, they must walk the talk. Their product and service quality must be par excellence; their behavior must be above reproach; their financial results must show consistent growth; and they must be likable and trustworthy. Companies as diverse as FedEx, Johnson & Johnson, and Harley-Davidson clearly have mastered the art.

Government officials and economists believe reputation is becoming an ever more significant asset. "In today's world, where ideas are increasingly displacing the physical in the production of economic value, competition for reputation becomes a significant driving force, propelling our economy forward," Federal Reserve chairman Alan Greenspan said in a 1999 commencement speech at Harvard University. "Manufactured goods often can be evaluated before the completion of a transaction. Service providers, on the other hand, usually can offer only their reputations."

Indeed, the accounting industry had been considering how to add corporate reputation to the asset side of the balance sheet. But in this post-Enron environment, there's been less talk of that lately. Perhaps accounting firms have decided they had better get their own reputations in order first.

What shapes corporate reputation? In these days of near daily scandals, many people mistakenly equate reputation with corporate social responsibility and ethical behavior. Though certainly of growing importance, ethics and social responsibility are but two elements of the equation. Financial performance, the workplace environment, the quality of products and services, corporate leadership, and vision also figure into reputation. There's also that elusive emotional bond between a company and its stakeholders that is central to the most enduring reputations. A company's good name can be affected for better or worse every time a customer sees a company truck, makes a phone call to a corporate office, or signs on to its Web site.

Of course, the CEO's own reputation affects a corporation's reputation, too. The imperial CEO may be a dying breed in this new era of greater accountability and corporate distrust. But the behavior of high-profile top dogs such as Bill Gates, Jeff Bezos, and Carly Fiorina still affects their companies' image. And who can forget Martha Stewart's devastating effect on her company's reputation? Or Dick Grasso's $139.5 million payday and the toll it took on the New York Stock Exchange's good name?

A 2003 survey by the public relations firm Burson-Marsteller found that respondents believe that fully half of a company's reputation is attributable to the CEO's reputation. That's up from 40 percent in 1997, when Burson first conducted its CEO survey with corporate executives, financial analysts, institutional investors, board members, the business media, and government officials. "The CEO is the ultimate spokesperson for the organization, the embodiment of the brand, and the official storyteller who knits together the company's past, present, and future," says Leslie Gaines-Ross, chief knowledge and research officer at Burson. "As reputations rise and fall dramatically today, CEOs are the designated guardians and are expected to pass that reputation along to the next generation of leaders in even better condition than they received it."

Boards of directors are giving more weight to reputation management skills when choosing new CEOs, and reputation is becoming a factor in measuring CEOs' performance and awarding compensation. Yet it is still the rare company that realizes the full value of its reputation. "Companies have to recognize that a diminishing reputation is a serious problem," says John Gilfeather, vice chairman of market research firm RoperASW. "But some CEOs still say this is fluff."

They do so at their peril. Never have companies needed guidance more in protecting their image. They are constantly exposed to scrutiny through the Internet and 24-hour all-news television channels. Business is truly global, and information, especially gossip, travels fast.

Some companies seem to bruise their reputations regularly. Ford Motor Company seriously damaged its reputation in the furor over the hazards of its Explorer sport-utility vehicles, which were equipped with Firestone tires. More recently, the company hurt its credibility with environmentalists after reporting that the fuel economy of its sport-utility vehicles had worsened. The disclosure was at odds with Ford's earlier pledge that it would reduce fuel consumption by the maligned, gas-guzzling SUVs. So much for Ford's "green" reputation.

Before the accounting trickery and other abuses surfaced, a few of the worst offenders had ironically fooled some people into believing they were quite reputable. In hindsight, such reputations were clearly bogus. Enron, for example, was ranked as the most innovative company in a survey of executives, directors, and securities analysts by *Fortune* magazine just months before the energy company was exposed as a fraud. Ahold, the Dutch supermarket company, placed first in a 2001 study of corporate reputation by Harris Interactive and the Reputation Institute but later came under government investigation for massive accounting irregularities.

More responsible corporate governance and more stringent accounting supervision may help reduce the public's skepticism about the business world. The Sarbanes-Oxley Act to improve corporate governance, the Public Company Accounting Oversight Board, and other regulatory policies and organizations are potentially significant because they should force companies to be more open and honest. After all, trust is

CORPORATE AMERICA'S FRAYED REPUTATION

How the general public responded to a Harris Interactive survey in late 2002 asking how corporate America's reputation had changed over the previous two years:

Declined a lot	48%
Declined a little	31%
Stayed the same	14%
Improved a little	6%
Improved a lot	1%

the cornerstone of reputation. But to attain a truly outstanding reputation, corporate America must aspire to go well beyond government regulations. What the law demands and what the public expects are often two very different things.

In fact, a strong reputation carries with it extra responsibility. Customers hold FedEx to a higher standard than some of its competitors. Slogging through to deliver packages in the worst weather is a badge of honor FedEx has earned through the years. But when it fails to live up to that image, customers judge it more harshly than they do other delivery services.

Carmakers face the same dilemma. Once they have earned a strong reputation for quality, they suffer more than other manufacturers when they must recall a model because of defects. A study by a doctoral student at Stanford University and a professor at the University of Texas found that market share drops following recall announcements, particularly for companies known for reliability, such as Toyota Motor Corporation and Honda Motor Company.

FOSTERING A REPUTATION-CONSCIOUS CULTURE

If they ever hope to maximize the value of their reputations, companies must make reputation management a fundamental part of their corporate culture and value system. Companies must spread the message of reputation management throughout the organization and make employees cognizant of how each and every one of them affects reputation on a daily basis. Reputation must be central to the corporate identity, not merely clever image advertising and manipulative public relations ploys.

A company that enjoys a rich heritage and revered leaders can successfully tap its past to instill a greater reputation consciousness among employees, whether it be General Electric and Thomas Alva Edison or IBM and Thomas J. Watson, Sr. A proud history can motivate employees to uphold the corporate reputation and continue the traditions. Indeed, in the 2002 Harris Interactive study of corporate reputation, most of the top ten companies had deep roots, with some, such as General Mills and Eastman Kodak, dating back more than one hundred years.

For reputation management to truly permeate the culture, companies need much more than a passive caretaker. No doubt the CEO must set the tone and be ultimately accountable for reputation. But reputation management is a 24/7 job. Companies must designate certain managers or departments to be the primary guardian, as FedEx has done with Bill Margaritis.

At GlaxoSmithKline, the reputation watchdog is Duncan Burke. "I'm trying to get people to think about reputation systematically, to remind them to take it seriously all the time," says Burke, vice president of corporate image and reputation. "People tend to focus on reputation when there are troubles and forget about it in good times." He works closely with the pharmaceutical company's media relations department and with employees throughout the company. He tries to keep employees informed of the company's perspective so they can answer tough questions about why executive pay seems so high, why Glaxo performs animal research, and why it charges more for medicine than many people can afford.

"Big pharmaceutical companies are seen as pariahs right now because of the issue of access to medicine at a reasonable price," says Burke. "So it's especially important that there's one person in my position to reflect on how the world thinks of Glaxo and how we want the world to see us."

Another company committed to a reputation-oriented culture is Alticor, the parent company of the Amway direct sales business. For years, it had suffered from negative media coverage as the Federal Trade Commission investigated its sales tactics and it became embroiled in a customs dispute with the Canadian government. But it wasn't until 1996 that Amway made image enhancement a top priority.

Still struggling to overcome misconceptions that it's a cult engaged in a pyramid-style selling scheme, Amway wanted to impress on its managers the importance of embracing reputation management. Amway began with corporate image conferences and progressed to a more thorough indoctrination at "Reputation University," an intensive three-day series of panels that attracted eighty senior managers from around the world.

Reputation University included lectures on reputation theory by academics and an explanation of the company's reputation measurement system. The highlight of the curriculum was a case study on how to build reputation in a fictitious country called Trevador. Through that exercise, Amway managers learned to deal with such reputation issues as the legality of its direct sales approach, perceptions that its salespeople are too pushy, and questions about the effectiveness and value of its products.

"Reputation University has had lasting impact," says Mark Bain, Alticor's vice president of corporate communications. "It's no longer necessary to explain the theory and process of reputation management; now we're simply doing it." He acknowledges that it isn't always easy to keep everybody working with the team. "You must work in a highly integrated and aligned manner across job functions and markets," Bain adds. "Not an easy task given budgets, turf, silos, and egos. But it is the only way. The alternative is as futile as herding cats."

THE PAYOFFS FROM A POSITIVE REPUTATION

Reputation is certainly something companies covet and brag about. "Our reputation stands behind them," an ad for Bose radios and CD players declares, while an ad for Knight Trading Group asserts that it is "committed to our clients, to earning a reputation of trust."

But how does the intangible asset called reputation produce tangible benefits? Some effects are quite clear-cut. Customers naturally gravitate to companies with a positive reputation for product and service quality. They become loyal consumers and are even willing to pay a premium price. It was Microsoft Corporation's reputation for top-quality computer software that helped it move into video-game systems against established players Sony Corporation and Nintendo Company.

A good reputation can also result in a higher credit rating and make it

---

REPUTATION REWARDS

These companies are reaping the greatest benefits from their strong reputations, according to a 2002 Harris Interactive survey. The largest percentage of respondents said they definitely intended to buy these companies' products and services or invest in these companies' stocks.

HIGHEST FUTURE PURCHASE INTENT

1. Wal-Mart
2. Home Depot
3. Johnson & Johnson
4. General Mills
5. Coca-Cola

HIGHEST FUTURE INVESTMENT INTENT

1. Johnson & Johnson
2. Sony
3. Wal-Mart
4. General Electric
5. Southwest Airlines/Harley-Davidson

---

easier—and cheaper—to tap the capital markets. Investors almost certainly will snap up the stock of a company with a good record of financial performance and leadership. It's difficult to accurately quantify, but companies have no doubt about the intangible asset's impact on Wall Street's perceptions. "You always have to deliver the numbers," says James Clippard, head of investor relations at FedEx. "But if your reputation is not good, the numbers will be suspect and marked down somewhat." FedEx periodically surveys investors to gauge their feelings about the company and detect any problems it needs to address.

Several academic studies have attempted to show a relationship between corporate reputation and investment appeal. An analysis of 216 companies found that there was a premium on the stock values of companies with stronger reputations for social responsibility. And a study of 10 portfolios of companies indicated that investors were willing to pay more for the companies with stronger reputations and presumably less risk, thus lowering the cost of capital.

Enduring corporate reputations also can bolster employee morale and performance, be a magnet for talented executives, and strengthen relationships with regulators, advocacy groups, and local communities where companies operate offices and plants. A case in point is Public Service Enterprise Group (PSEG). Its reputation precedes it when it acquires or builds new power plants. Having developed a positive environmental record in New Jersey, the company has found it can secure faster government approvals, stronger community support, and better tax treatment when it ventures into other states.

For example, when PSEG purchased the Albany steam generating station in Bethlehem, New York, along the Hudson River in 2000, it received support from a number of environmental organizations, including the American Lung Association of New York, the Natural Resources Defense Council, and Scenic Hudson. They endorsed the company's plan to replace the old power plant with a new facility that would reduce air emissions and Hudson River water usage. "I call it our environmental afterglow," says Mark Brownstein, director of environmental strategy and policy at PSEG. "Being able to move nimbly through the regulatory process is a significant competitive advantage."

A mighty corporate reputation also can trickle down to product brands. DuPont found that 24 percent of the people who felt very favorably about the company would definitely buy its Stainmaster brand of carpeting, compared with only 4 percent of those with less favorable feelings. Similarly, more than half of consumers in the "very favorable" camp were very likely to believe Stainmaster's advertising claims, compared with 22 percent of those less favorably disposed.

REPUTATION CAPITAL

When companies are firing on all cylinders, they build up "reputation capital" to tide them over in turbulent times. It's like opening a savings account for a rainy day. If a crisis strikes or profits shrink, reputation suffers less and rebounds more quickly. Ardent fans are always willing to overlook minor faults and forgive major offenses—as long as the company does the right thing. Bill Margaritis of FedEx puts it well: "A strong corporate reputation is a life preserver in a crisis and a tailwind when you have an opportunity."

A crisis or other negative development will certainly tax any reputation and rob a company of some of its stored-up reputation capital. But a long history of public goodwill enables companies to bounce back much faster from a calamity. That's why Coca-Cola rebounded so fast after its ham-handed response to a soft drink contamination scare in Europe, as well as a widely publicized racial discrimination lawsuit in 1999. Reputation capital also helped Volvo maintain its image for safety, even after being exposed for rigging a commercial in the early 1990s to try to demonstrate that its vehicles were virtually indestructible. The ad showed a monster truck rolling over a Volvo without crushing it, but the company later admitted that the ad had been faked. Nevertheless, the company continues today to capitalize successfully on its safety image with ads that promote its "SUV with a conscience" and tout such features as a gyroscopic sensor to detect an impending rollover and inflatable side curtains for head protection in an accident.

A surprise asbestos scare inflicted no lasting scars on the image of Binney & Smith and its century-old Crayola brand, thanks to plenty of reputation capital. When a news story in 2000 reported that tests had showed asbestos in Crayola crayons, it conjured up a frightening image: innocent children coloring pictures and being exposed to a serious health hazard. Binney & Smith's reputation was clearly on the line.

To head off widespread panic, the company issued press releases the day the story broke in the *Seattle Post-Intelligencer* and ended up in virtually every newspaper and on every television news program. Binney & Smith said its own testing hadn't detected any asbestos but vowed from the first to change the ingredients in its crayons if experts and government regulators deemed it necessary.

Even with Binney & Smith's rapid-fire response, some schools still decided to play it safe and pull Crayola crayons out of all of their students' desks. Worse, some schools and day care centers even issued press releases to allay parents' concerns. "We can never be too cautious when it comes to the safety and well-being of the more than 80,000 children in our care," Angie Dorrell, curriculum director of La Petite Academy, said in announcing the school's plans to remove all crayons from its classrooms.

Binney & Smith called in Cone, a crisis management communications firm in Boston, for help in monitoring the media, training employees for media interviews, and counseling the CEO. The company's vigorous response reassured people long enough for the U.S. Consumer Product Safety Commission to conduct its own tests and conclude that it could find only a scientifically insignificant trace amount of asbestos in two Crayola crayons. At the commission's suggestion, however, crayon makers did agree to reformulate their products to eliminate any asbestos traces and asbestos-like fibers. The combination of reputation capital and smart reputation management protected Binney & Smith during the crisis.

But reputations can crumble fast for companies without such a strong legacy. Many of the companies scarred by the accounting-fraud scandals may never fully recover. That's because they had little if any reputation capital to begin with, and whatever they might have had is now all used up. People won't be willing to give WorldCom the benefit of the doubt in the future. Never mind that it's now called MCI. They will still remember that it was dragged through the mud for its massive accounting fraud, filed for bankruptcy protection, and caused severe financial pain to its employees and stockholders.

THE COST OF REPUTATION NEGLECT
AND DAMAGE

Reputations can be lost in a flash. And companies that have failed to nurture and protect their reputations invariably learn a painful lesson: that a wounded reputation isn't easily or quickly repaired.

Companies simply can't be too watchful. They must always be alert to identify possible threats to their delicate reputations and develop defenses—policies, procedures, and allies—to preempt or quickly overcome them. New reputation challenges constantly arise. Who would have thought that fast-food restaurants and food manufacturers would be blamed—even sued—because someone became obese from wolfing down too many Oreo cookies and Big Macs? Although many people believe such litigation is ludicrous, the food industry nevertheless realizes that a serious reputation problem is in the making. Rather belatedly, McDonald's Corporation is concocting better-tasting salads, while Kraft Foods plans to cut the calorie content and portion sizes of such fattening fare as Oscar Mayer hot dogs and Velveeta cheese. Such moves at this point seem like defensive PR ploys and may not enhance reputation much.

But better late than never. The fallout from a seriously damaged reputation can be extensive and long-lasting. Following the Enron implo-

RESTORING REPUTATION

The Burson-Marsteller public relations firm surveyed "business influencers" in 2003 about the expected length of time to repair a damaged reputation. The average response was 3.65 years. Here are the estimates by different types of respondents.

CEOs	3.51 years
Other senior executives	3.81
Wall Street analysts and institutional investors	3.86
Business media representatives	2.96
Government officials	3.72
Board members	3.55

sion and revelations of questionable accounting and trading practices at other energy companies in 2002, the electric power industry's reputation sank and access to new capital was shut off. Investors were spooked and lacked confidence in many of the energy companies.

Even innocent employees can suffer from their company's battered reputation. People who have been laid off or resigned from scandal-plagued companies such as Enron and Arthur Andersen are finding corporate recruiters leery of hiring them.

How long does it take to recoup from reputation damage? Burson-Marsteller surveyed "business influencers" from companies, Wall Street, government, and the news media to estimate the recovery time and came up with an average of 3.65 years.

It is of course difficult to generalize in this fashion since the recovery time can be much longer. It took Audi a full decade to reverse a sales slide that began with reports about an alleged defect that caused its 5000 series models to surge out of control. Audi maintained that the unintended acceleration problem was a result of driver error, not mechanical problems. Nevertheless, Audi faced such pressure that it recalled the cars to install a mechanism to prevent the driver from shifting gears if his foot wasn't on the brake. Ultimately, Audi was vindicated when the government concluded that in fact drivers were mostly at fault for accidentally pressing the gas pedal rather than applying the brakes. But the reputation—and sales—damage was done. Audi would probably have fared better had it not blamed its customers but instead announced an immediate recall. Passing the buck to drivers clearly backfired.

No one can really predict how long it will take before a company can start reaping the benefits of its good name again. Every reputation problem is different. Yet some companies seem to believe they can declare that their reputations are on the mend with just a little positive news. Xerox Corporation CEO Anne Mulcahy announced in July 2003 that the embattled copier maker had turned the corner and its troubles were past. "The chapter is closed on our turnaround story," she said in releasing quarterly earnings that exceeded Wall Street expectations. But her statement followed by less than two months a decision by the Securities and Exchange Commission to force six former and current Xerox executives to pay $22 million in fines and other penalties to settle fraud charges. Many stock analysts, investors, and other stakeholders will need more proof before they'll begin to accord Xerox the benefits that come with a solid corporate reputation.

Know Thyself—Measure Your Reputation

"Merchants of Death": That ghastly epithet summed up DuPont's reputation back in 1930s America, on the eve of World War II. Having reaped huge profits from its munitions sales during World War I, the chemical company's top executives were called before a U.S. Senate committee investigating wartime profiteering. Although munitions had become an increasingly small portion of the company's overall sales, DuPont still bore the stigma.

How badly tainted was its reputation? When the company measured the public's pulse through survey research, it found that it did in fact face a very high hurdle in overcoming the death merchant image. The studies revealed that less than half of the American public held a favorable impression of DuPont. Company executives were dismayed and unsure of what to do next.

For advice, DuPont turned to the New York advertising firm Batten, Barton, Durstine & Osborn, known today as BBDO Worldwide. Bruce Barton, one of the agency partners, proposed a $500,000 campaign to fashion a new image. The cornerstone of the campaign would be the company's sponsorship of a new radio series called *The Cavalcade of America*.

Long, talky ads on the program promoted the nonexplosives part of

DuPont's business—products such as antifreeze, cellophane, and automobile finishes. At the same time, the agency created DuPont's famous slogan "Better things for better living . . . through chemistry." Progress was slow, but by the mid-1950s, surveys showed that the corporate reputation was on the mend: four out of five people reported positive feelings toward DuPont.

That success story illustrates DuPont's long commitment to reputation measurement and management. The company believes strongly in the importance of systematic research in monitoring the ups and downs of its reputation and guiding its reputation management strategies. It understands well that before a company can make a serious stab at changing the public's perceptions of it, it must have a clear and credible measure of those perceptions. Trying to navigate the reputation process without an accurate barometer is risky business.

It is perhaps fitting that a company steeped in scientific research saw the value early on of reputation research. DuPont may have French roots, but it proudly considers itself an integral part of American history and aims to protect its 200-year-old reputation. The company's roots date back to the early nineteenth century, when Eleuthere Irénée du Pont left France for the new nation and soon began producing gunpowder along the banks of the Brandywine River in Delaware. Among his first customers was Thomas Jefferson, who requested gunpowder for the U.S. War Department and later for hunting and blasting rock at his Monticello estate. Over the next two centuries, DuPont evolved into America's largest chemicals company and contributed heavily to American society, from nylon stockings to Kevlar bulletproof vests.

By tracking its reputation on a regular basis, the company has been able to react quickly to changing perceptions of itself and its industry. "We very systematically measure reputation to know what's resonating and what isn't," says Kathleen Forte, vice president of global public affairs. "We have been measuring many of the same attributes for decades."

DuPont was a pioneer in developing more sophisticated measures of reputation beyond standard public opinion and market research surveys. More than thirty years ago, when corporate reputation was barely spoken of, the company concocted one of the first detailed reputation-measuring methodologies.

The public relations department, along with the behavioral research section of the advertising department, undertook an ambitious study in

1971 that assessed how various demographic groups rated DuPont's corporate reputation. They asked "young adult influentials," educators, and students to evaluate DuPont on more than two dozen traits, including "makes high-quality products," "innovative," "a good stock to own," "smart, aggressive management," "good working conditions," "concerned with social ills," "pollutes," and "too rich and powerful." Respondents evaluated each trait on a good/bad scale and then told how important it was to them and how much they associated it with DuPont.

The study concluded that DuPont enjoyed a powerful reputation as a leader in research and technology and as a sound and growing company. But it fell short in the areas of making high-quality products and services, being a good place to work, and having concern for the environment and social issues. DuPont officials used the data in plotting public-relations strategies. But more significant than the results was the methodology. The research showed how far ahead of most companies DuPont was in its understanding of the reputation process.

Through the years, DuPont has tried a variety of measurement approaches, both quantitative and qualitative, including a study that valued the DuPont brand as being worth $11 billion to $14 billion, with a future potential value of $19 billion.

DuPont measures its reputation after major corporate changes such as its surprise entry into the oil business in 1981 with its purchase of Conoco. It must also monitor its reputation with the public to detect the impact of political and sociological trends. As American values have changed, so has DuPont's image.

Antibusiness, trust-busting sentiment in America threatened DuPont's reputation in the 1950s, prompting it to add ideological content to its advertising. The preachy commercials touted DuPont's economic contributions, advocated tax relief for research expenditures, and promoted the study of chemistry. Then, in the 1970s, the environmental movement focused attention on pollution by the chemical industry. By the late 1980s, DuPont found itself labeled the top polluter in America and in great need of repair to its reputation. Edgar Woolard, the CEO at the time, demanded more than cosmetic adjustments and immediately set the company on a course of more stringent environmental responsibility—reducing emissions and waste production while controlling energy consumption.

DuPont improved its environmental reputation, but image studies showed it still needed to change the public's perceptions of itself. In the mid-1990s, research with focus groups of investors, customers, employees, and government officials indicated that people viewed DuPont as a bunch of aloof scientists off in their ivory towers. Hoping to be seen as more caring, DuPont created an advertising campaign showing its human face through vignettes about individual scientists and their stories about developing plastic bridges and improved toothbrushes. Members of focus groups that viewed the commercials immediately said they felt better about DuPont.

DuPont also hoped to change its conservative reputation to one of dynamism and innovation, as well as escape perceptions of the chemical industry as cyclical, boring, and environmentally irresponsible.

"DuPont is a science company," declares Charles O. Holliday, Jr., chairman and chief executive officer. It needed "a new positioning that uniquely describes the essence of DuPont." Thus was born the current advertising slogan: "The miracles of science." "The key drivers of our reputation are scientific attributes," says Kathleen Forte. "Science is a wonderful association because it's very much connected with improving quality of life. That makes our message more personally relevant."

Before changing slogans, the company, in typical fashion, did its homework. It carefully researched public opinion because it feared that consumers might think "miracles" sounded too religious. But "The miracles of science" tested well with consumers, employees, and customers in six countries.

Now DuPont is hoping for miraculous reputation gains. Recent research found that nearly 60 percent of U.S. consumers have a favorable attitude toward DuPont, as do about three quarters of corporate executives. The company will be watching its research results closely to see how many of the "neutrals" and "negatives" it can convert through its "Miracles of science" campaign.

KEEP SCORE

The first step in managing reputation is measuring it. You can't manage what you can't measure. Companies must mine research data and learn how they are perceived by different audiences and which factors drive their reputations. Where are their strengths and weaknesses? How does their reputation compare with the image of their chief competitors?

Armed with those insights, they are then ready for the hard part—strengthening their reputations to attract customers, employees, and investors.

Increasingly, companies are following DuPont's example and monitoring their reputations. The recent corporate chicanery and the concomitant regulatory crackdown on accounting practices and corporate governance have certainly contributed to the growing interest in measuring reputation. But corporate reputation had begun attracting the attention of CEOs in the late 1990s, even before Enron's collapse.

"The corporate scandals raised the visibility of what we do, but most of our clients are not those associated with any scandals," says Joy Marie Sever, director of Harris Interactive's reputation practice. "Many began paying attention to their reputations before the scandals became public."

Sever's clients, however, are still in the minority. Fewer than half of companies—only 41 percent—said they have custom research programs in place to measure their reputations, according to a survey of senior executives by the public relations firm Hill & Knowlton and *Chief Executive* magazine. A surprising 73 percent depend on word of mouth, while 27 percent rely on reputation rankings published by the news media. Smaller businesses are much less likely to fund customized research studies, 32 percent compared with 48 percent of large companies. The energy and utilities, financial services, and health care industries are the most likely to hire research firms for customized projects.

One problem is that too many companies measure reputation only in times of trouble; most fail to check it on a methodical basis over time. "Some companies are always changing their research vendors or using one of their numerous ad agencies, but the real power of reputation measurement is the ability to follow it over time using a consistent methodology," says James Gregory, CEO of CoreBrand, a Stamford, Connecticut–based consulting firm.

Companies certainly have plenty of reputable measurement systems to choose from in tracking and managing reputation. The process isn't an exact science by any means, but many of the various methodologies have been finely tuned and measure a wide range of factors that combine to form a reputation. It's important, however, to understand each research firm's methodology, especially the stakeholders being surveyed and the attributes being studied.

Beware of the proliferation of ratings of customer satisfaction. A quick perusal of any edition of *The Wall Street Journal* will likely turn up three or four self-congratulatory ads hyping a top ranking in one of those surveys. While such beauty contests may influence consumers' purchases of cars, cell phones, and computers, they focus only on product and service quality and fall well short of being barometers of overall reputation.

Companies will find more merit in rankings such as Harris Interactive's Reputation Quotient and *Fortune* magazine's tally of the most admired companies. Such surveys are methodologically sound and provide a more complete gauge of corporate reputation. Other respected annual studies are CoreBrand's Brand Power rankings, based on senior executives' ratings of their familiarity with and favorable feelings toward companies, and *The Wall Street Journal* market research department's survey of subscribers' perceptions of the reputation, management quality, and investment potential of more than eight hundred companies.

But even the best of such rankings have limited value. Companies need far more than such one-size-fits-all surveys. They must periodically perform their own customized research through their internal market research department, their public relations or advertising agency, or an independent research firm such as Harris Interactive, Roper-ASW, Opinion Research Corporation, or Walker Information. "When I take a company's temperature, I like to ask open-ended questions about favorability," says John Gilfeather, vice chairman of RoperASW. "I want to know just how strongly positive and how strongly negative the feelings are."

Custom research allows corporate managers to focus on the reputation attributes that are most relevant to them, as well as gather intelligence on their competitors. Given the tumultuous, cutthroat nature of the telecommunications market, AT&T has moved to continuous customized reputation research, generating bimonthly results about how it's being perceived by employees, the general public, active investors, its own shareholders, and community activists. In addition, quarterly reports provide feedback about customers' experiences and perceptions. These days, everybody loves to hate the phone company. The more information, the better in trying to defuse customers' hostility.

"The publicly available rankings just give you bragging rights and don't really help manage the corporate brand," says Robert Atkyns, director of global brand and PR research and brand asset management at AT&T. "We prefer our own research because it allows us to get closer to our own issues. We always have research out in the field. Ongoing reputation tracking is necessary to monitor ongoing success in managing reputation rather than simply responding in damage control mode to crises."

Companies also need to slice the research data by demographic groups and other special features. Investors may be a more significant stakeholder group to some companies, while others may be more concerned about the attitudes of boycotters. Altria Group, for example, has stepped up its corporate brand research to study the attitudes of more of its audiences. It frequently surveys the general public but is also increasingly interested in measuring its reputation with women "opinion leaders." The tobacco and food company also focuses its research more on states where public policy issues have surfaced, such as a cigarette tax increase or restrictions on smoking in public places.

A few companies have grown so confident in their detailed measurement systems that they are making corporate reputation an element of performance appraisals and executive compensation. It's a bold move but one that gives senior executives a very tangible stake in this very intangible asset, as their reputations are on the line alongside the corporation's reputation. National Australia Bank built corporate reputation measures into its CEO's performance scorecard, along with financial results and other metrics. And Alticor, the parent company of the Amway direct sales business, has tied its corporate reputation directly to management performance and compensation. "We believe that what gets measured gets done," says Mark Bain, Alticor's vice president of corporate communications. "If reputation is part of a department's or a market's annual plan—and therefore part of a manager's total compensation—it will get focus and attention."

WHO'S MEASURING WHAT

Ever wonder why Johnson & Johnson is number 1 in the annual Reputation Quotient survey by Harris Interactive but ranks sixth in *Fortune* magazine's list of America's most admired companies and third in the CoreBrand Brand Power ranking? It all has to do with who's being surveyed about which corporate attributes.

Here is a guide to three of the best-known reputation studies, all of which have value as general indicators of how companies stack up and are a good starting point for more in-depth, customized research.

WHO'S ON FIRST?

Rankings of the best corporate reputations vary significantly depending on the survey respondents and other methodology differences. Here are the top ten lists from three reputation rankings:

THE REPUTATION QUOTIENT

Survey of 22,500 members of the general public by Harris Interactive and the Reputation Institute

1. Johnson & Johnson
2. Harley-Davidson
3. Coca-Cola
4. United Parcel Service
5. General Mills
6. Maytag
7. Eastman Kodak
8. Home Depot
9. Dell
10. 3M

AMERICA'S MOST ADMIRED COMPANIES

Poll of 10,000 executives, directors, and securities analysts by the Hay Group for *Fortune* magazine

1. Wal-Mart
2. Southwest Airlines
3. Berkshire Hathaway
4. Dell
5. General Electric
6. Johnson & Johnson
7. Microsoft
8. FedEx
9. Starbucks
10. Procter & Gamble

BRAND POWER

Survey of 10,000 senior executives at large companies by Core-Brand

1. Coca-Cola
2. United Parcel Service
3. Johnson & Johnson
4. Microsoft
5. Walt Disney
6. Campbell Soup
7. FedEx
8. PepsiCo
9. Harley-Davidson
10. General Electric

The Reputation Quotient

One of the most widely watched reputation rankings is the Reputation Quotient, or RQ, which was designed by Harris Interactive, best known for its Harris Poll of public opinion, and the Reputation Institute, a New York City–based research organization. That's because the RQ reflects overall American sentiment best and covers a variety of stakeholder groups. Many rankings are based only on the opinions of corporate executives and investment analysts, but Harris takes a much broader perspective, surveying more than 20,000 members of the general public in its annual online study. Harris also breaks down its findings by a number of subgroups, such as investors, customers, and corporate employees. The survey asks respondents to rate a pre-selected group of sixty of the "most visible" companies on twenty attributes in six categories: emotional appeal, products and services, financial performance, social responsibility, workplace environment, and vision and leadership. The RQ results are published each year in *The Wall Street Journal.*

Fortune's Most Admired Companies

Fortune magazine's annual report on America's most admired companies is based on the opinions of 10,000 executives, directors, and securities analysts surveyed by the Hay Group, a human resources consulting firm. For the overall top ten list, the respondents choose the ten companies that they admire most in any industry from a preselected list. For the industry rankings, they are asked to rate the largest companies in their own industry on eight criteria: social responsibility, innovation, long-term investment value, use of corporate assets, employee talent, financial soundness, quality of products and services, and quality of management.

CoreBrand

CoreBrand, a consulting firm, focuses on the opinions of senior executives at large corporations for its assessment of the strongest corporate reputations. Its Brand Power study ranks companies based on the ratings they receive for familiarity and favorability about reputation, management quality, and investment potential. Separately, CoreBrand has developed a brand equity methodology that goes a step beyond the reputation rating. It places a value on the corporate brand and then calculates it as a percentage of a company's total market capitalization. The Brand Power and Brand Equity rankings vary quite a bit: Microsoft, General Electric, and Wal-Mart have dominated the equity ranking, while Coca-Cola, United Parcel Service, and Johnson & Johnson are tops in the reputation survey.

NEW PLAYERS IN REPUTATION MEASUREMENT

Some intriguing new players have entered the reputation measurement field. A company called Rating Research is borrowing from the credit-rating industry for its scoring system. Not surprisingly, the founder was once a manager at Moody's Investors Service, and two of the other principals also previously worked at Moody's.

Rating Research assigns companies letter grades like Moody's—from AAA to C—and it ranks companies within rather than across industries. By 2003, the firm had rated companies in the electric power, banking, discount and department store, and pharmaceutical industries.

Johnson & Johnson, Merck & Company, and Pfizer led the pharmaceutical industry ranking with AAA ratings, while Forest Laboratories held the bottom spot with a BB rating. Among banking firms, Fifth Third Bancorp and Northern Trust Corporation topped the list with AA ratings, and six companies tied for the lowest rating of BB. Wal-Mart earned the highest rating of AA in the department and discount store ranking, while Kmart ended up in the cellar with a CCC. And in the electric power industry, the winners were Duke Energy Corporation and Southern Company (AA), with PG&E Corporation (CCC) at the bottom of the ranking.

"A credit rating is intended to be a long-term assessment of a company's ability to pay its debt, and our reputation rating is much the same," explains Jeffrey Resnick, chief research officer at Rating Research. "Very few companies go through life without controversies, and the question is whether they have built up enough reputation strength." Rating Research surveys senior executives and financial analysts, using a set of about two dozen overall attributes, supplemented with additional factors for issues that are germane to a specific industry. Rating Research believes that executives and analysts are most knowl-

THE MOODY'S OF REPUTATION

Here is Rating Research's ranking of pharmaceutical companies based on its surveys of executives and financial analysts.

AAA
Johnson & Johnson
Merck
Pfizer

AA
Amgen
Eli Lilly
GlaxoSmithKline

A
Astra Zeneca
Aventis
Bayer
Genentech
Novartis

BBB
Abbott Laboratories
Alcon
Allergan
Bristol-Myers Squibb
Roche
Schering-Plough
Wyeth

BB
Forest Laboratories

REPUTATIONS OF THE DJIA 30

NFO WorldGroup surveyed investors about corporate reputation and rated the thirty companies in the Dow Jones Industrial Average in three categories.

STRONG

Coca-Cola, Johnson & Johnson, Walt Disney, Intel, Microsoft, Procter & Gamble, General Electric, DuPont, Home Depot, United Technologies, Wal-Mart, Eastman Kodak

VULNERABLE

3M, Hewlett-Packard, IBM, McDonald's, International Paper, Merck, Boeing, Honeywell, Caterpillar, General Motors, Citigroup, American Express, AT&T, J. P. Morgan Chase, Exxon Mobil, Alcoa

AT RISK

SBC Communications, Altria Group (Philip Morris)

edgeable about reputation issues, but like some of the other rankings, it omits two major stakeholder groups, customers and employees.

Capitalizing on the post-Enron climate in corporate America, Rating Research has expanded into rating companies on their ethics reputations, using a combination of quantitative and qualitative research. Companies receive letter ratings on ethics, too, ranging from E1 to E5.

Another novel reputation measurement approach is NFO World-Group's Corporate Opinion, Reputation and Equity (CORE) Index. This reputation radar system has a narrower focus than most ratings—the thirty companies in the Dow Jones Industrial Average—and doesn't rank them numerically. Rather it categorizes them as resilient, strong, vulnerable, or at risk, based on their point scores in surveys of 2,250 individual investors.

For 2002, none of the companies was rated as resilient; twelve qualified as strong; sixteen scored in the vulnerable category; and two were classified as at risk. Investors graded the companies on more than twenty factors, and the most important qualities were a clear sign of the times: customer satisfaction, fair and ethical business practices, quality products and services, and trust and confidence.

THE POWER OF THE PRESS

Many people's only knowledge of a company comes from *The Wall Street Journal*, *BusinessWeek*, CNBC, or another media source. They have little if any direct experience with corporate America. That gives the news media plenty of power over corporate reputations.

But companies aren't powerless themselves. More are attempting to measure the news media's impact on their reputation and learn from the research. They realize that a scathing story on the front page of *The Wall Street Journal* or *The New York Times* can ruin a reputation. Less obvious is the cumulative impact of all those media mentions on corporate reputation.

Special tracking services keep count of how often a corporate name appears in the media, and a few research firms can perform more sophisticated analysis of the content and placement of media coverage.

Delahaye Medialink Worldwide and the Reputation Institute, for example, compile a media reputation index based on an analysis of more than 350,000 print and broadcast news items. Each company is scored based on how many positive and negative reputation-driving attributes are found in each story. In addition, Delahaye factors in the prominence of the story, the extent of the company's mention, the use of visuals, the size of the publication's circulation or the broadcast audience, and, most important, the tone of the news report. In 2002, the index showed that Microsoft, Wal-Mart, Walt Disney, General Motors, and IBM received the most reputation-enhancing media coverage.

"It's important to monitor how companies are featured in the media because any change in a company's media coverage can influence how people perceive the company, thereby affecting its reputation," says Charles Fombrun, founder of the Reputation Institute. Companies, in turn, can apply the media findings to their public relations campaigns and other branding strategies.

INTERNATIONAL INTELLIGENCE

For multinational corporations, measuring reputation is a global affair. Cultural differences mandate that companies monitor their reputations country by country. What matters most in one region of the world may be of much less significance elsewhere.

"Measuring investor attitudes involves pretty much the same reputation attributes everywhere—thought leadership, paying attention to customers, strong management, good financial results," says James Fink, the head of worldwide marketing research at Opinion Research Corporation in Princeton, New Jersey. "But other stakeholder groups vary more. Customers, for example, in Germany and France place more emphasis on how companies treat their employees than do people in the United Kingdom, the United States, and Canada."

As it expands in Asia and other regions of the world, Amway uses the same quantitative methodology from country to country but changes some of the questions. Its surveys of the general public track about forty reputation attributes in twenty countries.

In some countries, Amway faces government restrictions and misunderstandings about its direct sales approach. Many people still associate it with pyramid selling schemes, making Amway's worldwide reputation research essential. "As a large international company in a misunderstood industry, we still have progress to make in gaining acceptance," says Mark Bain of Amway's parent company, Alticor. "The regulatory, legal, and media challenges are not going to go away in the short term."

For IBM, the fast-moving, global nature of technology means that management must take a highly comprehensive approach to reputation measurement. The company conducts 12,000 telephone interviews annually with business customers in North America, Japan, and major European countries, from the heads of management information systems departments to entrepreneurs. Managers receive quarterly reports measuring more than two dozen attributes and learn the impact of financial performance, advertising, and public relations campaigns on the reputations of IBM and its major competitors in those countries.

AT&T also understands cultural variations well and adjusts its advertising and marketing based on the importance of reputation attributes in different countries. AT&T's corporate branding studies in Chile, for instance, found that people there valued dynamic, risk-taking companies. The result: "We make a world of difference" became the local advertising slogan. In Taiwan, on the other hand, consumers gave high ratings to companies whose products and services provide an advantage. "Get the edge" seemed the perfect pitch for that country.

Reputation research revealed that Mexican consumers highly value companies that demonstrate customer appreciation and "care enough to meet their needs," says Robert Atkyns, AT&T's global brand research director. "So in Mexico, we're trying to brand the AT&T customer service experience, much like the strategy at Nordstrom and Ritz-Carlton."

LAW THREE

LEARN TO PLAY TO
MANY AUDIENCES

"Nothing comes between me and my Calvins." When actress Brooke Shields purred those lines in a blue jeans commercial more than twenty years ago, she established designer Calvin Klein's reputation for steamy advertising that always pushed the envelope. The company's later ads featured or suggested nudity, group sex, and models who looked anorexic and drugged out. Everyone wondered: What will Calvin do next?

This reputation for the risqué served Klein and his major stakeholders, including his licensees and retailers, extraordinarily well. Retailers and the manufacturers to which Klein licensed his name happily reaped the revenues from his perfumes, underwear, and jeans. And of course the provocative tone of his marketing campaigns was pitch perfect for his young, hip consumers, his most important stakeholders.

The canny marketer had fashioned a positive reputation with all of the stakeholder groups that mattered most to his company. Never mind that older consumers were offended by the sexual advertising. They weren't his target audience anyway. He also didn't have to worry about the Wall Street investment community because his company was privately held.

Klein accomplished an amazing balancing act with his stakeholders,

36

given how much he was testing the limits of good taste with each successive marketing campaign. He demonstrated how to successfully maintain a strong reputation at the same time with various stakeholder groups. Creating that balance is essential to reputation management. While companies can't keep everyone happy all of the time, they must know who their most important stakeholders are at the moment and focus on them.

Sometimes, however, things get out of sync. Which is exactly what happened in 1995, when Calvin Klein finally miscalculated. He ended up damaging his reputation with some key stakeholders, as well as much of mainstream America.

His first and biggest misstep was a jeans campaign that resembled child pornography and caused a major uproar. Even President Bill Clinton criticized the creepy ads that showed teenagers posing for a leering photographer who made suggestive comments about their bodies and urged the boys to rip off their shirts. The U.S. Justice Department went so far as investigating the actors' backgrounds to determine whether they were underage but concluded that federal child pornography statutes had not been violated.

The controversial campaign, which received saturation media coverage, only boosted Klein's cool quotient with his teenage customers and sparked a surge in jeans sales. That may well have been his goal. But it was all too much for some retailers, a reaction he hadn't counted on. Target Corporation, for one, didn't approve and didn't want its name anywhere near the ads. The department store operator called them "too much of a lightning rod."

Klein clearly had crossed the line with his ads. Although there wasn't a peep of protest from his young customers, it's never a good idea to get the Justice Department after you. Most surprisingly, Klein didn't learn his lesson. Shortly after the kiddie porn flap, he offended Warnaco, his underwear licensee, with ads showing a hunky young man with his legs spread wide. Warnaco huffed that it was in business to sell underwear, "not to have problems." Next came complaints of appealing to pedophiles. Klein had created a line of children's underwear and depicted little boys and girls in their underpants jumping up and down on a sofa. Even Rudolph Giuliani, then mayor of New York City, accused Mr. Klein of behaving "in very bad taste."

In all three cases, Klein, acting surprised by all the fuss, scrapped the ad campaigns. But he and his brand were left with the taint of having gone beyond the boundaries of decency just to sell blue jeans and under-wear. His reputation with some of his key stakeholders and the general public would never be the same.

More recently, Klein has tamed down his ads and acknowledged a more conservative tilt in the United States. The old edginess is gone. He has even used the saccharine tune "What the World Needs Now Is Love" in recent perfume commercials. In the end, he failed in the challenging juggling act of managing his reputation so well with his many audiences.

THE BALANCING ACT

A company's many constituencies—shareholders, customers, employees, and others—pose a challenging test for any company trying to manage its reputation. Stakeholders may have different, even diametrically opposed, interests. The trick is to maintain a balance that produces an overall positive reputation.

First of all, it is critical to determine precisely who your stakeholders are and play to all of them in different ways at different times. While DaimlerChrysler traditionally focuses on car buyers, it launched a $90 million corporate image campaign in 2001 aimed mainly at investors and financial analysts to promote the corporate brand rather than individual automotive brands. The image advertising was necessary because it followed a corporate restructuring and conveyed DaimlerChrysler's new strategy.

Stakeholders typically are quite an eclectic cast of characters. Of course, employees, customers, and investors are the most visible. But don't forget about activists, regulatory officials, franchisees, licensees, suppliers, and the news media. It's also helpful to send departing employees out the door with positive feelings about the company. They can certainly influence people's perceptions of a company's reputation—and often for the worse.

Alumni of Procter & Gamble had gathered for several years for a reunion weekend in Chicago without the company's blessing or involvement. But in 2003, P&G finally decided to endorse the reunion and invite alumni to meet on its corporate turf in Cincinnati. P&G was smart to cozy up to its former employees, many of whom are in influential top jobs at companies such as General Electric, 3M, and Microsoft,

THE CAST OF CORPORATE STAKEHOLDERS

Companies have more stakeholders than they probably realize. While all of the stakeholder groups listed here don't apply to every company, they show just how complicated the reputation management process can be. Companies must manage their reputations with myriad stakeholders, who are both affected by and influence the corporate image:

The general public
Customers
Employees
Prospective employees
Retirees
Other former employees
Retailers
Distributors
Suppliers
Franchisees
Licensees
Shareholders
Potential investors
Financial analysts
Government officials
Regulatory agencies
Industry competitors
The news media
Social and environmental activists
Members of the local community

and can certainly affect its reputation. For one thing, P&G sees its alumni network as an untapped opportunity to help in its recruitment of top talent. The consumer products marketer even asked some of its star graduates, such as Meg Whitman, CEO of eBay, and Jeffrey Immelt, CEO of General Electric, to appear in a recruiting video.

P&G is also trying to be friendlier with another even more vital stakeholder group: retailers. Today, the company's relationship with retailers is complicated. P&G and its retailers are both partners and rivals because many stores sell their own private-label brands of detergents and diapers that compete with P&G's flagship Tide and Pampers brands. Rather than just haggle all the time with store managers over shelf space and price discounts, P&G also wants to increase cooperation with retailers. It is spending time trying to make shopping easier for consumers and boost sales for both itself and the retailers. For example, it worked with more than thirty retailers to simplify the shampoo department with its glut of brands and ended up generating sales growth of 10 to 44 percent. Such results are bound to boost the company's reputation.

Companies must remember, however, that they can't please all of the people all of the time. Know who likes you and who is less fond of you. Some industries, such as energy, are unlikely ever to be loved by consumers, so it makes sense for them to focus heavily on investors, employees, and regulatory officials in building their reputations. "To consumers, the energy industry is always a bunch of rapacious plunderers of the environment and their pockets," says Harlan Teller, who studies corporate reputation for the public relations firm Hill & Knowlton. "But energy companies that are financially successful are very much in favor with investors."

As with people, relationships among companies and their stakeholders are often complex and intertwined. Stakeholders have their own agendas and self-interest. What makes for a positive reputation with one audience may alienate another. If a company cuts costs to the bone to make stock analysts and investors admire its financial performance, it will most likely damage its reputation with its employees, who will bear the brunt of the cost savings. That's where the tricky balancing act comes in.

One danger is sending competing signals to different constituencies. Health maintenance organizations, for example, have made conflicting promises. Many HMOs reassured doctors that they would have independence, promised corporate clients that medical costs would be controlled, and told patients they would receive the finest care at the lowest cost. Soon all three constituencies felt deceived, and the reputations of HMOs plummeted.

Recently, Aetna broke ranks with other health insurers and announced a truce with physicians, many of whom had complained that it had unfairly cut reimbursements to them and interfered in their treatment decisions. In settling the lawsuit, involving some 700,000 doctors, Aetna trumpeted it as "a new era of cooperation in health care."

Managing your reputation well with one stakeholder group can produce an exponential payoff with some of your other audiences. In Aetna's case, its more harmonious relationship with doctors may strengthen its reputation with another important stakeholder group: corporate customers. They may be more inclined to choose Aetna now because they want to avoid the kinds of rancorous relations between doctors and insurers that typically lead to unhappy employees.

Positive stakeholder relationships also can protect reputation during turbulent times. FedEx enjoys a good reputation with Williams-Sonoma because of FedEx's timely delivery of its mail-order household products. So Williams-Sonoma was happy to help out when FedEx faced the threat of a pilots' strike. In media interviews, Williams-Sonoma officials expressed confidence in FedEx's ability to weather a strike well. That helped reassure investors and other customers about FedEx's continued reliability in the event of a pilot walkout.

On the other hand, Coca-Cola may not be able to count on such support from a key stakeholder that it offended. Coke damaged its relationship with a major customer—Burger King—when it admitted that some employees had improperly influenced the results of a marketing test aimed at winning more business from the fast-food company. The employees had paid a consultant to recruit children to buy a large number of meals at Burger King featuring a coupon for a Frozen Coke slushy drink, which was being tested before its expansion to more restaurants.

Coke executives expressed their regret and made a multimillion-dollar payment to Burger King as part of its apology. But Burger King officials still publicly rebuked the company. "We expect and demand the highest standards of conduct and integrity in all our vendor relationships and will not tolerate any deviation from these standards," said Brad Blum, CEO of Burger King. Not only did Coke anger a major stakeholder, but it also risked jeopardizing its relationship with other fountain customers, who account for about a third of the company's U.S. sales.

KEEPING YOUR PRIORITIES STRAIGHT

Companies should prioritize stakeholders by importance. It's like a pyramid with the most important stakeholders at the top and others ranked in descending order. This pyramid will vary by company and industry, and for multinational companies, the most significant stakeholders may not be the same in all countries.

Stakeholder priorities got out of whack during the 1990s when quarterly earnings growth and an ever-rising stock price became the obsession of companies, stock analysts, and investors. Shareholders and analysts took precedence, and companies neglected other important constituencies. Though investors are a key audience for most companies, customers and employees, the lifeblood of any business, must be at the top of list.

Indeed, employees are ultimately the key stakeholder group because reputation is built from the inside out. A positive reputation creates a sense of pride and motivates employees to help maintain it. It's also a powerful lure for new hires. In a 2002 survey by the Burson-Masteller public relations agency and *PR Week* magazine, 61 percent of CEOs said they were increasing internal communications with their employees. The stepped-up communication coincided with studies showing a decline in employee loyalty and corporate credibility.

As for customers, they really are king. Some of the best-regarded companies continue to give their customers priority. Johnson & Johnson, for example, still lives by its Credo, written back in 1943, that declares, "Our first responsibility is to the doctors, nurses and patients, to mothers and fathers and all others who use our products and services." Next come employees, then the community, and last, stockholders.

Of course, you need to distinguish your core customers from other consumers. When Levi Strauss cut off philanthropic support for the Boy Scouts of America because of its antigay policies, the jeans maker was deluged with more than 100,000 letters and postcards from people threatening a boycott. Levi, which has a long history of commitment to civil rights, had no intention of backing down. But it was still concerned about the potential impact on its business. Had it damaged its reputation with many of its loyal customers?

The company proceeded to research the zip codes of the postcard senders and determined that they were not stakeholders who would significantly affect Levi's bottom line. They were largely concentrated in rural, politically conservative areas and not in the company's more critical urban markets. The demographic data for the protesters were also skewed to older and more blue-collar people than Levi's typical customer.

SILVER-HAIRED STAKEHOLDERS

Retirees may be out of sight, but they should never be out of mind. Once retirees leave the workplace, their power to affect corporate reputation may lessen, but it's still formidable. Unfortunately, most companies don't appreciate their clout.

Businesses must remember that retirees can be their best friends or worst enemies, depending on how they feel they are being treated. They can burnish the reputation of an employer they feel fondly about and sully the image of a company they feel has wronged them. These days, retirees are especially vigilant about possible cutbacks in their medical benefits and pensions. Some are taking aim at what they consider excessive pay, perks, and severance benefits for senior executives at such companies as Delta Air Lines and Verizon Communications.

With so many retirees concerned about cutbacks in their benefits, some companies are taking pains to reassure them. Gillette Company, for example, organizes a gathering for retirees each fall, and the CEO spends as much time as necessary answering their questions, from how to fill out medical benefit forms to how safe their pensions are.

As a result of such meetings, Gillette retirees feel a bond with one another—and the company. They are much more likely to write to their legislators about a proposed bill that could affect Gillette or to support the company during a crisis. "Retirees are an extremely important audience, and you must have a constant dialogue with them," says Eric Kraus, vice president of corporate communications. "You certainly don't want the people who played a pivotal role at the company to have negative perceptions of it."

Some retirees are giving Gillette valuable exposure in the community through their local volunteer activities. As part of the Gillette Retiree Outreach Program, they work at food pantries and blood banks, read to the disabled, and donate their time to literacy programs. Recently, the group was honored by the Greater Boston Food Bank. "That kind of recognition certainly helps Gillette's reputation," says Kraus.

Pfizer also views its retirees as a critical stakeholder group in reputation management. The pharmaceutical company keeps in close touch with them through communication programs and regional retiree meetings. "Seniors vote and can affect policies important to Pfizer," says John Santoro, executive director for leadership communications. Given senior citizens' hostility toward high drug prices these days, Pfizer can use all of the elderly friends it can find.

REGULATORS AND REPUTATION

The gambling industry suffers from one of the most negative reputations in America. But Harrah's Entertainment has managed to stand out from its competitors and forge a largely positive reputation with all-important regulatory officials, as well as employees, customers, and even the general public.

In essence, Harrah's took the high road. It pointed out its positive contributions and showed how it tries to prevent some of the negative consequences of legalized gambling. In its casinos, the company has long communicated its focus on responsible gambling. It refuses to cash welfare or unemployment checks, displays toll-free "help line" numbers for compulsive gamblers, and honors requests from gambling addicts that they be denied access to the casino. Harrah's also avoids promoting gambling to young people by not advertising in certain media, such as college newspapers and on comics pages, and by not licensing its logo on children's clothing, toys, and game equipment.

Only recently did Harrah's go public with the responsible gambling message in a television commercial meant to bolster its reputation with people beyond customers and employees. In the ad, Chairman Phil Satre discusses the times when people should *not* gamble—if they're drunk, lonely or depressed, underage, or unable to limit their betting. Satre believes that the company's integrity attracts customers and employees and improves its reputation with regulators and politicians. Indeed, he says, the responsible gambling program has clearly helped Harrah's win approval to build casinos.

To further boost its reputation with regulators and the public, Harrah's also promotes its positive impact on local communities. In Louisiana, it created commercials showing how it helps the state by employing people and providing business to print shops and other small firms. Satre credits the campaign at least partly for Harrah's success in winning a $50 million tax cut for its New Orleans casino. "The images of small-business owners and employees told our story best to regulators," says Satre. "The greatest threat to the growth of casino gambling is the industry's bad reputation with some people. And those negative perceptions die hard."

THE LOCAL AND GLOBAL COMMUNITIES

Companies are paying more attention to certain stakeholder groups because of the growing importance of corporate citizenship in the reputation equation. Many realize that they have neglected two audiences: the local communities in which they operate and the broader world community of activist organization.

Ignoring activists can be very dangerous. They learn a company's business inside and out and sometimes use moles within the company to disrupt operations, such as its Web site and internal e-mail system. Making peace with activists is almost always in a company's interest.

Fast-food companies, besieged by many militant groups over the years regarding environmental and nutrition issues, seem finally to be catching on to how to manage their relationships with activist groups. They have become allies, for example, with organizations concerned about the welfare of the farm animals that end up on the dinner table. McDonald's and other companies are pressuring their suppliers to treat livestock and chickens more humanely by putting them in larger pens and reducing the use of electrical prods. Even People for the Ethical Treatment of Animals (PETA), one of the most confrontational groups, has been impressed by the fast-food industry's response.

At the local level, many companies haven't given back enough to the towns where they operate their plants and offices—which is a serious omission. Harris Interactive's research shows that perceptions of a company's community responsibility appear to be as important to overall corporate reputation as perceptions about its products and services.

You don't have to convince Ronald Sargent of the significance of community stakeholders. When he became president and chief executive officer of Staples in early 2002, he soon realized that the office supplies retailer had emphasized customers and employees to the neglect of community relations. "We needed to become more active with our community stakeholders," says Sargent, "by focusing on a cause and really dedicating ourselves to it."

Under Sargent, the company has made youth and education its philanthropic focus. In summer 2002, the company launched the Staples Foundation for Learning to fund job-training and education programs, particularly for the disadvantaged. It also works with Boys & Girls Clubs of America to provide safe, supervised havens for youngsters during after-school hours and on weekends. The latter cause is especially

---

COMMUNITY LEADERS

In Harris Interactive's study of corporate reputation in fall 2002, it found that the companies in the first list scored highest for community support. The second list includes the companies that showed the most improvement in their community responsibility scores between 2001 and 2002.

HIGHEST RATED

1. United Parcel Service
2. Home Depot
3. Wal-Mart
4. FedEx
5. McDonald's

MOST IMPROVED

1. Home Depot
2. Sears
3. DaimlerChrysler
4. Johnson & Johnson
5. Xerox

---

meaningful to Sargent. "I grew up two doors away from a motorcycle gang and became a Boys and Girls Club kid," he says. "It provided a good foundation for me. I ended up attending Harvard College and Harvard Business School."

GETTING TO KNOW YOU

"P&G needs more corporate awareness. I don't really know what they make or what they do."

"It seems they don't reach out to people like me; all of their ads are for housewives."

"There is not a single product that makes me think, 'Yes, this is P&G.'"

Those comments from public opinion surveys clearly show that Procter & Gamble's corporate reputation needs attention. Many companies bear the same name as their major product brand—the Coca-Colas and Nikes of the world. Ads for their soft drinks and sneakers also affect their corporate reputations. But other companies, such as P&G, are more invisible and don't enjoy a strong reputation with some of their stakeholder groups. When people see a commercial for Crest toothpaste, for instance, there's no mention of P&G.

Consumers are often surprised to learn that P&G makes many of the products that are part of their everyday lives. P&G thus misses the reputation rub-off that could come from shoppers' satisfaction with its brands. For example, its Swiffer floor duster has been a huge hit, but many people don't know that they have P&G to thank for making their lives a little easier.

So P&G is applying its classic product branding skills to the corporate brand. In essence, it wants more of its stakeholders to get to know it better. P&G's research told it that since the September 11, 2001, terrorist attacks and the corporate accounting skullduggery, stakeholders want to know much more about the companies they're investing in, working for, and doing business with. "We will more actively manage and leverage the P&G brand with employees, customers, suppliers, and in some markets, consumers," says A. G. Lafley, chairman and CEO. In addition, the company plans to build stronger relationships with financial analysts, the media, activist organizations, and government officials.

The corporate branding project is a work in progress. P&G has developed a "brand ambassador" program, identifying about a thousand "thought leaders in the trenches" to help it bring the corporate brand to life both inside the company and with external stakeholders. The company also has created a corporate brand equity survey to monitor its reputation.

"We are trying to define what we want the P&G brand to stand for," says Kelly Brown, marketing director for the corporate branding project. "It's a classic branding problem. We're treating this as we would a new business and applying the same branding approach that we use with our products."

Employees are the most critical component of the branding project. "We're reaffirming our corporate values with our employees," Brown says, "because P&G's reputation is formed by the Procter people with whom you interact."

In promoting its corporate brand more aggressively, P&G faces some risks, including fueling the satanism rumors that still bedevil the company. For decades, the company has been fighting rumors that its logo showing the man in the moon and a constellation of stars represented satanism. P&G has even posted a denial of the rumor on its corporate Web site, with supporting statements from such religious leaders as evangelist Billy Graham and the Roman Catholic archbishop of Cincinnati.

To try to kill the rumor once and for all, the company has replaced the old logo with a new design using its P&G initials. "Some employees mourned the loss of the moon and stars," says Brown, "but it's an unfortunate distraction." Even with the simpler blue logo, she concedes that the rumors could catch fire again. "We go through peaks and valleys," she adds. "It's very unpredictable and very aggravating."

INTERNATIONAL STAKEHOLDERS

Multinational companies face the additional challenge of managing their reputations with stakeholders in many countries. They must understand and cater to country-by-country differences regarding which constituencies are most significant and what matters most to them. Europeans tend to value corporate social responsibility more than Americans, for example.

Companies sometimes realize their reputations are weak with foreign stakeholders only after they encounter problems abroad. When the European Commission blocked its acquisition of Honeywell, for example, General Electric realized it needed to bolster its reputation with government officials in Europe and created a corporate image campaign there.

As Procter & Gamble develops its corporate branding program, it's clear that a cookie-cutter approach won't work. Its model is "a global template" customized to meet regional and country differences. In China, for example, P&G understands that it's very important for stakeholders to know and trust the company behind the products.

DuPont has learned that certain attributes matter more to stakeholders outside the United States. For instance, the chemical company plays up the fact that it is more than two hundred years old with stakeholders in Asia, particularly regulatory officials, who value heritage. To demonstrate its longevity, DuPont executives have even given Asian officials tours of the Hagley Museum, the site of the company's first powder works on the Brandywine River. Visitors see massive stone mills, a water wheel, the original du Pont family homestead, and a nineteenth-century machine shop.

In Europe, it's a different story. There, DuPont is especially sensitive to activist stakeholders, who are more strongly opposed to animal research and biotechnology than their counterparts in other countries.

Gillette finds that certain constituencies matter more in some countries. Financial analysts, for example, are a more important stakeholder group in the United States, while retailers carry more weight in some foreign countries. Gillette believes it benefits from the fact that it has operated abroad for nearly a hundred years and isn't viewed so much as an American company but more as part of the local culture in countries such as France and Germany. That's especially advantageous these days in the aftermath of the war in Iraq, when stakeholders in some countries may harbor anti-American bias toward U.S.-based multinationals.

A SHIFT IN THE PECKING ORDER

The stakeholder pyramid isn't a static structure. It's vital to understand which audiences are most important to a company at any given time. At the pace of change today, a company needs to frequently reevaluate which stakeholder group matters most at the moment.

For Public Service Enterprise Group (PSEG), investors have moved ahead of regulatory authorities and consumers in its stakeholder hierarchy. Founded a century ago as a New Jersey utility company, PSEG has evolved in recent years into a much more deregulated and diverse energy business. When it was primarily a regulated entity with relatively predictable financial results, PSEG's stock price was fairly stable. No longer; with the majority of its operations unregulated now, the energy company must cope with a more volatile stock price and must manage its reputation with investors much more closely.

Nowadays, PSEG advertises in *The Wall Street Journal* and business magazines, promoting its diversified "power portfolio" of both domestic and international energy generation and delivery systems. "We're more like a regular company, and we need to explain what the company is now," says Paul Rosengren, manager of public information. "It's not as simple anymore. It's really important to be classified properly and to develop a good reputation on Wall Street." During the California energy crisis, PSEG didn't want to risk getting lumped with the West Coast and suffering reputation damage. It dispatched a report to investors pointing out how its New Jersey market was much different, with higher power reserves and a more diverse fuel mix.

Although its priorities have shifted, PSEG doesn't by any means ignore state regulatory officials. They still set utility rates and grant PSEG approval to build power plants. So PSEG advertises on the New Jersey Network to reach "opinion leaders" and places ads in local sports arenas and stadiums. "We still want to be seen by legislators as a New Jersey company," says Rosengren. "If the head of a legislative committee is involved in a golf tournament, then we might sponsor it."

Corporate upheaval is another reason that stakeholder priorities sometimes shift. During its severe financial troubles, Lucent Technologies put a higher priority on two stakeholders: employees and customers. As the company's workforce shrank from more than 100,000 to a mere 35,000, many employees worried if they would be next and what the company's near-term future looked like. CEO Patricia Russo communicated regularly with employees through in-house broadcasts and internal e-mail messages, reassuring them that the telecommunications company would survive its ordeal.

"I know it is difficult to stay focused when you see our stock price dip below one dollar and constantly hear and read negative news about our industry," she stated in one letter to employees. "But the messages about the industry and the players in it are not likely to change until there is some evidence of stability and then recovery. And it is important to remember that stock price follows performance."

As rumors swirled about a liquidity crisis, Russo and other Lucent executives also kept major customers informed of the company's tribulations by preparing special reports on its financial condition and business strategy.

Lucent kept in close contact with stock analysts, credit-rating agencies, and its bankers, too. "The most important thing was to try to convey to our stakeholders a sense of stability," says Kathleen Fitzgerald, former senior vice president for public relations and advertising. "We went from being a darling to being a dog. So many people have been angry with us because of the money they lost on Lucent stock."

Many pharmaceutical companies have failed to respond successfully to a shift in stakeholder importance that, ironically, they themselves initiated. They have succeeded in creating a more powerful stakeholder in the consumer, but one that holds a largely negative opinion of them. And they have only themselves to blame for the dilemma.

It used to be that physicians and to a lesser degree pharmacists were among their most important stakeholders because they most directly influenced the choice of prescription drugs for patients. But through the explosion of direct-to-consumer advertising of prescription medications, the drug industry has made patients a much more important stakeholder group. Yet they have fared poorly in creating a positive corporate reputation and linking their individual drug brands to the corporate brand through advertising and public relations. Many consumers simply lump most pharmaceutical companies together as greedy bandits that overcharge them for vital medicines.

LAW FOUR

LIVE YOUR VALUES
AND ETHICS

Walk into the corporate headquarters of Johnson & Johnson, and you come face to face with an eight-foot-tall limestone pillar of words. There, literally carved in stone, is the company's cherished Credo. Written sixty years ago by former chairman Robert Wood Johnson, the Credo lays out J&J's values in twenty-five simple but eloquent sentences.

But the Credo isn't just a showpiece in the headquarters lobby in New Brunswick, New Jersey. It has become a vibrant part of J&J's day-to-day business operations throughout the world—from mundane decisions about corporate facilities to major crises involving the safety of its drugs. Employees treat the Credo with all the reverence they would give to a religious creed. "The Credo is the glue that holds this highly decentralized company together," says William Weldon, chairman and CEO of Johnson & Johnson. "We can miss a numbers target occasionally, but the Credo cannot be compromised."

The Credo certainly sets J&J apart in this era of corporate distrust and shows how much an ethical culture can influence reputation. The pharmaceutical and consumer products company lives its values statement and enjoys one of the best reputations in the world. For four consecutive years, J&J was ranked number 1 in Harris Interactive's annual

52

list of global companies with the best corporate reputations. The 2002 ranking, based on a public opinion survey conducted in the fall, showed that J&J is viewed as one of the most trusted, most ethical companies in the world.

"Johnson & Johnson has just always been a very trustworthy company, and trust is extremely important to me," says Margaret Buettner, a Census Bureau field representative in Imperial, Missouri, who has been loyal to the company's baby powder and shampoo for more than forty years. "Their ads are honest," says Buettner, who gave J&J a high rating in the Harris ranking. "They don't talk down to me." Indeed, the company avoids playing on consumers' fears and other emotions in advertising. J&J considers its ubiquitous red script logo much more than a trademark—it's a "trustmark."

The Credo's message was farsighted and hasn't changed much through the years. But it has been revised slightly to reflect societal trends—with the addition of "protecting the environment and natural resources" in 1979 and references to fathers and employees' family responsibilities in 1987.

J&J reinforces the Credo on a regular basis with its entire workforce of 106,000. It is displayed on walls and tabletops throughout J&J offices in more than fifty countries and has been translated into thirty-six languages. Every two years, all employees must rate the company on how well it has lived up to the Credo. More frequently, managers debate the values statement at "Credo Challenge" meetings and apply it to real-world case studies during "Living our Credo Values" sessions. Should J&J, for example, close an inefficient plant and move the operations to a lower-cost developing country? Or should it put the welfare of the employees who would lose their jobs first?

"We worry about a level of complacency setting in," says Russell Deyo, vice president, administration. "We have to earn our reputation every day." He notes that the company tries to make people think carefully about their decisions by asking them if they would be comfortable explaining their actions to the CEO, talking about them with their mother and father, or seeing them described on the front page of *The Wall Street Journal.*

You can be sure that the Credo will figure into the debate over any substantive issue, including the company's decision to stay in South Africa during the era of apartheid for the sake of its black employees there. In 1975, the Credo's pronouncements about community respon-

JOHNSON & JOHNSON'S VALUES STATEMENT

OUR CREDO

We believe our first responsibility is to the doctors, nurses and patients, to mothers and fathers and all others who use our products and services. In meeting their needs everything we do must be of high quality. We must constantly strive to reduce our costs in order to maintain reasonable prices. Customers' orders must be serviced promptly and accurately. Our suppliers and distributors must have an opportunity to make a fair profit.

We are responsible to our employees, the men and women who work with us throughout the world. Everyone must be considered as an individual. We must respect their dignity and recognize their merit. They must have a sense of security in their jobs. Compensation must be fair and adequate, and working conditions clean, orderly and safe. We must be mindful of ways to help our employees fulfill their family responsibilities. Employees must feel free to make suggestions and complaints. There must be equal opportunity for employment, development and advancement for those qualified. We must provide competent management, and their actions must be just and ethical.

We are responsible to the communities in which we live and work and to the world community as well. We must be good citizens—support good works and charities and bear our fair share of taxes. We must encourage civic improvements and better health and education. We must maintain in good order the property we are privileged to use, protecting the environment and natural resources.

Our final responsibility is to our stockholders. Business must make a sound profit. We must experiment with new ideas. Research must be carried on, innovative programs developed and mistakes paid for. New equipment must be purchased, new facilities provided and new products launched. Reserves must be created to provide for adverse times. When we operate according to these principles, the stockholders should realize a fair return.

sibility prompted J&J to keep its headquarters in New Brunswick rather than relocate to a smaller, more pastoral town. It concluded that it should be part of solving the local urban problems.

Sometimes executives disagree over whether a particular business decision is truly a Credo issue, but at least it becomes part of the give-and-take. For example, there was conflict when the company decided to put sprinkler systems in all of its facilities. J&J executives considered its fire-safety strategy very significant in meeting the Credo's call for safe working conditions. But managers in some countries objected because of the expense. They argued—to no avail—that the project cost would put them at a competitive disadvantage with other companies that don't have sprinkler systems.

As a health care company, J&J faces crises on a regular basis that test the Credo. Because of the Credo, the company's response to the Tylenol poisonings in 1982 and 1986 was pretty straightforward. To live up to its pledge to put customers first, it had little choice but to remove Tylenol from store shelves. In return for putting them first, customers gave J&J back its Tylenol business when it reintroduced the analgesic in a tamper-resistant package.

More recently, J&J also invoked the Credo when it withdrew its heartburn drug Propulsid from the market and made it available on a restricted-access basis only. Ralph Larsen, chairman and CEO at the time of the decision in 2000, told analysts that the company was disappointed with the loss of $660 million of Propulsid sales but that "it was, in the final analysis, the right thing to do for the patients." Propulsid had been linked to heart rhythm irregularities and some deaths and was being investigated by the Food and Drug Administration.

"It took moral courage to do what we did," says Roger Fine, vice president and general counsel. "Not only were there lost sales, but we also knew there would be a feeding frenzy by lawyers"—suing the company on behalf of people who had used Propulsid.

Such actions don't mean that J&J isn't a scrappy competitor and that it doesn't sometimes fall short of the Credo's principles. The Credo isn't foolproof. That was clearly shown when J&J's Ortho Pharmaceutical subsidiary pleaded guilty to obstruction of justice in 1995 because documents had been destroyed during an FDA investigation of the company's marketing of its Retin-A acne drug as a wrinkle remover. At the time, the company called the document destruction "deplorable" and said it took full responsibility. "The key thing is to own up to our mistakes," says Deyo, "and learn from a distressing experience like Retin-A so it never happens again."

WHOM DO YOU TRUST?

Never have corporate ethics and values been more scrutinized. As a result, integrity has become perhaps the most critical element of a strong reputation. People want trust more than anything after the past two years of fraud, manipulation, and lying. The public's message is loud and clear: Honesty isn't the best policy, it's the only policy. That may sound simplistic, but it has apparently been very difficult for many companies and many of their executives to grasp.

A Wall Street Journal/NBC News poll in 2002 found that fully 70 percent of Americans didn't trust the word of brokers and corporations. One third of the respondents said they had "hardly any confidence" in big-company executives—the highest proportion in more than three decades.

"Business ethics is an oxymoron," says Paul Major, an addiction counselor in Carmel Valley, Calif. He watched as the value of his 401(k) plan fell by 30 percent in 2002, at least partly because of companies that had cooked their books. "People flat-out lied, and no one wants to take responsibility," he adds. "Companies don't even bother to say they're sorry about what happened. "

But now ethics has become the hot buzzword inside both the executive suite and the business school classroom. The Ethics Officer Association attracted 150 new member companies in the second half of 2002. Many companies are setting up ethics hotlines for whistle-blowers and beefing up their codes of conduct following the Enron debacle. But it's too soon to tell whether this is a revolution or simply another corporate fad.

The current rush to jump on the ethics bandwagon isn't surprising. Ethics programs have often resulted from crises like the recent string of accounting scandals. It was the billing and kickback scandals of the 1980s that caused military contractors to draft ethics statements and hire ethics officers. The Defense Industry Initiative on Business Ethics and Conduct was created in 1986 to clean up such abuses as charging $600 for toilet seats and billing the federal government for executives' country club memberships and dog kennel fees.

Defense contractors also developed their own in-house ethics programs. "You have to have the resources to investigate and the commitment to discipline people," says Patricia Ellis, vice president for business ethics and compliance at Raytheon Company, a defense and aerospace company that has about twenty full-time employees in its ethics program. She has been involved in several recent investigations of Raytheon by the Securities and Exchange Commission, including an embarrassing sanction of the company and its chief financial officer for alleged violation of federal fair-disclosure laws.

Integrity policies come in many shapes and sizes. Some companies, such as Johnson & Johnson, call theirs a credo. Many have written a values statement; for others, it's called a code of ethics. And some companies have both. Values statements promote commitment, integrity, respect, trust, teamwork, and other noble virtues. Ethics codes tend to be less visionary and are more oriented toward compliance with laws and regulations. They typically deal with such issues as bribery, insider trading, sexual harassment, privacy, and conflicts of interest. The best approach is a mix of inspirational thoughts about integrity and legalistic language about company policies. General Electric's integrity program is called "The Spirit and the Letter" because GE wants its employees not just to follow the law but also to make ethics a part of their regular routine.

"I preach to everyone that you're never going to do away with sin," says Ben Heineman, GE's general counsel. "But you have to handle compliance problems with dispatch and integrity." Of course, what constitutes ethical behavior can still be subjective. Some environmentalists have criticized GE for being less than ethical over the PCB pollution it caused in New York's Hudson River. But Heineman says the PCB case was simply a difference of opinion with the U.S. Environmental Protection Agency. In the end, GE agreed to the EPA's PCB dredging project. "It was a public policy disagreement," says Heineman, "not an issue of legal compliance or anything unethical."

PLATITUDES AND "PAPER PROGRAMS"

Sadly, at many companies ethics and values are just for show. They amount to a lot of paperwork and little more than platitudes. Companies may post their ethics and values statements on bulletin boards and require employees to sign an annual document declaring that they haven't violated the principles. But that doesn't mean the statements have any substance. Even after all of the scandals of the past two years, it's still the rare company that makes ethics and values a part of its culture and day-to-day decision making.

Even some of the most scandal-ridden companies made superficial attempts at appearing ethical. Tyco International, whose former chief executive and chief financial officers have been charged with looting the company of about $600 million, was actually a member of the Ethics Officer Association. Not surprisingly, Tyco representatives failed to attend the association's meetings. Such window dressing doesn't fool anybody for long, and certainly not regulatory officials. "The government has gotten more savvy about companies that have nothing more than paper programs," says Ed Petry, executive director of the ethics association. As for Tyco, it has rejoined the association and its new senior executives are expected to take a more active interest in learning how to create a serious ethics program.

Even disgraced Enron had developed an extensive ethics code and set of values: "respect, integrity, communication and excellence." Certainly, many Enron employees acted quite responsibly. But the code still seems like a bad joke now that the company's deceptive and fraudulent accounting practices have been exposed. An Enron spokesman notes that top executives had clashed over making the company's values and ethics code part of employees' performance ratings and compensation. Instead, some corporate officers believed that employees should be judged simply on their trading successes, regardless of how they achieved them. It was a culture of "anything goes" as long as it had a financial payoff.

How much was Enron's ethics code worth in the end? A copy of the 63-page document was being peddled for $8.99 on eBay's auction site, and novelty collectors could add the "Values and Vision" videotape to their shopping cart for an additional $12.95. That about says it all for the value placed on ethics at the once revered energy-trading company.

Knowing now about Enron's downfall and how its top executives really did business, you feel as if you're reading not the actual ethics code but rather the script for a *Saturday Night Live* parody. Here are a few excerpts from the code and cover letter that truly give new meaning to the expression "empty words":

"We want to be proud of Enron and to know that it enjoys a reputation for fairness and honesty and that it is respected. . . . Let's keep that reputation high."
"Ruthlessness, callousness and arrogance don't belong here."
"We work with customers and prospects openly, honestly and sincerely."

"We are dedicated to conducting business according to all applicable local and international laws and regulations . . . and with the highest professional and ethical standards."

Even the Smithsonian Institution in Washington, D.C., has acquired the Enron ethics code for its collection of historical memorabilia.

CREATING A CULTURE OF MORALITY

A sterile museum piece is the last thing you want your ethics and values statements to become. To enhance your corporate reputation, values must become an entrenched part of the culture. Ethics are the corporate DNA, not just the fashion of the day, for companies with outstanding reputations.

Academic studies of some of America's largest companies have shown that a strong reputation for ethical behavior pays off financially, too. Curtis Verschoor, an accounting professor at DePaul University in Chicago, found that companies expressing a strong commitment to their ethics code performed better than others on such measures as investment return, sales and profit growth, and return on equity. On another measure—market value added, or the excess value of a company beyond its shareholders' investments—Verschoor's study determined that the average was $10.6 billion more than that of companies that didn't mention a code of ethics.

"The most critical factors appear to be the nature of the values upon which the corporate culture is based," says Verschoor, "and the strength of top management's commitment to the ethical treatment of stakeholders, which are expressed in actions and not just in words."

The challenge is to inculcate ethics and values into each and every employee. Which is no easy feat, especially in organizations with tens of thousands of employees spread around the world. Indeed, Jeffrey Immelt, chairman and CEO of General Electric, says he loses sleep fretting about whether all of the company's 300,000 employees are following the code of conduct. "You always worry that somebody doesn't get it," he says. "We can survive bad markets. What you can't live through is anybody who takes from the company or does something wrong in the community."

It's Immelt and other CEOs who set the tone for the rest of the company. Integrity "is the core of who we are," he remarks in GE's ethics training video. "You can count on me to have leaders who never look the other way" when ethics violations come to light.

Equally important is the establishment of a full-fledged ethics program led by an ethics officer. An effective ethics officer sends a powerful message to the company about the importance of integrity. Generally, they report to the CEO or another very senior executive, as well as the board of directors' audit committee. But despite all of the scandals, many companies still don't have such full-time officers and assign ethics issues instead to the legal department.

"I'm concerned that the ethics movement hasn't picked up more momentum after Enron and that there aren't more people like me," says Alan Yuspeh, senior vice president for ethics, compliance, and corporate responsibility at the hospital company HCA. Charges of Medicare fraud in the mid-1990s prompted Columbia/HCA Healthcare Corporation to create an ethics department and hire Yuspeh, who had been one of the key players involved in the defense industry's ethics reforms.

Yuspeh's concerns about the future of ethics management may be well founded. After corporate America's latest round of workforce reductions, ethics programs may receive even less attention. Employees at thinned-down companies are now doing the jobs of laid-off workers, and their managers may not be able to find time to provide ethics training.

Instead, companies need to get the word out about ethical standards with more vigor than ever. At the very least, employees need an annual refresher course on ethics. Companies should also post their value statements and ethics codes throughout the workplace and on their internal and external Web sites for all to see. Staples, the office supplies retailer, gives employees wallet-size brochures detailing its values. Pricewater-houseCoopers recently put up posters in its accounting offices that asked, "Who is responsible for ethics at PwC?" As employees come closer, they see themselves in a mirror on the poster.

Some companies are trumpeting their ethical principles in advertising. A few financial services companies, in particular, have tried to separate themselves from the Wall Street scandal over analysts' conflicts of interest. In a folksy ad entitled "American Values," American Century Investment Services says that two things have remained constant: its values and its founder's daily peanut butter sandwich lunch.

But such self-congratulatory ads can be risky. They may come across

ETHICS LEADERS AND LAGGARDS

Here are the top ten and bottom ten companies in Harris Interactive's rating of companies for "maintaining high ethical standards." The rankings are based on an online public opinion survey in fall 2002.

TOP 10
1. Johnson & Johnson
2. United Parcel Service
3. Harley-Davidson
4. Home Depot
5. General Mills
6. Walt Disney
7. FedEx
8. Maytag
9. Wal-Mart
10. Southwest Airlines

BOTTOM 10
1. Enron
2. WorldCom (now MCI)
3. Andersen Worldwide
4. Global Crossing
5. Adelphia Communications
6. Philip Morris (now Altria Group)
7. Bridgestone/Firestone
8. Qwest Communications
9. AOL Time Warner
10. Kmart

as a manipulative attempt to capitalize on competitors' misdeeds, and may ultimately backfire. Charles Schwab & Company has portrayed itself as more principled than other brokerage firms in a hard-hitting ad campaign that says that avoiding conflicts of interest is "at the heart of our values," and that "from day one, the individual investor has been at the center of what we do." But by November 2003, the holier-than-thou ad claims had lost credibility as Schwab found itself caught up in the mutual fund trading scandals.

PricewaterhouseCoopers developed an advertising campaign in 2002 touting its integrity and announcing that it will resign from accounts if it can't resolve concerns about the quality of financial information and the integrity of the client's management team. It sounds admirable, but the positive effects on the accounting firm's reputation were surely diminished by continuing media coverage of its troubles. At the same time as the ads were running, news stories reported on PwC's multimillion-dollar payments to resolve lawsuits over alleged audit failures and about continuing regulatory scrutiny related to its prior audits of Tyco International.

Ideally, ethics and values should be integrated into performance appraisals and compensation plans. Companies should reward employees who abide by their standards and punish offenders. It's very disconcerting when employees see their colleagues skirting or violating standards but still receiving pay raises and promotions. The ethics code then looks hollow, and employees no longer have much incentive to abide by it.

A survey of corporate ethics officers by the Conference Board, a New York research organization, found that companies too often look the other way. When asked what happens to great performers who don't live up to corporate values, 23 percent said that companies tolerate them, nearly 30 percent said that they receive "coaching," and 8 percent said that they even get promoted. About 22 percent said that the violators are penalized, but only 18 percent said that they get fired.

Not so at GE, says Ben Heineman, the general counsel. GE disciplines not only the employee violating its ethics code but also people who are aware of the violation but don't report it. Such failure to report might mean no salary increases for two years. "The sanctions become more severe the higher you go in the organization," says Heineman. "The chiefs have to be disciplined, not just the Indians." And anyone, he adds, "who touches a hair on the head of a whistle-blower is gone."

A VIRTUOUS TOBACCO COMPANY?

Guess which company has been the most active on the ethics front over the last few years? The answer is Altria Group, the new name for Philip Morris, which will probably surprise people who believe that behaving ethically and selling cigarettes are completely incompatible.

Altria clearly has its work cut out for it. It continues to be plagued by lawsuits accusing the company of concealing information about the health hazards and addictive nature of cigarettes. In a Harris Interactive survey in 2002 before its name change, Philip Morris ranked fifty-fifth out of sixty companies for maintaining high ethical standards. "How can you improve the reputation of a company selling time bombs to consumers in the form of tobacco products?" asks Tracy Tiffany, a survey respondent from Saint Joseph, Michigan. "Forget it."

But Altria isn't deterred by cynics who consider an ethical tobacco company a contradiction of terms. It has taken ethics responsibilities away from the legal department and placed them in a separate office under David Greenberg, senior vice president and chief compliance officer. He has a seat on the corporate management committee and reports to the senior vice president for corporate affairs and the audit committee of the board of directors. His office is located on the twenty-second floor of Altria Group's headquarters building in New York along with those of the CEO and other top managers. "I can walk down the hall to (Chairman and CEO) Louis Camilleri's office and resolve in thirty seconds what would take someone at a lower level two weeks," says Greenberg.

The forty-page Altria Code of Conduct for Compliance and Integrity details how to deal with such issues as competitive intelligence, investment conflicts of interest, privacy of customer data, and responsible marketing. Operating companies and corporate-level departments must submit annual compliance plans to Greenberg, who is accountable to the board's audit committee to ensure that the plans are in place and carried out.

Employees will be trained via the Internet. They will be presented with ethical problems that fall into the gray area and asked to make choices. Can a supplier invite you to stay at his home for the weekend? Can you ship a product right at the end of a quarter and book it in order to make your numbers? If people pick the wrong course of action, they will be tutored on the right response.

Some ethics codes and values programs are so general that they don't have much punch and are hard to follow. It's far better to be specific and try to tailor them to your company and industry. That's what Greenberg has accomplished with a risk assessment matrix to help Altria's managers determine the probability of certain risks and their potential impact on the company. Among the risks in the detailed matrix: manipulation of financial statements, embezzlement, insider trading, tobacco taxes, industrial espionage, trademark infringement, drug and alcohol abuse or weapons in the workplace, and defamation or harassment in employee e-mails.

The ethics program coincides with a growing focus on corporate responsibility and the name change to Altria. But employees still wondered if some nefarious act sparked it. "People asked whether we did something really wrong and whether the code is because of Enron," Greenberg says. Some employees also complained because Altria had put its new "integrity helpline" number at the bottom of every page of the code. "It looked like we wanted people to rat on everyone," Greenberg says. "We overdid it a bit."

ONE SIZE DOES *NOT* FIT ALL

Ethics codes must be elastic for companies doing business around the globe. Multinational companies have discovered that they must be sensitive to foreign cultures and customize their ethics policies to fit local customs. That isn't to say they can condone bribery or other illegal conduct. But U.S. mores don't necessarily apply in every country. A gift may be an ethical violation in some countries but merely a kind gesture in others.

PricewaterhouseCoopers learned that lesson recently as it developed its first global code of conduct, extending its six-year-old U.S. ethics program to offices around the world. Barbara Kipp, global leader for ethics and business conduct, recalls a female employee from Britain, who considered it unwanted attention when a partner in France took her to dinner and gave her a gift. But the Frenchman would have considered it rude to do otherwise. "We can't say to people in France and Japan to never give a gift," says Kipp. "We say we will avoid conflicts of interest and favoritism, but the details are left in the hands of the people in each country."

The accounting firm also decided against a global hotline because its international employees were unlikely to call, especially if they knew an American would answer. With loyalty to the local team of paramount importance in some countries, foreign employees are more likely to take ethical concerns to one of their colleagues.

Altria Group sought input from both U.S. and international employees as it crafted its ethics code. After meeting with employees in twenty focus groups in the United States, the Philippines, Ukraine, France, and Switzerland, Altria realized that the perspective was too American. It had used the example of a gift of Super Bowl tickets in one ethics situation and changed it to World Cup tickets. There was also a vignette about an employee returning from lunch with alcohol on his breath, but that didn't fly in France, where wine is frequently served at meals. So the anecdote was changed to describe a man looking impaired when he arrives at work in the morning.

"We also had to make our sexual harassment case more blatant," says Altria's Greenberg, "because in some countries it's okay to comment on a woman's appearance."

REAFFIRM, REINFORCE, REVISE

Take every opportunity to reaffirm and reinforce your corporate values and ethics. They also should be revisited regularly so they can be updated or strengthened to reflect changes in the company and in society. Values and ethics aren't the Ten Commandments; they shouldn't be preserved unchanged for centuries.

General Electric updated its integrity statement a few years go to add new policies and make it more global. More recently, in the wake of Arthur Andersen's notorious shredding of Enron files, GE revised its rules for document management. For example, it is dropping its automatic e-mail deletion system and telling employees to use their discretion and save anything that might be important on their computer's hard drive.

It's especially important to reaffirm or revise the corporate values and ethics when the company has undergone major strategic and management changes. Such turmoil can cause employees to doubt the company's continued commitment to its longtime principles.

In his annual state-of-the-business address to employees in early 2003, A. G. Lafley, chairman and CEO of Procter & Gamble, reaffirmed the company's values of leadership, ownership, integrity, passion for winning, and trust. It seemed especially necessary in the wake of his successful but sometimes painful restructuring of the consumer products company, which had included thousands of layoffs.

He said that executives had considered whether the company's "purpose, values and principles" should be changed but decided firmly against it. "They are an unchanging compass," he told employees, "that guides us through even the most volatile changes."

Levi Strauss has also been reassuring its employees that its dedication to integrity and social responsibility hasn't wavered. The philosophy of sharing the company's prosperity dates back to founder Levi Strauss's donation of five dollars to a San Francisco orphanage in 1854. But nearly 150 years later, some employees had started to worry that the jeans maker's "profits with principles" business strategy might be endangered. The company had been losing the market share battle in the jeans business, and for the first time, the CEO had been chosen from outside the founding family.

It seemed an appropriate time to renew Levi's commitment to ethical behavior. The company issued a brand new "Values and Vision" statement, which focuses on four primary attributes—empathy, originality, integrity, and courage—and Philip Marineau, the new CEO, pledged his support.

"Employees were concerned because they knew some of the new leadership had come from companies where values weren't as strong," says Robert Haas, the company's chairman and great-great-grandnephew of Levi Strauss. "But now they see an intensified recommitment to the values that make them proud to work here."

BE ENTERTAINING AND ENGAGING

Ethics can be fun. Yeah, right. Many people would do anything to get out of a meeting or training session about ethics compliance. Their immediate reaction: boring!

How can you make serious subjects such as sexual harassment and bribery entertaining? Well, just consider what some of the companies with the most comprehensive ethics programs are doing to engage their employees and motivate them to do the right thing.

General Electric's NBC television network created a videotape for employees that is quite candid about its ethical lapses. NBC News reporter Ann Curry reports on GE's ethics policies much as she would handle a story for the NBC program *Dateline*. She describes several cases of unethical behavior at GE, including a bogus contract for aircraft engines with the Israeli Air Force that involved an Israeli general and a senior marketing manager at GE. The pair diverted $11 million into a

Swiss bank account. There are also intriguing stories about a failed attempt to launder money by purchasing $40,000 of GE air conditioners and a government bribery case involving a joint venture in Japan. "Vice sometimes works better than virtue in connecting with your employees," says GE's Heineman.

Greenberg, the ethics chief at Altria Group, is also well aware of "the boredom factor" when the subject is ethics. So he often resorts to humor. When he was making a presentation to a group of lawyers, an actor in a superhero costume suddenly jumped onstage and started looking over his notes. Next, in a parody of the old television show *The Twilight Zone*, a Rod Serling–like character appeared and announced that everyone was about to enter the "Compliance Zone." Actors then presented ethical dilemmas, and the audience voted on solutions.

Raytheon's ethics training may be the most entertaining. Raytheon enlisted movie critic Roger Ebert and created a parody of his long-running movie-review program. But in this case, his partner in the balcony isn't another film critic; it's Patty Ellis, Raytheon's ethics guru. Instead of actual movies, they watch film clips of workplace dramas and critique the actors' responses to unethical conduct.

How would you rate the handling of this ethics quandary from the training video? When a young woman asks for time off, her supervisor takes her hand and tries to talk her into going out on a date. She firmly refuses, and he backs down after persuading her to let the matter drop. Thumbs up or thumbs down? Ebert gave it a thumbs-up because the woman resisted her boss's romantic overtures. But for Ellis, it's thumbs down: the employee should have reported the sexual harassment to her supervisors to prevent her boss from bothering other women.

Some Raytheon employees were skeptical at first when they heard about the training video because they felt that ethical issues aren't exactly a laughing matter. "But now they absolutely love it," says Ellis. "And we hand out microwave popcorn to add to the fun." But more important, the Ebert-Ellis show made a strong impression on employees.

LAW FIVE

BE A MODEL CITIZEN

Jeffrey Swartz, the president of Timberland Company, was getting lambasted. Virginia Kent, a member of Timberland's board of directors, was dressing him down for what she perceived to be a failure to publicize the company's many socially responsible activities in its own stores.

Suddenly, Swartz started chuckling. Kent, taken aback at his response, demanded to know what was so funny. It isn't that your criticisms aren't justified, Swartz told her. "I'm just pleasantly surprised to find you're such an advocate of our social justice strategy."

For Swartz, that boardroom exchange marked a major breakthrough. Most Timberland employees had long ago embraced the company's vision of making the world a better place. Now his directors—"red-blooded capitalists," Swartz calls them—were signing on, too. "I worked so hard for the day," he says, "when an independent outside director would yell because there was not enough evidence of our social justice programs in the stores."

Jeffrey Swartz is the poster boy for corporate citizenship. He doesn't do it just because it's the right thing. He's made social and environmental responsibility an integral part of the company's identity and one of the most significant elements of its reputation. Timberland's dedication to socially responsible activities motivates its workers and wins praise from customers, retailers, and investors. Swartz says that he includes discussion of social responsibility in his conference calls and meetings with securities analysts and seeks institutional support from mutual funds with a social and environmental focus.

Timberland's model-citizen image also opens doors to new business. Not long ago, Swartz attended a White House event with Robert Nardelli, chairman and CEO of Home Depot. In talking about their companies' commitments to social and environmental issues and other business matters, Swartz wasn't shy. He took the opportunity to make a business pitch: Might Home Depot be interested in stocking Timberland's PRO line of boots? he wondered. In no time, Nardelli had put Home Depot's merchandising managers in touch with Timberland.

Timberland's social responsibility agenda includes monitoring labor conditions at its contractors' overseas factories, improving energy efficiency at its facilities, and reducing leather waste and the use of chemical solvents. But most distinctive is its focus on volunteerism, dating back to 1989, when the company became a founding sponsor of a youth service organization called City Year. Inspired by the young volunteers, Swartz decided to bring the concept inside the company. In 1992, he created a Social Enterprise department at Timberland and began offering employees sixteen hours of paid leave a year to do volunteer work.

The idea was to give people the opportunity to do community service but not tell them what to do—let them "discover the goodness inside themselves," as Swartz puts it. The sixteen hours have gradually expanded to forty, and Timberland has also begun offering employees six-month paid sabbaticals to work with nonprofit organizations, including an orphanage in Peru and a community food bank in Somersworth, New Hampshire. "It matters to me to work for a company with humanity and integrity," says Maureen Franzosa, a senior merchandise analyst who took a sabbatical to help out at a sexual assault support agency in Portsmouth, New Hampshire. "We're not saving the world every day, but the desire to do so permeates the atmosphere at Timberland."

Corporate citizenship is still a work in progress at Timberland. There is dissent and discourse about how far to carry it, but if you don't believe social responsibility is part of the business, you don't really belong at Timberland.

Swartz is far from satisfied with Timberland's overall performance, however. He says he takes it as a personal failure when employees don't join in the volunteer programs. The company isn't happy that few employees use all forty hours of paid community service time and that volunteerism hasn't taken hold more strongly among senior managers and foreign employees. "I want social responsibility to become embodied in the company, part of our corporate DNA," Swartz declares. "I'm not just a limousine liberal."

HEART AND SOUL

Over the past decade, corporate citizenship has become much more than a line in a company's values statement. It is now one of the key elements of the reputation equation. It's not a choice anymore; it's part of the cost of doing business in the new millennium.

Companies are increasingly being judged on their treatment of the environment, their involvement in the communities where factories and offices are located, their support of charities and social causes, and their respect for the natural environment. They need to demonstrate that they have heart and soul, especially at a time when the public is so distrustful of corporate America.

That's why Weyerhaeuser runs full-page newspaper ads pointing out that it plants 100 million seedlings a year as part of the "special responsibility of managing a resource as precious as trees"; why Toyota advertises its hydrogen-powered fuel-cell vehicles and support of family literacy programs; why the banking company HSBC Holdings encourages employees to apply to become environmental fellows and venture from their offices for two weeks to track jaguars in Brazil or observe dolphins in New Zealand; and why General Electric and other companies let the world know about their multimillion-dollar donations following the September 11, 2001, terrorist attacks on the World Trade Center and the Pentagon.

If you still think such activities don't matter much, consider these statistics. More than three quarters of respondents to a 2002 survey by the public relations firm Cone said that a company's commitment to social issues is important in deciding where they work, who does business in their communities, and which products and services they recommend to other people. About two thirds also said that social responsibility affects which stocks they buy. Indeed, in 2002, even as some mutual

---

SEPTEMBER 11 REPUTATION BOOST

Corporate America clearly improved its reputation with its outpouring of support following the terrorist attacks of September 11, 2001. A survey by Harris Interactive found people both impressed and surprised by the magnitude of the corporate response. Unfortunately, the Enron debacle, Wall Street conflicts of interest, and other corporate scandals followed soon after and certainly diminished the positive effects of the September 11 relief effort.

Percentage of people impressed by the corporate response to 9/11:
Very: 46%
Somewhat: 42%
Not very/not at all: 12%

Percentage of people surprised by the corporate response to 9/11:
Very: 18%
Somewhat: 40%
Not very/not at all: 42%

---

funds suffered sharp withdrawals, socially responsible funds attracted more money.

Corporate virtue goes by many names these days: social responsibility, environmental stewardship, sustainable development, and the triple bottom line, among others. Corporate citizenship seems best, however, because it's an umbrella term that covers all the bases.

To be sure, there is still debate over where a company's primary responsibility lies. A Harris Interactive public opinion poll found people split on how far citizenship should reach. More than half believe companies' responsibility should be limited to employees, customers, and local communities, as well as shareholders. About 45 percent, however, feel that companies must address global social problems, too.

Only 1 percent said a company's responsibility is simply to generate profits for its shareholders. That small minority sides with economist Milton Friedman and his famous declaration that the notion of social responsibility is "a fundamentally subversive doctrine" in a free society. He went on to say, "There is one and only one social responsibility of business—to use its resources and engage in activities designed to increase its profits so long as it stays within the rules of the game."

But such thinking won't fly today at any company interested in cultivating a positive reputation. Multinational companies can't afford to limit the reach of their philanthropy to their own backyards at a time when antiglobalization forces routinely charge them with irresponsible behavior—from trashing the environment to exploiting cheap labor. The heat is definitely being turned up. More and more activists, battling everything from genetically engineered food to wood from endangered forests, are swooping down on companies with demands for corporate reform. A coalition of religious groups is even invoking God's name in advertisements that ask "What would Jesus drive?" and argue for more fuel-efficient vehicles that pollute less.

That doesn't mean that companies must make social activism their obsession, as gourmet ice cream marketer Ben & Jerry's Homemade and Body Shop International did in the 1980s. But it must become a core part of the business and must be communicated regularly to all of the company's constituencies. The trick is to make your corporate citizenship powerful and highly visible without looking as if you're just out for glory.

Being a do-gooder will surely gain in importance. Business schools are paying much more attention to it in grooming MBA students. They are establishing full-blown programs in corporate citizenship and running business-plan competitions for socially responsible new ventures. Ford Motor Company, for instance, donated $3 million to Northwestern University's Kellogg School of Management to establish the Center for Global Citizenship. There's even a Web site that offers professors case studies on social and environmental matters for their MBA courses.

OWN THE CAUSE

Avon Products, IBM, Johnson & Johnson, and Levi Strauss each "owns" one of the following causes: education, AIDS, nursing, and breast cancer. Can you guess which company goes with which cause? If the companies have succeeded in their corporate citizenship strategies, you would have matched Avon with breast cancer, IBM with education, J&J with nursing, and Levi Strauss with AIDS.

Many of you probably made the correct choices because owning a major cause is by far the best way to develop a strong reputation for

CAUSE DU JOUR

Many companies poll employees, shareholder, customers, or sometimes all three to determine which causes resonate most with their stakeholder groups. But they need to repeat the survey frequently because people's preferences change with world events. These results from surveys of American adults by the public relations firm Cone show the most popular causes in recent years. Only medical research is consistently listed as a top priority.

March 2001
1. Crime
2. Medical research
3. Hunger/poverty
4. Drug and alcohol abuse
5. Environment

October 2001
1. National tragedy (September 11)
2. Medical research
3. Education
4. Support for military
5. Homelessness

July 2002
1. Education
2. Medical research
3. Poverty
4. Environment
5. College scholarships

social responsibility. Even Andrew Carnegie practiced this approach with his contributions to building libraries and increasing literacy.

Companies that support a potpourri of philanthropic organizations aren't closely linked to any in the public's mind, and their social responsibility activities tend to blur. But by championing one issue and channeling most of its money and talent into it, a company can become almost synonymous with it.

When women think of breast cancer, Avon's name comes quickly to mind. Never mind that many other companies, including archrival

Revlon, also raise funds for the breast cancer cause. The strong connection hit home not long ago for Robert Corti, Avon's chief financial officer. He delivered a speech at the College of the Holy Cross in Worcester, Massachusetts, where his son is a student, and a physician came up afterward to thank him for Avon's funding of breast cancer research.

Social responsibility is nothing new at Avon; just the strategy has changed. In fact, David McConnell, who founded California Perfume Company, the predecessor of Avon, in 1886, included in his list of corporate principles: "to meet fully the obligations of corporate citizenship by contributing to the well-being of society, and the environment in which it functions."

A primary global cause is especially important for a multinational company like Avon, which sells its cosmetics in 143 countries. "It's easier when you have a single focus," says Andrea Jung, Avon's chairman and CEO, who lost her grandmother to breast cancer. "Our shareholders and every sales associate around the world know what we're trying to achieve. It's a very galvanizing cause for them."

Avon's breast cancer campaign began more than a decade ago in Britain as a grassroots program based on what saleswomen and consumers nominated as the most important cause to them. From a pink-ribbon pin and other pink products, the campaign evolved to include fund-raising walks and more personal connections with women. Sales representatives hand out pamphlets to their customers showing how to do a self-exam, and Avon's Web site includes online support groups for women with breast cancer.

Altogether, the Avon Breast Cancer Crusade has generated more than $250 million for an array of international programs. The company helps fund medical research, buys mammogram machines, and pays transportation and child care costs for low-income women receiving treatment.

Owning a cause doesn't mean saying no to every other needy organization. While the breast cancer crusade is global, Avon allows for local markets to focus on other issues. In Asia, for example, elder care is a major concern, while Europeans are interested in recycling. Avon also donates fashion accessories and money to Dress for Success, a global organization that provides interview outfits and career coaching to low-income women.

Avon is counting on its strong reputation, including the breast cancer crusade, to help it make its new push into the teen market. Parents, it hopes, will be more willing to let their daughters sell Avon products because they know they can trust the company to be responsible. "We walk the talk," says Jung, "and people know it."

GET IN FRONT OF THE PARADE

There's a place in this world for activists, no doubt about it. Without them, this country would still be lagging on civil rights, a cleaner environment, and other worthy causes. But never forget: Most activists are your enemy. You have to beat them to the punch, or you may find your company on the painful end of a boycott or, at the very least, a lot of bad publicity. And when you're in that position, it's pretty certain you're going to lose.

The wisest strategy is to take the lead in your industry in reacting to controversial issues. Avon, for example, moved quickly to halt the use of laboratory animals in its cosmetics testing in 1989, and in 1991 Levi Strauss became the first multinational to establish a comprehensive code of ethical conduct for its overseas manufacturing and finishing contractors. Today, both companies enjoy good relations with activist organizations.

But you can't chalk up many reputation points if the public perceives you as a reluctant corporate citizen publicly harassed into behaving nobly. Home Depot learned that lesson, even though it enjoys an overall positive reputation for social responsibility. It works with young people who have never completed high school to transform abandoned buildings into affordable housing. It has sponsored a road-trip exhibit of an original copy of the Declaration of Independence. And it is always on the scene at disasters with building materials to help make repairs.

But its halo got tarnished when it became the target of protests during the 1990s because of its sale of products made of "old-growth wood" from endangered ancient forests. Activists grilled executives at annual meetings and staged well-publicized stunts at Home Depot stores, including a takeover of their intercom systems. On St. Patrick's Day, 1999, environmentalists obtained the access codes for the intercoms and announced to stunned store managers and customers: "Attention, shoppers. On aisle seven you'll find mahogany ripped from the heart of the Amazon."

To its credit, the company pledged later that year to gradually stop selling products containing wood from endangered forests. But how much better Home Depot would have looked had it taken the initiative earlier and settled with the forest preservation groups before they resorted to noisy protests. Even today, Web sites still call for "stopping Home Depot's theft of our rain forests."

ACTIONS SPEAK LOUDER THAN MONEY

If you want to boost your reputation for corporate citizenship, don't just reach for your checkbook. The best way is to provide products and services to a good cause rather than simply money. People are much more impressed. It's like comparing a handmade gift with a check. One requires personal attention, planning, and labor; the other, just a fat wallet.

So it was at Ground Zero in Manhattan after September 11, 2001, that McDonald's, which supplied burgers and chicken nuggets to rescue workers around the clock, received far more enthusiastic kudos than any of the companies that donated cash. Somehow it seemed more heartfelt and humanitarian to be on the scene helping out. What's more, McDonald's good deeds were chronicled in the extensive television coverage of the tragedy, so that the company didn't need to crow about its own kindness.

IBM, one of the staunchest opponents of checkbook charity, uses its technological prowess to help solve societal problems rather than just throw money at them. IBM decided to focus primarily on education based on feedback from employees, shareholders, and community leaders, and in 1995, it launched Reinventing Education to improve students' achievement. "Money in and of itself doesn't solve problems," says Stanley Litow, president of the IBM Foundation and vice president of the corporate community relations program. He knows all too well about money and troubled schools as former deputy chancellor and chief operating officer of the New York City Board of Education, the nation's largest school system and one of its most distressed.

To date, IBM has invested some $70 million in its education initiative. Among the projects: a summer camp to encourage girls' interest in math and science, voice recognition technology for learning to read, an online system for conducting parent-teacher conferences, and a distance-learning theater program for high school students in remote areas far from Broadway.

What's the payoff for all that effort? It's difficult for companies to measure the bottom-line results of most of their benevolent deeds. IBM does note that its community projects lead to new products and services that clearly will benefit the company, including more than twenty new patents in such areas as digital library and voice recognition technology. The company also sees improvements in the skills and morale of employees who serve as project managers and technology advisers in the schools.

The intangible rewards, however, will prove most meaningful over the long run. IBM has received a slew of honors from government and philanthropic organizations for its largesse, and in an independent survey of teachers, it was named most often as America's top corporate supporter of education. The company expects such recognition to translate into reputation benefits that will influence public officials and attract new customers and investors for years to come.

CHIEF CORPORATE CITIZEN

Too many CEOs farm out their philanthropic activities to a foundation director and get involved only if they have a pet cause to push. But the CEO must assume the role of chief corporate citizen if social responsibility is to permeate the culture and become one of the company's chief reputation attributes. That's the role taken by leaders like Andrea Jung at Avon, Louis Gerstner at IBM, and Jeffrey Swartz at Timberland.

Jung participates in breast cancer walks, cuts the ribbon at health clinic openings in developing countries, and is chairman of Avon's new Corporate Social Responsibility Council. While CEO of IBM, Gerstner played host to national education summits at the company's Armonk, New York, headquarters. And Swartz makes his good deeds a family affair, taking his young sons along to shelters for homeless veterans.

Levi Strauss Chairman Robert Haas demonstrated especially courageous leadership back in 1982, when the mysterious AIDS virus was ravaging the gay community in Levi's hometown of San Francisco. The disease was still little understood, and some employees wanted to hand out fliers warning others at the company about it. But these lower-level employees were afraid of being stigmatized and hurting their job prospects if they publicly associated themselves with AIDS. So Haas himself, along with other senior executives, manned an information table and distributed the fliers. The company foundation also became a pioneer in the AIDS fight, with its contributions to date exceeding $25 million. "Being committed to doing the right thing means taking risks," says Haas.

In taking the lead, the CEO should avoid the temptation to enrich his pet charity or his alma mater or use philanthropy to get his wife on the board of the local ballet company. More enlightened companies, such as Avon, survey their employees periodically to find out the causes that matter most to them. It's a great morale booster and a tool for attracting and retaining the best and brightest workers.

And of course, the CEO shouldn't even think about tying philanthropy to a payback. Just look at what happened to Citigroup's reputation in the philanthropic community in the heat of the scandals over Wall Street analysts' conflicts of interest. E-mails surfaced in the press suggesting that Jack Grubman, the former top telecommunications analyst at Citigroup's Salomon Smith Barney securities unit, had raised his rating of AT&T's stock partly to secure help from Citigroup CEO Sandy Weill in getting his twins admitted to a prestigious New York preschool. It turned out that the twins made it in, and around the same time, Citigroup's philanthropic arm generously pledged a $1 million donation to the 92nd Street Y, which runs the preschool. The 92nd Street Y and Citigroup denied there had been any quid pro quo, but the episode certainly planted the perception that Citigroup's charitable contributions could be obtained in exchange for personal favors.

MIXING CHARITY WITH COMMERCE

Some companies practice what they call "strategic philanthropy," which links their good deeds to corporate goals. They believe this helps appease shareholders who are more interested in short-term profits than in long-term social benefits.

For example, State Farm Insurance Companies often makes contributions to increase public safety, such as offering free inspections of child safety seats and providing up to $120,000 for safety studies and improvements to a particularly dangerous traffic intersection. Fewer car accidents and serious injuries and fatalities are certainly in the best interest of both the public and State Farm's bottom line.

To boost its women's shoe and apparel business, Timberland teamed with Macy's and Dillard's department stores on a promotion that included a customer sweepstakes and a $10,000 donation to Share Our Strength, an organization that fights hunger and poverty in America. Macy's and Timberland employees also performed a day of community service at a center for pregnant teenagers in New York.

And Johnson & Johnson is a major supporter of nurses, who obviously play a big part in its business success. It has partnered with the Wharton School at the University of Pennsylvania for three weeks of management training for nurses and created a Web site and advertising campaign to attract more people to the nursing profession.

There's nothing wrong with such strategic business thinking as long as altruism remains a strong driving force. But another popular approach—cause-related marketing—has become much less effective in reputation enhancement. With cause-related marketing, companies donate all or a portion of their product sales to a charity. For one thing, it isn't as purely philanthropic because of the close commercial connection. What's more, cause-related campaigns have been greatly overdone. Back in 1983, it was a fresh concept when American Express donated a penny for every credit card transaction and $1 for every new card issued to help pay for the restoration of the Statue of Liberty. Transactions increased by 30%, while the number of new cards issued rose 15%.

Since then, however, literally hundreds of companies have linked marketing and charity. It's a hackneyed technique. But if you still feel you want to connect product sales to charitable donations, at least don't be chintzy. Give away the lion's share of the revenue you raise. Newman's Own, actor Paul Newman's food company, owes its stellar reputation to the fact that it donates all of its aftertax profits to education and charity—a total to date of more than $125 million.

MEASURE THE RESULTS

As important as it is to reputation, corporate citizenship is still a hard sell to stubborn shareholders and skeptical employees. Some of your stakeholders will never sway from their belief that only profits and stock price matter, but you may succeed in winning some converts if you can demonstrate accountability. Smart companies provide detailed, public information on how their philanthropic programs are working. Such transparency adds to the credibility of corporate citizenship activities and further enhances reputation. It demonstrates the company's dedication to making sure its contributions are actually doing some good and to monitoring the performance of its beneficiaries. Accountability is just good business and should impress many of your employees and shareholders.

Merck, the pharmaceutical manufacturer, underscored the success of its program to improve science teaching with third-party validation by the Consortium for Policy Research in Education at the University of Pennsylvania. The consortium found that the Merck program has significantly strengthened teachers' skills and science knowledge in four public school districts in New Jersey and Pennsylvania. It has even managed to make science careers appealing to girls and minority students who had never previously expressed an interest in the study of science.

"We evaluate our community relations work just as we would other parts of our business," says IBM's Litow. A three-year study by an independent organization called the Center for Children and Technology provided evidence of improvement in students' performance, teaching quality, and school management in the districts that are part of the company's Reinventing Education program.

Some companies keep very close track of exactly where the money goes. At Avon, for example, the results of its breast cancer contributions are listed in striking detail on its Web site, including 201,890,000 free educational fliers distributed in twenty-one countries, 36,000 free mammograms in Argentina, 6,421,380 clinical exams in 360 cities in Mexico, and 1,300,000 women educated about the cancer in Ukraine.

THE PERILS OF PROMOTING PHILANTHROPY

Is it philanthropy or profiteering? Americans tend to be highly skeptical about the motivation behind messages of social and environmental responsibility, and they aren't very forgiving if a company fails to live up to the good neighbor image it projects.

The typical reaction is "Hmm, there must be something in it for the company." Many people also suspect that philanthropy is an attempt to deflect attention away from negative news. That was the public reaction to both Philip Morris (now named Altria Group) and Microsoft when they promoted their good deeds.

General Electric's ads also met with some skepticism. For the first time, GE's corporate advertising campaign included messages about its $30 million "college bound" program for students and employee volunteers who serve pancakes to the elderly, clean playgrounds, and read to kindergartners. The positive message in those ads, however, was certainly offset for many people by GE's protracted battle with regulators over cleaning up its extensive pollution of the Hudson River, as well as news of the lavish retirement package of former CEO John F. Welch, Jr. Indeed, Jobs with Justice, a worker advocacy group, named GE its National Grinch of the Year in 2002 because it said the company was trying to shift more health care costs to its workers after giving Welch such a swell going-away package.

So scandal-scarred companies such as MCI and Tyco International needn't waste their time and money talking up any philanthropic activities. At this point, the public doesn't want to hear it.

But for the vast majority of companies, the public does crave information about their records on social and environmental responsibility to help decide which to buy from, invest in, and work for. Yet many people find themselves in the dark. Of twenty attributes in an annual corporate reputation survey by Harris Interactive, the question of whether a company supports good causes usually elicits the largest percentage of "not sure" responses.

Corporate communications officials are understandably confused about how best to publicize their good works, given that the public itself is split over the best approach. About half of the respondents to the Harris survey believe that advertising and press releases are appropriate, but 40 percent prefer a less splashy message and recommend using annual reports and corporate Web sites for philanthropic information.

Sarah Marcus, a survey respondent from Madison, Wisconsin, is in the latter camp. "I wish companies would just back off and stop flaunting their donations in newspaper and television ads that I have to see whether I want to or not," she says. "Companies hope I'll end up feeling more warmly about them and will buy their products, but advertising defeats the altruism in my mind."

How do you reap reputation points for your social responsibility? It isn't easy. Merck, for example, has been stumped about how best to get some credit for its benevolence. It would like to change the perception of pharmaceutical companies from cold-blooded profiteers to compassionate seekers of medical cures. Merck and other drug companies have come under heavy attack for the surging prices of pharmaceuticals and their limited availability to people in need, whether America's poor or Africa's AIDS victims.

But Merck does have positive stories to tell, including annual philanthropic contributions of $340 million in cash and products. Since 1987, for example, the company has provided more than 700 million tablets of Mectizan to people at risk for developing so-called river blindness in some of the poorest countries in the world.

Merck traditionally was more concerned about communicating with physicians than with consumers. But now company executives acknowledge that they must pay more attention to Merck's public reputation because politicians are lumping the pharmaceutical industry with the tobacco industry as just another bunch of unethical, greedy companies. Merck recently did post a social responsibility report on its Web site, but that reaches only people who care enough to search out such information.

Companies often find they're damned if they do and damned if they don't. Some companies decide to take the high road and let their actions speak for themselves. But silence can be as risky as boastfulness. Such companies as Procter & Gamble, Johnson & Johnson, and Toyota, which didn't widely promote their September 11 philanthropy, were criticized by some people who assumed they hadn't pitched in to help. J&J sent a straightforward advisory to the news media listing its donations of cash and products to the relief effort, but only as a defensive move. Investors and employees were firing off e-mails complaining that they hadn't read or heard about anything that J&J was doing to help the survivors and rescue workers.

During tragic events such as the terrorist attacks, people become particularly sensitive about companies' motives for promoting their good deeds. Verizon Communications informed its customers of its charitable donations and its efforts to provide telecommunications services in downtown Manhattan through a letter rather than advertising. But even that approach offended a few people, who complained to Verizon that they found it boastful and felt the company was taking advantage of the tragedy to promote itself.

Some companies say they took great pains to avoid appearing self-serving after September 11. For example, Avon tried not to seem mercenary in full-page newspaper ads that thanked its sales representatives for raising more than $7 million in charitable contributions through the sale of a heart-shaped American flag pin. The company was very careful not to include a phone number or Web site address in the ad to avoid appearing as if it were trying to sell something.

To communicate its breast cancer program and other social responsibility activities, Avon is more interested in creating buzz in the market than in counting press clippings. So it capitalizes on the credibility its sales reps enjoy when they visit their customers' homes. The saleswomen chat about Avon's philanthropic ventures or include printed information with the orders they deliver.

Some companies believe that advertising can succeed if it is handled sensitively. Ronald McDonald House Charities for the first time recently developed documentary-style commercials to showcase its camp for children with cancer, a baseball field for special needs children, and lodging facilities for the families of seriously ill children in nearby hospitals. McDonald's, on the other hand, released its first global social responsibility report on its Web site. "We wanted to be transparent on these issues but not do a lot of self-promotion," says Walt Riker, corporate vice president for communications.

Media coverage of philanthropy provides the most credible publicity. It's usually safe to let the beneficiaries do the talking to the media and work in a plug for the company. Best of all is making your projects so interesting that they're a natural for media publicity.

That has been IBM's strategy. The company has created only a couple of low-key ads tying corporate philanthropy, such as a disaster relief Web site it helped develop for the Red Cross, with its e-business brand campaign. But it has sparked lots of media stories about such projects as the digital replication of Michelangelo's second Pietà statue and the creation of a virtual State Hermitage Museum on the Web for people who can't travel all the way to Saint Petersburg, Russia. IBM may have played second fiddle to the art projects, but it couldn't ever have bought the credibility the media coverage delivered.

LAW SIX

CONVEY A COMPELLING CORPORATE VISION

It almost seemed meant to be. BP—Beyond Petroleum. The energy giant's name lent itself perfectly to its new slogan and new vision. It was a striking change for a company whose initials had originally stood for British Petroleum. But then, BP's vision for the twenty-first century was striking indeed—and a bit puzzling—coming from the world's second largest oil company.

What BP aims to do is seize the moral high ground. It is making a major effort to position itself as a new breed of energy company, one that is environmentally friendly, with alternative energy projects and other green initiatives.

BP understands that vision is one of the most essential ingredients in the reputation recipe. A visionary company inspires confidence about the future and takes a leadership position in its industry. Although BP is part of an unpopular industry, its well-articulated vision may succeed in elevating it above many of its competitors. Other companies such as Royal Dutch/Shell Group are also trying to communicate a "green" vision. But none has put its name on the line to the degree that BP has with its Beyond Petroleum mantra.

The new vision coincided with an urgent need to rebrand BP. The company had gone on an acquisitions spree in the 1990s, scooping up

Amoco, Atlantic Richfield, and Castrol. It needed a new corporate brand to unite all these companies. British Petroleum was much too provincial for a business operating in more than a hundred countries. More significantly, BP wanted an identity that was more about energy and the future than about its roots in the dirty oil business.

The Beyond Petroleum vision didn't materialize out of nowhere. BP proudly points out that it was the first major oil company—in 1997—to publicly recognize the risks of global warming. It is also ahead of government mandates and its own schedule in reducing the sulfur content in its fuel and keeping its promise to cut "greenhouse gas" emissions. As for new energy sources, BP expects its solar business to produce revenues of $1 billion by 2007 (still just a sliver of its total annual revenues of $179 billion), and it is building gas stations powered partly by solar panels.

"I believe people expect a company like BP to offer answers, not excuses," says John Browne, BP's group chief executive. "They expect successful companies to take on challenges, to apply skills and technology and to give them better choices. Well, we are ready to do our part—to reinvent the energy business and stabilize our emissions." Lord Browne has pledged to keep greenhouse gas emissions at the company's 2002 levels even though BP plans to increase its oil and gas production by 5.5 percent a year. The 2002 emissions level is 10 percent less than in 1990, an achievement BP made eight years ahead of its original plan.

Beyond Petroleum clearly is more than just sizzle. Whether or not all stakeholders buy into BP's vision, it's still a powerful statement. The company and its communications agencies have created an unusually comprehensive vision plan. There's no confusion about BP's stated mission—and no way to miss it either. If people didn't catch the long-running ad campaign, they're almost certain to drive by one of the redesigned BP gas stations.

BP's vision of moving beyond the energy source that has been its lifeblood represents such a dramatic change that the company needed groundbreaking ads, as well. Marketing officials believed their advertising would be dismissed if it followed the typical corporate approach of showing oil workers on offshore drilling rigs or alongside pipelines in the Alaskan wilderness. "We decided let's give a voice to consumers," says Patricia Wright, vice president of external affairs for BP North America.

It seemed most appropriate that the advertising capture the public's skepticism about Big Oil. So BP representatives wandered through the streets of major cities with video cameras in hand and interviewed more than four hundred people about their thoughts on oil companies, global warming, alternative energy, and the environment. As expected, the responses were mostly cynical. "I figure that the oil companies pay the motor companies not to put out a vehicle that's cleaner, healthier for our environment," Alfred Espinosa, a heavy-equipment operator, says in one ad. In another, Miranda Richardson, a ballet teacher, asks, "What are the oil companies' priorities? Their biggest priority is to make money. There's got to be a balance and maybe their balance is a little bit off."

BP also created a new corporate look, replacing its well-recognized BP shield with a new logo. Called the Helios trademark after the mythological god of the sun, the green and yellow circle is meant to represent a burst of energy but also resemble a sunflower. BP is careful that its sponsorships and other marketing fit its new vision, as well. Instead of sponsoring a car race, for example, it put its name on a sailing event.

But Beyond Petroleum involves much more than marketing and design. BP has put together a reputation management team of people from corporate communications, human resources, advertising, investor relations, and government relations. BP also created brand games and books to impress its new vision on its employees. "We focused heavily on employee communications to make workers proud of our new vision," Wright says. "Our new reputation also is helping BP recruit students on campus and attract experienced technical employees."

A survey after the internal branding campaign showed that 76 percent of employees felt favorably toward the BP–Beyond Petroleum positioning and 90 percent believed the company was moving in the right direction.

On the one hand, BP has embraced a popular vision that has great potential to burnish its corporate reputation. But it also has set itself up for intense scrutiny. If it retreats from its commitment to alternative fuels, the critics will be waiting to pounce. Even worse, an oil spill or other major environmental accident could seriously undermine BP's credibility and reputation. The skeptics in BP's own ads are mild compared with the news media and environmental watchdog groups.

Already, activists call the Beyond Petroleum vision mostly rhetoric and one of the most blatant examples ever of "greenwashing." Greenpeace labels BP one of the "corporate culprits" behind global warming and mocks its image campaign. "The truth behind BP's campaign is that the company is spending paltry sums on renewable energy while spending billions grabbing up oil wherever it can," Greenpeace scolds. "BP pays generous lip service to the global warming threat."

BP also came under attack for being part of the major lobbying group pushing to open the Arctic National Wildlife Refuge in Alaska to oil drilling. But in late 2002, it pulled out of the Arctic Power organization.

Beyond the environmental issues, the news media and other skeptics have pointed out that it's disingenuous for BP to claim that it's beyond petroleum, when its revenues and profits flow primarily from fossil fuels.

BP's response to its many skeptics is contained in its advertising tagline: It's a start. "We're saying we don't have it all figured out, but we're trying," says David Welch, director of global retail communications.

The company isn't surprised by the barbs from the media and environmentalists. "Any leader puts itself at risk," says Wright. "Anybody in our industry has the opportunity for accidents." Indeed, BP's safety record in Alaska was blemished by an oil well explosion in 2002 that seriously injured a worker. In addition, California regulators sued BP in 2003 for $319 million for alleged air pollution violations at an oil refinery.

Such trouble may be common for energy companies, but BP is positioning itself as a promising new kind of energy producer. It must convincingly resolve these problems to minimize damage to its vision and reputation.

It can be done. Two of the most socially and environmentally responsible companies of the 1980s came under fire for not living up to their mission—and survived the assault. Body Shop International, the British marketer of skin care products, and Ben & Jerry's Homemade, the Vermont ice cream company, were widely admired for their commitment to the environment and social justice. But in the 1990s, skeptics accused them of not living up to their pledges to buy raw materials from small suppliers in rainforests and other Third World communities. The companies lost some credibility with the public. But both survived with their reputations intact and today remain highly focused on corporate responsibility.

Whether BP's vision can withstand intense scrutiny is uncertain. BP has promoted an incredibly bold vision and put its corporate reputation on the line as never before. The big question over the next few years will be: Was Beyond Petroleum the slickest PR ploy ever by an embattled oil giant or the sincere new vision of a futuristic energy company?

VISION AND LEADERSHIP

Every company needs a dreamer. Usually, it's the founder, who has a passion and a plan when launching the business. And the aspirations are about much more than becoming rich and famous. They might be revolutionary—such as the invention of the telephone or the development of the personal computer. More likely they're more modest. A company may be driven to treat disease, provide more efficient and comfortable transportation service, or make technology more user-friendly and affordable.

Whatever the precise vision, it should give the company a clear sense of direction and purpose. The company stands for something that can be clearly articulated. The CEO must champion the vision, and employees must believe in it. The more compelling the vision, the more it will lift a company's reputation with its many stakeholders. They will perceive a visionary company to be well prepared to adapt to a fickle marketplace and volatile economy. If it is seen as a leader in its industry, it will almost certainly earn the public's admiration. In a recent survey by the Judge Institute of Management at the University of Cambridge, multinational CEOs named vision and leadership as the number one factors in preserving a positive corporate reputation.

"A computer on every desk and in every home." That's what Microsoft founders Bill Gates and Paul Allen said when the company set off on its journey to become the world's dominant software company. Underlying that ambitious but simple statement, of course, were more complex technologies and marketplace strategies. But what mattered most was that Gates and Allen were true visionaries. Although many critics scoffed at their dream of the ubiquitous computer, they saw the potential to turn a hobbyist's toy into an essential part of most people's daily lives.

For four straight years, Microsoft was ranked number 1 for vision and leadership by the Harris Interactive corporate reputation survey. Microsoft's vision has enabled it to foresee changes in the marketplace, adapt to them, and capitalize on them more quickly than the competi-

---

FARSIGHTED COMPANIES

These are the companies the public rated most positively for showing vision and leadership and offering strong prospects for future growth in the 2002 Harris Interactive study of corporate reputation.

VISION AND LEADERSHIP

1. Microsoft
2. Harley-Davidson
3. Johnson & Johnson
4. Dell
5. Coca-Cola
6. Wal-Mart
7. Anheuser-Busch
8. PepsiCo
9. United Parcel Service
10. Walt Disney

STRONG PROSPECTS FOR FUTURE GROWTH

1. Johnson & Johnson
2. Wal-Mart
3. Dell
4. Microsoft
5. Home Depot
6. Harley-Davidson
7. Coca-Cola
8. United Parcel Service
9. Sony
10. Walt Disney

---

tion. Even people slinging arrows at Microsoft wouldn't deny its powerful vision and leadership. In bringing its antitrust suit, the federal government considered the company's vision too monopolistic. Microsoft, of course, didn't see it that way.

Recently, Microsoft said that while clinging to its vision of technology, it had embraced a broader mission: "to enable people and businesses throughout the world to realize their full potential." The company added, "it's our belief that the true measure of our success is not in the power of our software, but in the power it unleashes in us all." Such declarations may sound pretentious to some people, but such vision statements, backed up by solid strategies, can inspire both employees and customers.

Sometimes the corporate vision represents a break from the past, as in BP's case. Other companies embrace a vision that has survived the test of time. Consider Merck, which has followed for more than fifty years George Merck's pronouncement "We try never to forget that medicine is for the people. It is not for the profits. The profits follow, and if we have remembered that, they have never failed to appear." The statement is succinct but memorable.

L. L. Bean still adheres to founder Leon Leonwood Bean's "golden rule." When he started his boot business in 1912, his fundamental philosophy was "Sell good merchandise at a reasonable profit, treat your customers like human beings, and they will always come back for more."

More recently, another company was born from a vision based on people's humanity. An upstart with the cool name JetBlue Airways entered the brutally competitive airline industry in 2000 with the mission "to bring humanity back to air travel." It was the right vision at the right time. The flying experience had deteriorated to the point that coach passengers complained that they felt like cattle being herded into ever-tighter seats.

To be sure, JetBlue's vision of a low-fare, high-service airline wasn't exactly original. Southwest Airlines had already made a name for itself for friendly, consistent service. But David Neeleman, JetBlue's founder, made comfort and frills a bigger part of his strategy. The airline offers such amenities as leather seats, live satellite television programming, and an in-flight yoga program.

People have flocked to JetBlue, which reported net earnings of $54.9 million in 2002, up 43 percent from the year before. But there's trouble on the horizon. Already, Delta Air Lines is trying to copy JetBlue's vision with a new airline of its own with the catchy name Song. It, too, boasts leather seats and low fares. But Song hopes to be even more "humanizing" than JetBlue by offering more entertainment choices and selling treats ranging from Cinnabon coffee cakes to Cosmopolitan cocktails.

How successfully the airlines follow their vision will ultimately separate the winners and the losers. Perfect adherence to one's vision is virtually an impossible dream. But companies must remain closely aligned with their vision and progress toward it. They shouldn't always be trying to latch on to the next big thing.

Some companies drift, however, as the executive suite changes and they expand into new businesses. Walt Disney Company, which focused for years on the Disney magic of family-oriented entertainment, has moved in new directions as it has acquired and developed new media properties, from the ABC television network to Miramax Films. Its vision no longer seems quite so clear to some stakeholders.

Although the general public still perceives the company's entertainment focus to be strong, some consumers complain that the company is growing too far away from its roots as a company dedicated to families. They don't like the movies being produced by the company's adult-oriented studios, and they object to the rising theme-park prices, which are out of reach for many Americans. Even the archbishop of Canterbury in Britain has attacked the company for excessive commercialism and marketing to children. To which Disney replied in a prepared statement that skirted the issue: "Since the release of *Snow White and the Seven Dwarfs* and the opening of the Disneyland theme park decades ago, Walt Disney's vision has been to provide quality entertainment and experiences for parents and children to enjoy together. Community decency and optimism are the centerpiece of what the Walt Disney Company strives to achieve in all that we create."

Clearly, Disney has an enviable heritage. But it needs to ponder its vision for the future as it struggles to improve its financial performance and stock price, hurt in recent years by its weak television and theme-park businesses.

THE CHARISMATIC CEO

A charismatic, visionary CEO can have enormous impact on a company's reputation. Just consider what Frank Perdue did for chicken and Victor Kiam for electric shavers. Indeed, research has found that one of the key determinants of CEOs' failure is the lack of a clearly communicated vision.

The technology industry has produced a large crop of visionary CEOs. Of course, there's Bill Gates, whose title is now chairman and chief software architect. Michael Dell, the founder of Dell, Inc., also ranks among the CEOs with the strongest reputations for vision and leadership. He developed a philosophy called the "the soul of Dell," that includes "a passion for winning in everything we do."

The corporate vision often becomes closely linked to the CEO's personality. After all, the chief executive officer is a company's most visible symbol, its personification. But a truly great company continues to thrive even after its stellar CEO leaves. That isn't to say the death or departure of an especially engaging CEO doesn't affect corporate reputation. But companies like General Electric survive their legendary leaders, at least partly because the best CEOs make sure they develop exceptional bench strength.

At GE, Jeffrey Immelt, who succeeded management whiz Jack Welch, is already making his mark. GE's vision has evolved to put renewed emphasis on research, the bedrock of the company that was cofounded by Thomas Edison. Immelt recently invested $100 million to upgrade GE's research center in upstate New York, and GE even replaced its familiar corporate slogan "We bring good things to life" with "Imagination at work."

Some companies, however, don't prepare as well for the loss of a visionary leader. Wendy's International felt the absence so strongly of founder Dave Thomas, who died in 2002, that it used his name posthumously in advertising. Thomas's persona is still very much part of the Wendy's culture and is a prominent part of the company's Web site, which describes his "humble beginning," his values and his "folk hero" status. While companies such as Wendy's want to continue their patriarch's vision after their leaders are gone, they shouldn't dwell in the past too long. The business world is so competitive that companies must be constantly innovating and focusing on the future. Instead of promoting Thomas's contributions, Wendy's needs to cook up an exotic new burger and speed up service. That would be a winning vision for a fast-food joint.

PRACTICAL AND POETIC

So how do you articulate your vision in an official corporate statement? Vision can be a rather fuzzy concept, but the writing process may help you flesh it out.

At the very least, a vision statement helps convey a company's mission to both employees and external stakeholders. The corporate vision

VISIONARY WORDS

Here are excerpts from a variety of corporate vision statements. Some are more inspiring than others, but each attempts to capture the essence of the company.

"To honor God in all we do. To help people develop. To pursue excellence. To grow profitably."—ServiceMaster Corporation

"Be the world's beer company. Enrich and entertain a global audience. Deliver superior returns to our shareholders."—Anheuser-Busch

"To dedicate our business to the pursuit of social and environmental change. To creatively balance the financial and human needs of our stakeholders. To tirelessly work to narrow the gap between principle and practice, whilst making fun, passion and care part of our daily lives."—Body Shop International

"To make the finest quality all natural ice cream and euphoric concoctions . . . to operate the company on a sustainable financial basis of profitable growth . . . to operate the company in a way that actively recognizes the central role that business plays in society."—Ben & Jerry's Homemade Holdings

"Dedication to the highest quality of customer service delivered with a sense of warmth, friendliness, individual pride, and company spirit."—Southwest Airlines Company

"To bring inspiration and innovation to every athlete* in the world." [*"If you have a body, you are an athlete."]—Nike

"We exist to benefit and refresh everyone who is touched by our business. When we bring refreshment, value, joy and fun to our stakeholders, then we successfully nurture and protect our brands. That is the key to fulfilling our ultimate obligation to provide consistently attractive returns to the owners of our business."—Coca-Cola Company

"Respect for the individual. Service to our customers. Strive for excellence."—Wal-Mart Stores

"We dedicate ourselves daily to the work of improving life on our planet. We have the curiosity to go farther, the imagination to think bigger, the determination to try harder and the conscience to care more. Our solutions will be bold. Our methods will be our obsession. Our tools are our minds. Our success will be ensured. Our principles are sacred."—DuPont

"Our strategic intent is to help people find better ways to do great work—by constantly leading in document technologies, products and services that improve our customers' work processes and business results."—Xerox Corporation

"The ambition of the Northwestern is less to be large than to be safe; its aim is to rank first in benefits to policy owners rather than first in size."—Northwestern Mutual

"With pride, passion and performance, we create the world's best home appliances, which make life easier and more enjoyable for all people. Our goal is a Whirlpool product in every home, everywhere."—Whirlpool Corporation

"We demand integrity. Our people come first. We take great care of our customers. We make 'perfect 10' pizzas every day. We operate with smart hustle and positive energy."—Domino's Pizza

should be ambitious and challenge employees. It ought to be broad enough to give the business room to expand but not filled with vague generalities. Some corporate visions are so simple as to be meaningless. Too many blandly call for becoming the best in the industry and rewarding shareholders. Here's a yawner on one company's Web site: "People working together as a global enterprise for leadership." This one won't exactly motivate employees either: "To feed, clothe and care for consumers." And there's this less than rousing theme: "Making people's lives better by unleashing our corporate power." Even Ford Motor Company, the century-old industrial icon, offers up a disappointingly obvious vision: "To become the world's leading consumer company for automotive products and services."

The ideal is to hit a balance between practical and poetic. Keep in mind that the corporate vision should touch people, especially employees, on an emotional level. Employees need to feel passion for the vision; an inspirational tone in a vision statement can stoke that passion. Brevity is also a virtue in making the vision more memorable.

Most companies have created vision or mission statements. A survey by the consulting firm Bain & Company found that 70 percent of companies have drafted one. But based on a search of corporate Web sites, many companies seem to be keeping their vision statements a secret. Maybe they have not yet achieved a consensus within the organization or are embarrassed by what they've committed to paper. Whatever the case, a company must communicate its vision to its many stakeholders if it is to contribute to reputation.

Of course, the vision statement should come from the top. It may well be based on input the CEO has received over time from other managers and employees. But it must not be a group effort because committees often simply dumb down a strong statement. The CEO should write and communicate it—perhaps with the help of a skilled wordsmith at the company.

There are some new options for truly uninspired CEOs. Sensing a marketing opportunity, some Internet sites have sprung up that offer to write quickie vision statements. The One Page Business Plan Company recommends that companies use its "fill-in-the-blanks" form. Applied Learning Labs provides an eight-step map to a vision statement. But any CEO who takes such companies up on their offers can hardly be considered visionary and is likely to get a "paint-by-the-numbers" result.

FAILED VISION

You can certainly stumble in trying to fulfill your vision, but you can't afford to bomb. Just look at Vivendi Universal and Time Warner. Both companies hoped to prove that the whole is greater than the sum of its parts. They combined a host of media and Internet properties and expected to produce extraordinary media content and delivery synergies.

But media synergy has turned out to be one of the most misguided corporate visions of the new millennium. The concept sounds fine, but execution so far has been lousy. Both Time Warner and Vivendi Universal paid the price for their failed visions. Their reputations are ailing, some of their executives have been forced out, business units have been sold, and their stock prices have plummeted.

Both companies borrowed and spent heavily, but reality fell far short of their expansive visions. The Internet didn't turn out to be the great distribution pipeline for media and entertainment content that the companies had expected. What's more, melding the diverse corporate cultures proved to be extremely difficult, with divisiveness and resentment among the various media and Internet companies.

Vivendi Universal and Time Warner have been forced to scale back their grand schemes. They have been struggling to formulate a new vision that will win back the confidence of investors and other stakeholders and help repair their reputations. It won't be easy.

At least Jean-René Fourtou, who replaced Jean-Marie Messier as chairman of Vivendi Universal, appears to know what he's up against. He called the attempt by his ousted predecessor to build a media giant out of a sleepy French water company "not coherent" and "a mess."

As for Time Warner and its merger with America Online, once hailed as the ultimate marriage between old and new media, it will take plenty of soul-searching to find a more authentic vision. But Time Warner's first step was to get its finances in order by selling off assets. Understandably so—it reported a net loss of $98.7 billion for 2002, the biggest annual corporate loss in history. It also dropped AOL from the corporate name—a cosmetic move unlikely to make people forget the America Online half of the troubled marriage.

BACK TO BASICS

Sometimes corporate vision simply gets blurred. Companies lose sight of their founders' mission and wander off in all directions. Their reputations suffer because they are no longer serving their primary customers well, and they have confused and perhaps even alienated employees, investors, and other stakeholders.

That's when it's time to stop and get one's bearings straight. Retailers seem especially vulnerable to losing focus as they try to respond to new competition and be all things to all people.

That happened to Staples, the office supplies retailer. It kept opening new stores and adding new products at a furious pace. But it got its wake-up call in 2001, when growth slowed and it realized how much it had strayed from its original vision. The solution was a strategy dubbed "Back to Brighton." The company had opened its first store in Brighton, Massachusetts, in 1986, catering to small businesses and home offices. Its strategy: to provide smaller businesses the same low prices previously enjoyed only by large companies. But as it expanded to more than 1,500 stores worldwide, it became more and more consumer-oriented, and the merchandise mix grew too eclectic.

So Staples began weeding out gimmicky products such as Britney Spears backpacks, cartoon-themed notepads, and novelty pens adorned with feathers and shaped like vegetables. It dropped a $99 shredder and began stocking a more durable $300 shredder instead. And $699 computers went out the door, replaced by more profitable, built-to-order models. Altogether, Staples eliminated 700 consumer items and added back about 450 business-oriented products.

The office superstore also realized it had been disappointing small businesses and its home-office customers by failing to provide speedy, pleasant service. Customer service had lapsed over time even though it had been a critical part of Staples's original vision. The company's vision statement encourages employees to "strive to exceed our customers' expectations and provide a courteous, efficient shopping experience" and tells them to "remember, without customers, we have nothing."

Staples understands that customers take its lower prices and convenient locations for granted. What they really put a premium on is time. They expect Staples employees to be like librarians who know where all the merchandise is located—and to be courteous and friendly as well.

"We can run the most brilliant marketing strategy," says Shira Goodman, executive vice president for marketing. "But it's a waste of money if people don't find the merchandise and good service when they come into the stores or go online. We have to shift from a task-oriented to a customer-oriented culture."

To improve service, Staples instituted a pay system for its sales clerks based on performance and made customer service a more significant part of management bonus plans. "The easiest way to change the culture is with financial incentives," says Ronald Sargent, president and CEO. "We used to have pizza parties for employees on Friday but realized that our sales associates would rather have money to put gas in the car." The "Back to Brighton" vision showed results by the fourth quarter, ending on February 1, 2003, when profits jumped by 75 percent from the year before and sales rose by 14 percent.

REFOCUSING YOUR VISION

Companies must adapt to the accelerating pace of change in the world. Which may mean refocusing their vision from time to time.

Two major Japanese companies have recently made some major adjustments while remaining true to their fundamental vision. Sony, the consumer electronics king, is as committed as ever to innovation and quality. But now the creator of the Walkman and PlayStation sees its future in a "networked" world. It is banking on the spread of broadband high-speed technology and the rebirth of television as the center of broadband entertainment. Sony firmly believes that its many consumer products—from televisions and computers to mobile phones and game consoles—will be connected via the Internet. Consumers will be able to obtain Sony music, movies, and games at home, in the office, in the car, on the street corner.

"Sony's vision for this new era is what I call the Ubiquitous Value Network, a world where digital devices are seamlessly connected to each other and broadband networks," says Kunitake Ando, president. "People will be able to enjoy content and services anytime, anywhere on a global basis." Already, Sony is developing a line of products named Cocoon, short for Connected Community on Network. "Cocoon will transform television into an interactive, intelligent experience, changing people's lifestyles," Ando promises.

If Sony's vision proves prophetic, its reputation for innovation, vision, and leadership will grow even stronger.

Toyota Motor Corporation is also heading down a new road. In 2002, it announced a revised strategy with a heavy emphasis on the environment, materials, recycling, and new information technology to make driving safer and more comfortable. The "new corporate image for Toyota to pursue" includes four elements: "kind to the Earth, excitement for the world, respect for all people and comfort of life."

Above all, Toyota's 2010 Global Vision stresses the importance of balancing its growth with environmental responsibility. Fujio Cho, Toyota's president, predicts that "motorization will advance on a global scale" as the automobile industry increases its penetration of large emerging markets such as China and India. But that growth will require the company to accelerate its environmental action plan, including early introduction of ultra-low-emission vehicles and increased production of hybrid vehicles. Toyota unveiled the Prius, the world's first mass-produced gasoline-electric hybrid, in Japan in December 1997. It also has begun selling a hydrogen-powered fuel cell sport-utility vehicle whose only emission is water.

Toyota clearly recognizes the importance of an adaptable vision. In the company's 2002 annual report, Chairman Hiroshi Okuda puts it well: "The automobile industry has entered an era of megacompetition, which is focused on global motorization and next-generation technologies. Those companies that are unable to respond to the changing needs of modern society and present a firm vision for the future will be left behind."

A UNIQUE VISION

How do you write your corporate vision when you're deliberately taking steps that could ultimately destroy your primary business? Does that sound too bizarre to be true? Well, that's exactly what Altria Group is attempting. Altria, formerly called Philip Morris, intends to craft a new vision statement that will articulate what it means to be a responsible tobacco company. It promises to be unlike any other vision statement.

In setting its vision down in writing, Altria is struggling to reconcile the seeming inconsistencies of its actions. It is the only major tobacco company urging the U.S. Food and Drug Administration to regulate the contents of cigarettes. Its Philip Morris Web site bluntly states that kicking the habit is the best way to reduce the risks of lung cancer, heart disease, and emphysema. What's more, the company's Youth Smoking Prevention Department creates advertising encouraging parents to talk to their kids about the dangers of cigarettes and supports programs to help young people avoid smoking and other risky behavior.

At the same time, some 40 million American adults continue to smoke, and Altria's Philip Morris unit aggressively markets its cigarette brands to them. As a result, in 2002 Philip Morris USA reported an operating profit of $5 billion. Altria holds to the position that "it is important to preserve an environment in which adults can continue to make their own decisions about smoking."

Steven Parrish, senior vice president for corporate affairs, relishes the challenge of writing a new vision statement. Altria must first show its own employees and then the outside world, he says, "that there is a responsible way to carry out our business." He expects people to be skeptical at first because it's so counterintuitive. "It will be even harder for some people to understand and trust us," he says, "if we start doing more work on smoking cessation programs."

CREATE EMOTIONAL APPEAL

When Sue McHarness learned that one of her favorite employees at the local Wawa convenience store was moving away, she got busy in her kitchen. First she whipped up some cranberry orange and blueberry muffins to take to him, then a batch of sugar cookies. On his last day at work, she presented him with a cake decorated with white frosting and pastel sprinkles.

"I come to know these people quite well since I'm in there all the time buying cappuccino," says McHarness, a retiree in Woodstown, New Jersey. "It's kind of a little Wawa groupie thing. The employees even call me Nana because my stepgranddaughter works there."

What's going on here? Warm, fuzzy feelings about the local convenience store? Such devotion may seem strange, but it's just business as usual for Wawa. The family-run company with more than 500 convenience stores in the mid-Atlantic states has come to enjoy cultlike loyalty from many of its customers. People feel so strongly they talk about "My Wawa" and say they visit one of the stores at least once a day. "My Wawa" has become the focus of all of the company's advertising, which shows customers describing the stores as "the heart of the neighborhood" and "part of the family." One man says he visits Wawa several times daily because "I'm a bachelor, and Wawa is my kitchen." When longtime customers move out of Wawa's marketing territory, they insist that relatives and friends bring the store's hoagies when they visit.

Cheerful, attentive employees and consistent product quality have combined to produce this intense emotional bond. If you are in retailing or almost any consumer-oriented business, creating emotional appeal with your customers can make an enormous difference. The passion people feel about your company plays an invaluable role in shaping reputation.

Headquartered in suburban Philadelphia, Wawa has won an unusually positive reputation for an industry often associated with loud, loitering teenagers and frequent armed robberies. Like other convenience stores, Wawa has faced such negative publicity itself. Two Wawa clerks in Maryland were shot to death in 1999, and some Wawa stores in New Jersey became the target of bomb threats two years later.

But Wawa's customers seem to remember it more for its freshly made hoagies and neighborly employees. McHarness was especially touched when her church was rounding up Christmas gifts for needy families and Wawa workers went shopping for some of the toys on the list. When the church honored local police officers, firefighters, and ambulance drivers with a special dinner, Wawa supplied ice cream for dessert.

Wawa's quirky name just seems to add to the company's appeal. Unbeknown to most people, Wawa is the Lenni Lenape Indian word for the Canada goose, whose image has become part of the corporate logo. Wawa officials like to compare their corporate culture of teamwork to the way a flock of geese work together to increase their flying range.

It's been a long journey for Wawa. The company was founded some two hundred years ago, but not to sell groceries. It began life as an iron foundry and over the years evolved into a dairy and textile business. The dairy operation delivered "doctor-certified" milk to people's home by horse-drawn wagons. But as the milkman became a relic of the past, Wawa needed to change again. The company opened its first convenience store in Folsom, Pennsylvania, in 1964, hoping to capitalize on Wawa's reputation for fresh milk and personal service.

Along the way, Wawa made its share of mistakes. It ventured into the fast-food business with three Wawa Kitchens that all closed within a year. Later, it introduced brand-name products such as Pizza Hut and Dunkin' Donuts into its stores with great fanfare. "They were later quietly removed under the cover of night," says Richard D. Wood, Jr., president and CEO. Wawa learned that instead of offering other companies' brands, it should expand and create its own. Thus were born Shorti hoagies, Sizzli breakfast sandwiches, and Wawa Wraps.

Company executives say they have succeeded in making Wawa "a habit-forming daily routine" through their personal touch. Now their aim is "to become the retail brand customers can't live without." That's a lofty goal. It means keeping their sights constantly trained on the customer. Success is in the small details.

For example, Wawa hires retirees who are seeking a little extra money and companionship to work as coffee hosts and hostesses. They keep the counter clean and the brew warm and fresh—and, most important, make small talk with the customers while they fill their cups and stir in the cream and sugar.

To build trust, Wawa guarantees that its gasoline is "good as gold" and will pay for any mechanical problems that a qualified technician says were caused by the gas.

Clean, well-lit stores also add to Wawa's appeal. That's because the company religiously remodels about fifty stores a year. "One of the colossal strategic errors of retailers is to let their existing facilities become outdated and obsolete," says Wood. "This leads to a downward spiral that is nearly impossible to reverse."

Convenience and simplifying people's lives are Wawa's reasons for being, and the company never forgets it. The company's operations engineering department is always striving to shave seconds off customers' transactions by making the "runway," or cash register area, more efficient. For example, Wawa separated its deli and sandwich-making area from the checkout counter to reduce waiting time. And unlike most small retailers, Wawa doesn't sell state lottery tickets. If jackpots get big, the lines of ticket buyers grow so long that people buying coffee or sandwiches become annoyed by their long wait.

Wawa scored perhaps its biggest coup with customers in the late 1990s, when banks began charging fees to noncustomers who used their ATMs. Wawa said "No way!" to PNC Financial Services Group, which puts its machines in the company's stores. No matter where you keep your banking accounts, you can use a PNC machine at Wawa free of charge. "We had a debate over the surcharge but decided customers expect fairness and convenience from us," says Howard Stoeckel, Wawa's executive vice president. "This built both goodwill and customer traffic for us." Wawa even considered running ads based on the playful headline "Bank Robs Man," but PNC officials weren't amused.

Wawa opted for the less provocative slogan "Get your money for nothin'."

The ATM policy has won Wawa some lifetime customers. "I'll never go anywhere but Wawa," says Laura Castellano, corporate social responsibility manager at Avon Products. "I loved how they put their customers first and stood up to the bank."

Wawa doesn't take itself too seriously, and that adds to its emotional appeal. For example, Wawa draws attention to itself during the annual July 4 festivities in Philadelphia with Wawa hoagie day. A couple of years ago, it unveiled a record-breaking 10,000-foot-long hoagie that had required 300 employees to create and took more than 30,000 people less than thirty minutes to devour. A Wawa store has even doubled as a wedding chapel. An assistant manager was wed in front of the produce case at his Wawa in Yardley, Pennsylvania, where he had met his fiancée.

"It's a real neighborhood place where the morale is good and people are always laughing," says John Cronin of Drexel Hill, Pennsylvania, who is partial to Wawa's hoagies and precooked dinners. The retired college history teacher is especially fond of his local Wawa because the store manager is a former student of his.

To retain its emotional link with customers like Cronin, Wawa executives spend time at all of their stores. They visit some of the chain's stores every week to talk with shoppers and store clerks to learn what's going well and what isn't. Senior managers stop by each store about twice a year.

At one point Wawa executives noticed a growing pattern of accidents in which customers' cars had run into their storefronts. So to show its concern for customer and employee safety, Wawa is retrofitting all of its stores with barriers to prevent cars from crashing into the stores. "We were seeing cars hit the stores about once a month," says Richard Wood, the CEO, "and I became convinced someone would get killed if we didn't take action. We earn our reputation by doing the right thing." Some evenings, Wood himself has wheeled a cart of snacks and coffee around Children's Hospital of Philadelphia and handed out free coffee to worried, waiting parents. He is also a good sport with employees. He has dressed up as a matador and pirate at parties to induct top-performing employees into the "President's Club."

Wawa never forgets the fragility of its respected reputation. It wasted little time apologizing for a major misstep shortly after the terrorist attacks of September 11, 2001. When it raised its gasoline prices, customers and government officials were irate and accused Wawa of price gouging. The company admitted its error and took its licks.

Wawa also inadvertently stirred up a tempest when it proposed chopping down a stately, sixty-foot white oak tree to make way for parking spaces for tractor-trailer trucks at a store in Millville, New Jersey. Local residents and the high school ecology club protested that the two-hundred-year-old oak was a natural treasure. Although Wawa had the legal right to clear the tree, it redesigned its plans to eliminate some parking spaces. Wawa thus became a hero. A fence was erected around the tree with a plaque thanking Wawa for letting the tree stand.

"The thing about our customers is that they feel empowered to speak up," says Stoeckel. "If they don't like something we do, they yell at us rather than go to the competition."

IGNITING THE EMOTIONAL SPARK

Wawa has succeeded more than most companies in tapping into the secret of an enduringly good corporate reputation. Financial performance, leadership, corporate responsibility, and product quality are all essential, but emotion is the primary driver of reputation. It's a feeling of excitement and engagement that makes customers drive out of their way to buy your product and to recommend your company and its brands to other people.

Emotional appeal isn't easy to define, but you know it when you see it. It's the homeowner who absolutely loves Home Depot and says, "I get lost in there for hours and always buy more than I intended." Or the Yahoo! user who declares that "Yahoo! is home for me" and takes "me places I only dream about." Or the man who says that his "Toyota family" owns a Camry with 300,000 miles on it and would buy another Toyota "in a heartbeat."

It's worth remembering that feelings about companies aren't entirely rational. Ken Roberts, chairman and CEO of Lippincott Mercer, a brand identity consultancy, recalls that simply redesigning the seat upholstery and flight attendant uniforms for Continental Airlines improved people's feelings about the company in general. "People actually thought the food tasted better," he says, "even though only the seat fabric they were sitting on was different."

Whether or not it always makes sense, emotional appeal produces an

---

EMOTIONAL APPEAL

These ten companies received the highest scores from the general public for their "emotional appeal" in the 2002 Harris Interactive study of corporate reputation:

1. Johnson & Johnson
2. Harley-Davidson
3. United Parcel Service
4. General Mills
5. Home Depot
6. FedEx
7. Eastman Kodak
8. Maytag
9. Dell
10. Coca-Cola

---

intense loyalty that should be protected at all costs. That elusive emotional spark between a company and its stakeholders makes some reputations soar and never lose altitude. Maytag Corporation may possess many admirable qualities, but the image of the lonely repairman and reliable Maytag appliances is what accounts for its special halo. Although the Walt Disney Company faces strategic and financial challenges galore, Mickey Mouse and the rest of the Disney menagerie still lend the company a special aura. And the fun, friendly employees, as much as the low fares, keep passengers flying on Southwest Airlines.

The recent corporate scandals and publicity about executive greed have conspired to badly damage the emotional bond people had felt with many companies. In a 2002 study of corporate reputation by Harris Interactive, emotional appeal was the attribute that showed the most significant decline.

Emotional appeal is a complex concept. In the Harris survey, it is defined as good feelings about a company, admiration and respect for it, and trust in it. But emotions aren't that simple. Many experiences feed into people's feelings about a company and create the nostalgia that helps sustain emotional appeal and corporate reputation. Most important are people's interactions with a company's employees and its products and services over time. Corporate advertising and media publicity also influence people's feelings. And companies sometimes develop close ties with the local communities where they do business.

Corporate Web sites offer companies a perfect opportunity to deepen their connections, but surprisingly few take advantage of the electronic emotional link. Coca-Cola, however, has made its Web site a sentimental journey. There are old recipes for making Coca-Cola ham and Chocolate Cola cake, information about Coca-Cola collectibles, memories of classic commercials, and consumers' stories about everything from how they survived the New Coke fiasco to how Coke figured into their romances and life in the military.

One contributor tells how he had admired his future wife from afar for nearly three years and finally went to the restaurant where she worked and asked, "Can I have a large Coke and your phone number?" She gave him both. In another story, a member of the U.S. Army says, "When things were at their worst in jungle or desert, Coke brought me home to family and memories. It's America in a bottle."

More locally, some companies strive to get close to the communities where they operate. That's especially important for some industries, especially ones that provide service, like banks. Citizens Financial Group recognizes the importance of emotional appeal and aims to keep its small-town, community bank image even as it grows large. Citizens, owned by the Royal Bank of Scotland Group, has expanded from its New England home base into the mid-Atlantic states and become one of the largest commercial bank holding companies in America. But it still promotes itself as "not your typical bank" because of its personalized, community-oriented approach.

On opening day for the Boston Red Sox, Citizens is a big presence around town, distributing free game tickets, bags of caramel-covered popcorn, and transit tokens. When Citizens acquired nearly 350 bank branches from Mellon Financial Corporation in Pennsylvania, Delaware, and New Jersey, it made a big splash with the local communities. Some 500,000 public transit riders traveled free on Citizens' opening day in Philadelphia and Pittsburgh. At one branch, tellers greeted customers with a song. Some employees washed customers' car windows, and others delivered breakfast to business customers' offices.

"Usually, the places that delight me are little, like the local hardware store or the dry cleaner," says Larry Fish, Citizens' chairman and CEO. "My dry cleaner knows me and if I say they lost one of my shirts, they replace it. That's what Citizens wants to be like."

The company's annual report provides a strong indicator that the little things do indeed matter. Along with all of the financial data, Citizens includes two other statistics: "We set another record for the seventh consecutive year. Our branches distributed 6.2 million lollipops and 294,100 dog biscuits last year. (Not that we have anything against cats.)"

ADVERTISING THAT TOUCHES THE HEART

The first job of advertising is to sell a product. But don't underestimate how much it can contribute to corporate reputation, especially in sparking emotional appeal. Whether charming, heartrending, or hilarious, advertising can strike a powerful emotional chord. Eastman Kodak's commercials, for example, have long captivated viewers with their lush photography and heart tugging, if saccharine, jingles.

Unfortunately, some companies have lost the emotional bond their advertising once engendered. Many consumers fondly remember ads like AT&T's "Reach out and touch someone" campaign. Although AT&T still enjoys lingering reputation benefits from its past heartwarming ads, their impact has faded as more recent ads failed to produce the same emotional resonance.

Advertising agencies go to great lengths to forge an emotional connection. They hire anthropologists, sociologists, and psychologists to probe the subconscious feelings people have about companies and their brands. They might, for example, ask consumers to write an obituary about a corporate brand and then analyze whether the deceased company is described as young and virile and the victim of a tragic accident, or as worn-out and succumbing to old age.

Saatchi & Saatchi researchers once did a psychological analysis of the fast-food industry. It seems that a quick meal ordered at a drive-through window is a much deeper experience than anyone ever suspected. The researchers found that fast-food chains fulfill basic human needs for immediate oral gratification, regression to a carefree, childlike state, and dependency on someone else. People look to fast food, the Saatchi analysts concluded, almost as "a surrogate mom."

When a psychologist asked a female bank employee to describe McDonald's and Burger King as animal characters in a cartoon, she characterized McDonald's as a cute baby chick and Burger King as a sly cat. She also proposed that a Burger King ad might feature aliens from outer space, an image the psychologists found rich with subconscious meaning. To them, the aliens suggested that consumers felt emotionally distant from Burger King.

Whether or not you buy into such psychological probing, there's no question that companies enjoy varying degrees of emotional appeal. Financial services and technology advertising, in particular, seems to leave many people cold. Consumer product marketers clearly have the edge in understanding how to create emotionally touching advertising.

Consider Johnson & Johnson, which typically ranks first in emotional appeal in corporate reputation surveys. Although baby powder and other infant care products make up a small part of Johnson & Johnson's sales today, the wonder of babies remains the focus of its corporate advertising. Recent ads continue to charm consumers with the theme "Having a baby changes everything." One ad asks, "Who'd have ever thought the love of your life would be short and bald?" as a mother bathes her baby in the kitchen sink.

"We are and always will be, first and foremost, known as 'the baby company,'" says Andrea Alstrup, J&J's corporate vice president for advertising. "This comes from the emotional and everyday experiences people have with our products. They remember the fragrance of Johnson's Baby Powder. They remember bathing their babies. This reminds consumers that we at J&J understand the mother-infant bond and the importance of families."

THE DELIGHT FACTOR

Creating emotional appeal means more than simply exceeding people's expectations. It means delighting them. Indeed, "delight" has become the latest catchphrase for companies aiming for a special relationship with their customers.

It's certainly a worthy goal. But it runs the risk of overuse. While every company can treat its customers better, it's a much bigger challenge to delight them. Even Toys 'R' Us talks these days about "guest delight" and making its stores fun again. The toy retailer may be providing better service, but many of its stores are still far from delightful.

Some companies, however, do go well beyond the ordinary to delight people and engender strong emotional appeal. That's the mission of

CUSTOMER CARE

Whole Foods Market recognizes that its customers are its most important stakeholders. The Austin, Texas–based retailer of natural and organic foods has developed a set of customer service beliefs to make its stores so "delightful" that they become community meeting places where people come to join friends and make new ones:

- Customers are the lifeblood of our business and we are interdependent on each other.
- Customers are the primary motivation for our work; they are not an interruption of our work.
- Customers are people who bring us their wants and desires and our primary objective is to satisfy them as best we can. They are *not* people to argue or match wits with.
- Customers are fellow human beings with feelings and emotions like our own; they are equals to be treated with courtesy and respect at all times.

Whole Foods Market, a chain of about 150 stores that sell natural and organic foods and offer a complete refund if customers don't experience "100% product satisfaction." The company recognizes that by treating customers as special and providing a "delightful" experience, they become more than regular shoppers. They are transformed into Whole Foods evangelists who rave about the store to their friends, neighbors, and coworkers. Nothing is more powerful than word-of-mouth promotion.

Whole Foods creates such advocates not just by offering distinctive products and a high level of service but also by staging special events. For example, the Whole Foods store in Winston-Salem, North Carolina, organized an aromatherapy class and a tasting of Spanish and Italian wines, while one in Madison, New Jersey, provided $1-a-minute massage therapy and one in Cambridge, Massachusetts, sponsored a Mother's Day poetry contest.

Of course, some companies owe their enthusiastic following to the nature of the product. Harley-Davidson, for example, enjoys an almost euphoric connection with its bikers. More than 700,000 people belong to H.O.G. (Harley Owners Group) clubs, and the company boasts that

TOTAL DELIGHT

Strategic Vision, a San Diego research firm, has developed a survey to rate vehicles that truly delight drivers. Here are the top two vehicles in each category of the 2002 Total Delight Index:

SMALL CAR: Honda Insight, Suzuki Aerio
COMPACT CAR: Chrysler PT Cruiser, Volkswagen Jetta
MIDSIZE CAR: Volkswagen Passat, Nissan Altima
LARGER CAR: Oldsmobile Aurora, Chrysler Concorde
SMALL SPECIALTY CAR: Mini Cooper, Volkswagen Beetle
MIDSIZE SPECIALTY CAR: Honda Accord Coupe, Mercury Cougar
NEAR-LUXURY CAR: BMW 3-series, Lexus ES 300
LUXURY CAR: BMW 7-series, BMW 5-series
CONVERTIBLE (under $30,000): Pontiac Firebird, Chevrolet Camaro
CONVERTIBLE (over $30,000): Audi TT, Lexus SC 430
MINIVAN: Honda Odyssey, Kia Sedona
SMALL SUV: Honda CR-V, Hyundai Santa Fe
MEDIUM SUV: Land Rover Discovery Series II, GMC Envoy
LARGE SUV: Toyota Sequoia, Ford Excursion
LUXURY SUV: BMW X5, Cadillac Escalade
COMPACT PICKUP: Toyota Tacoma, Dodge Dakota
FULL-SIZE PICKUP: Toyota Tundra, Dodge Ram 1500

more than 90 percent of its motorcycle buyers intend to repurchase a Harley. "First and foremost, we sell a very good product," says Jim Ziemer, a vice president at Harley-Davidson. "But we also fulfill dreams through the experience of motorcycling."

Creating customer delight is becoming so important to companies that there is now even an actual measurement tool. A research firm called Strategic Vision in San Diego recently created a car-rating index based entirely on emotional appeal. Called the Total Delight Index, it is calculated from the responses of more than 75,000 new-car owners. Unlike the many other measures of automotive satisfaction today, the new delight index taps into the emotional thrill people experience with a car. Strategic Vision believes that especially in the crowded auto marketplace, creating delight is crucial to success.

The delight index goes well beyond simple satisfaction and manufacturing excellence. A company can build an outstanding car without delighting drivers. "An excellent vehicle is done exceedingly well, but a delightful vehicle creates a strong positive emotional spark that lifts the spirits and emotionally moves the customer," says Darrell Edwards, president of Strategic Vision. "Delight leads to commitment; commitment leads to loyalty."

Japanese and European companies dominate Strategic Vision's list of most delightful cars, but several Chrysler and General Motors models also made the cut. BMW monopolizes the luxury categories, while Honda, Toyota, and Volkswagen fare well in a variety of categories. Retro cars such as the PT Cruiser and the VW Beetle also scored high on delight.

CLOSE TO THE CUSTOMER

In today's fast, faceless world, the personal touch carries more emotional punch than ever. But few companies make any effort to connect with their consumers and other stakeholders in any meaningful way. The only corporate contact most people receive is an annoying telemarketing call during dinner or at the kids' bedtime. And now some companies are even creating virtual phone representatives (read: computer programs with human voices) to answer your complaints.

Such annoying high-tech gimmickry only increases the impact of personal treatment. When the Banana Republic clothing chain mails small black leather picture frames and thank-you notes to its most frequent shoppers, it makes a strong impression. Or when Southwest Airlines employees crack jokes with the passengers, they remember the special experience.

In fact, people sorely missed the airborne levity when Southwest decided to tone it down after the September 11, 2001, terrorist attacks. There were fewer jokes, no Halloween costumes, and no gag playing. But after receiving letters from passengers asking for a return to Southwest's stand-up comedy routines, the airline slowly began bringing back the fun. By the beginning of 2003, Southwest was in good form again with flight attendants cracking lines like "OK, people, it's open seating, just like at church—saints up front, sinners in back."

More companies are trying to move closer to their customers and sincerely listen to what they have to say. Citizens Bank places about 40,000 telephone calls each month to customers to gauge their satisfaction and find new ways to enhance service. Ultimately, the bank intends to contact each of its customers at least once a year.

Citizens stresses that it is determined to act on the customer feedback whenever possible. For example, it heard complaints about long waits at one of its Massachusetts branches and made three improvements: It added one more human teller, installed a teller terminal for noncash deposits, and hired a "service champion" to greet customers and expedite their transactions.

Goody's Family Clothing, a low-price clothing-store chain that needed a boost to its profits and reputation, sent its CEO, Bob Goodfriend, on a "good friend" bus tour through the Midwest and South to learn what women really want. Television commercials announced his local appearances and encouraged women to come down and tell Bob what was on their minds. He told them he wanted to learn "how we can make our store your store."

Women turned out in droves and told Bob they'd like everything from "plus size" lingerie for more ample bodies to wider store aisles, lounges for "parking" their husbands, bigger dressing rooms, "hipper" clothes, and up-close parking spaces for pregnant women and mothers with strollers. They loved being heard. One woman told Bob, "It sure is nice to finally find a man who's willing to listen."

To sustain the connection with customers, Goody's Web site now includes a section entitled "Tell Bob What You Want." Consumers can make suggestions about store improvements or vote on a list of possible improvements such as coffee bars, more cashiers, and kids' play areas.

"Women want to bond to a corporate brand, and if you give them a reason, they will," says Faith Popcorn, a marketing consultant whose specialties include the women's market. She advised Goody's on its bus tour and visited some of Goody's shoppers in their homes to learn more about their lifestyles and fashion preferences. In these ethnographical studies, Popcorn interviewed women with annual household incomes of less than $50,000 and observed their houses, closets, and clothing for clues that could help Goody's relate better to them.

One woman she visited was Tammy, a middle-aged factory worker in Tennessee, who considers her closets her "playground" and has built six closets in her home, each with a different theme: casual, dressy, shoes, coats, "Harley" biker, and attic storage. "I learned that Tammy believes clothes can affect her mood and that the shopping experience is very important to her," says Popcorn. Tammy also said she would never buy clothes on the Internet, and she equated finding a good fashion deal to winning the lottery.

"Executives need to get out and meet customers like Tammy and feel their pulse," says Popcorn. And that includes some of her biggest clients: Procter & Gamble and Campbell Soup. "A. G. Lafley, [P&G's CEO] should go into the laundry rooms of America and talk to women about their detergent and clothing stains," says Popcorn. "Doug Conant [Campbell's CEO] ought to be visiting women in their kitchens and snooping in their cupboards."

Part Two

Keeping That Good Reputation

Glass, china, and reputation are easily cracked, and never well mended.

—Benjamin Franklin

RECOGNIZE YOUR SHORTCOMINGS

For many consumers, shopping at a Home Depot store had become harder than actually doing their remodeling projects.

Do-it-yourselfers came to dread going to the hardware superstores. They felt as if they were roaming through an endless maze. As they wandered through aisle after aisle of the cavernous stores, they searched high and low, unable to find that needed hammer or bathroom faucet. Worse, they couldn't even find any employees wearing the company's trademark orange aprons. Most of the clerks they did finally encounter were clueless when asked for help. And after their torturous search, consumers often ended up leaving empty-handed anyway because products were out of stock.

Home Depot's reputation took a bruising. In Harris Interactive's annual corporate reputation study, the company plummeted to nineteenth place in 2001 from fourth the year before, when consumers had gushed about Home Depot and called it a toy store for adults.

But by the 2001 survey, Home Depot wasn't much fun anymore. One respondent recalled several exasperating trips to the store: "It took three calls to get someone to help us with flooring supplies. Another time we were purchasing fencing material and we had to load all of the material ourselves. It was impossible to get an employee to help."

Another consumer ranted, "It is impossible to get waited on. I have spent forty-five minutes in line just to purchase a single item!"

Home Depot had strayed far from its roots. After more than two decades of rapid growth, the retailer was no longer living up to its founders' promise of attentive, expert customer service. On top of the service snafus, Home Depot had become the target of negative publicity and lawsuits over injuries and deaths caused by merchandise tumbling from its shelves and forklifts.

The timing for all the dreadful news couldn't have been worse: Its reputation was weakening just as Lowe's, its chief competitor in the home improvement center business, was coming on strong, breathing down Home Depot's neck.

To its credit, Home Depot was on the case fast. It immediately began to take steps to improve service and safety, and it never tried to dismiss customers' complaints. Home Depot realized an important lesson: that companies must own up to their shortcomings before they can ever hope to improve their reputations. Strength comes from knowing your weaknesses.

Home Depot wasn't bold enough to address its shortcomings in advertising. But in news media interviews, corporate executives acknowledged the problem of inadequate service and explained their plans to take corrective action. "Our business proposition is and always has been to provide a high degree of service," says Gary Jusela, a vice president at Home Depot. "We've got to sweat the details on getting customer service just right." It's a tall order: Home Depot says that 22.3 million customers visit its more than 1,500 stores each week.

To improve service, Home Depot put more salespeople on the floor during peak shopping periods and reassigned shelf-stocking tasks to late at night. The company also realized that it had hired far too many inexperienced part-time workers and increased its full-time staff. In response to complaints about unfriendly clerks, the company's human resources department has made a point of hiring more "outgoing people."

Staff training also clearly needed lots of improvement. Jusela came on board as vice president of learning and was charged with making Home Depot's 300,000 clerks more knowledgeable about its 30,000-plus products. Store managers were told that they are responsible for one-on-one coaching of employees. In addition, Jusela instituted e-learning. Through interactive computer technology, he is teaching employees how to demonstrate products and answer customers' questions intelli-

---

AT YOUR SERVICE

Home Depot made a strong rebound in its customer service score in Harris Interactive's annual corporate reputation ranking. Here are the top ten companies rated by survey respondents as "providing excellent customer service" in 2001 and 2002.

2002	2001
1. United Parcel Service	1. FedEx
2. Maytag	2. Maytag
3. Home Depot	3. United Parcel Service
4. Johnson & Johnson	4. Target
5. Eastman Kodak	5. Walt Disney
6. FedEx	6. General Electric
7. Harley-Davidson	7. Hewlett-Packard
8. Sony	8. Sony
9. Walt Disney	9. Johnson & Johnson
10. Dell	10. Coca-Cola

---

gently. They are learning how to properly use cash registers, operate newfangled garden trimmers, and, most important, treat customers politely. "We use videos in which actors treat people rudely and resist taking a product back," says Jusela. "Then we turn around and demonstrate how to treat people with respect and not make them feel guilty for making a return."

Home Depot believes its house is sufficiently in order that it can begin to advertise its service quality once again. It created an image campaign in 2003—"You can do it. We can help"—touting its advisers, who can teach shoppers how to fix up their homes, and salespeople who really know where the merchandise is located. "People view Home Depot as more than a store," says John Costello, executive vice president and chief marketing officer. "Home Depot was always a trusted resource for information about home improvement projects. Now, we're trying to strengthen that emotional bond."

By 2002, Home Depot's overall reputation ranking had bounced back to eighth place in the Harris survey, and it was rated third for delivering excellent customer service. But it's clearly still a work in progress, as many customers can attest. Home Depot may be taking action, but by 2003 it still hadn't resolved all of its service shortcomings, by any means. Many clerks still just point customers in the general direction of merchandise rather than escorting them to the right location. Consumers still complain about messy, poorly lit stores, and the new self-service checkout registers can behave quite sluggishly.

Aware of its persistent shortcomings, Home Depot announced that it would increase capital spending in 2003 by 21 percent to $4 billion to further spruce up stores and enhance service. The company is also actively seeking consumer feedback: at the bottom of its cash register receipts is an invitation to participate in an online opinion survey and rate the helpfulness of employees, the amount of time required to check out, and the store's layout and cleanliness.

"Customers have high expectations of Home Depot," says Costello. "We need to strive harder to meet those expectations. For us, it's going to be a journey, not a destination."

FACE UP TO YOUR FOIBLES

Like Home Depot, any company with an ailing reputation must take an honest look at the reasons why. That doesn't mean the solutions will be easy, but self-awareness is the first step toward self-improvement.

Unfortunately, too many companies have managed to survive by living in denial. The major airlines have been slow to address shortcomings in everything from high fares to employee courtesy. Now they are paying the price as carriers such as Southwest Airlines and JetBlue win the loyalty of many disillusioned travelers.

How do companies discern their shortcomings? It doesn't take a corporate shrink. Often, a company's flaws are obvious to insiders; executives simply choose to ignore them. But for weaknesses that aren't so apparent, market research and reputation studies often provide enlightening clues to the corporate Achilles' heel. There's also probably nothing better than firsthand contact. CEOs and their lieutenants need to get out of their corner offices more often and stroll around offices, factories, and stores, talking with workers and customers about their concerns.

In this era of corporate scrutiny and distrust, companies will benefit even more from being honest about their shortcomings. People are inclined to like companies that admit their faults. Of course, they also must demonstrate that they intend to fix the problems—and fast.

Companies that acknowledge their failures and promise to try harder will repair their reputations much more quickly than those that play down their faults. Just consider the contrasting approaches taken by the heads of two leading financial institutions tainted by the abuses on Wall Street.

At the annual shareholder meeting in 2003, William Harrison, CEO of J. P. Morgan Chase & Co., owned up to the bank's disappointing financial performance and its role in the Wall Street research scandal. "Financial institutions, including J. P. Morgan Chase, must take their share of responsibility," he told shareholders. "We cannot undo what has been done, but we can express genuine regret and learn from the past." When a shareholder asked him who had been responsible for the bank's troubled dealings with Enron, he replied. "Accountability would start with me. I accept that."

At about the same time, Philip Purcell, the CEO at Morgan Stanley, was acting as if his firm hadn't slipped up at all. Commenting on the $1.4 billion Wall Street settlement of charges of misleading investors with overly optimistic stock research, Purcell took a holier-than-thou attitude and played down the company's role in the scandals. "I don't see anything in the settlement that will concern the retail investor about Morgan Stanley," he declared at a conference of institutional investors.

Eventually, Purcell backed down, after William Donaldson, chairman of the Securities and Exchange Commission, publicly scolded him. Donaldson said that Purcell's statements "reflect a disturbing and misguided perspective" on Morgan Stanley's alleged misconduct. Purcell's attempt to brush Morgan Stanley's misdeeds under the carpet thus had backfired badly and left the firm's halo even more tarnished.

Throughout the recent series of corporate financial scandals, many companies concealed the truth about shortcomings in their businesses through aggressive accounting practices that eventually caught up with them. Meeting the Street's earnings expectations meant hiding your shortcomings. Due to "inappropriate" accounting, Bristol-Myers Squibb, for example, inflated sales and earnings. At the same time, it faced serious weak spots in its business. Laboratory researchers had failed to fill the pipeline with potential blockbusters at the same time that the drug company was battling growing competition from less expensive generic versions of its leading pharmaceuticals.

Companies don't have unlimited time to discover and work on their shortcomings. It's late in the game, for instance, for Gateway to deal with its deficiencies. The computer marketer once enjoyed an extremely positive reputation with consumers, who praised everything from its customer service to the silly cow-spot design on its boxes. But its market share and reputation quickly eroded, and the company finally conceded that a lack of accountability and discipline had hurt its performance. It said it had failed to match its high-flying archrival Dell on "focus, discipline and metrics."

Gateway is trying to change its spots with help from the consulting firm Bain & Company. In addition to adding more discipline to its personal computer operations, Gateway is moving away from its PC roots into digital television and other consumer electronics products. Gateway will certainly need all the focus and discipline it can muster if it goes head to head with Sony and the other entrenched consumer electronics marketers.

A DISSERVICE TO YOUR REPUTATION

As Home Depot so painfully realized, poor customer service is one of the chief shortcomings that undermine corporate reputation. Rude treatment is damaging, too, of course. But it's slow, inept service that really makes customers fume because it costs them that most precious of commodities these days: time.

Lousy service afflicts thousands of businesses, many of which can't—or won't—come to grips with the problem. It's largely to blame for the sorry state of many retailers, restaurants, telecommunications and cable television companies, and other service-oriented businesses. Consumers gripe about the endless waits and recorded messages they must cope with when they call companies for help. They have lowered their expectations of service quality but still are surprised by how rotten it can be these days.

That's why Sheraton Hotels & Resorts offers a "service promise." It had come to terms with the fact that it suffered from the stigma of inattentive service and shabby digs. But with so many people skeptical about claims of service improvement, the hotel chain, owned by Starwood Hotels & Resorts Worldwide, decided it couldn't just announce a new commitment to service. It had to put its money on the line.

Your steak dinner arrived a full hour after you ordered? A cockroach has made itself at home in your bathroom? No sweat—Sheraton will compensate you with a free meal or room discount.

Admitting that service has deteriorated is the first step, of course. But companies must make improvements at once, as well as develop a strategy to identify the underlying causes and to make more far-reaching changes.

Listen closely to your customers. McDonald's is hyping its new salads with chicken, but chicken isn't uppermost in many of its customers' minds. What did shareholders complain about at McDonald's last annual meeting? Dirty restrooms.

McDonald's has long recognized that it frequently fails to live up to its ill-considered advertising slogan, "We love to see you smile." Interminable waits are nothing to smile about at a fast-food joint. Not to mention surly workers, unsanitary restrooms, and bungled food orders. Customers have even arrived home with takeout orders to find only buns and no burgers. "Service is so bad at McDonald's that now I check my bag thoroughly before I leave the drive-through window; you just never know what you might get," says Paul Houck of Lake George, New York, who once arrived home with a meatless Big Mac. "My wife is allergic to tomatoes, so I ask them to hold the tomatoes. Of course," he sighs, "there are always tomatoes on the burger."

Although well aware of such fiascos, McDonald's has far from solved the problem. Indeed, it was humbled in the fourth quarter of 2002 by its first quarterly loss since it went public nearly forty years ago.

To find out how abysmal the McDonald's experience can be, the company sent "mystery shoppers" into its restaurants to order lunch from unsuspecting employees. It also created a national toll-free consumer comment line; promised to train employees to be faster, nicer, and more accurate; and tested self-serve kiosks to speed up service. After all, the fast-food chain's reason for being is speed.

Recently, McDonald's wisely scrapped the "smile" theme in its ad campaign. Alas, its current slogan—"I'm lovin' it"—probably won't ring any truer with customers. People are impatient with McDonald's for not dealing more quickly and effectively with its service shortcomings. It had better hurry up and give people more reasons to love it.

REALITY BITES

That was the title of a 1994 movie about recent college graduates struggling to come to terms with the realities of the workaday world. Facing reality is painful for corporate executives in the workplace, too. It's always tempting to believe that looming problems will fade away. But accepting the truth and making hard decisions are what separate good managers from bad.

The longer problems fester, the more intractable they become and the more reputation harm they inflict. AT&T took far too long in coming to terms with a systemic service problem and sacrificed customer trust. In early 1990, a nine-hour network failure that knocked out telecommunication service in much of the United States posed a serious threat to AT&T's corporate brand. The company blamed the disruption on a software glitch and, to make amends, gave customers discounted long-distance service on Valentine's Day. People seemed to give AT&T the benefit of the doubt.

A year later, an AT&T crew cut a cable and crippled long distance service in the New York area, including the Federal Aviation Administration's communication system. Both air traffic and trading in some financial markets were delayed. AT&T's reputation was on shaky ground.

Then came the third strike: a combination of mechanical and human errors contributed to yet another network outage in New York in September 1991. At that point, industry regulators, congressional leaders, and corporate executives alike expressed outrage.

The service outages—all within less than two years—were a spinmeister's worst nightmare. Marilyn Laurie, who was AT&T's head of communications, recalls that the company's executives were loath to confront the depth of the problem. At a dinner for senior executives, she finally told CEO Robert Allen that they must talk about the service failures then and there. Reluctantly, they left their spouses and convened behind closed doors.

"The core of our identity was reliability," Laurie recalled later in a speech to the Arthur W. Page Society, an organization of public relations directors. "Our personal pride was built around flawless service. We were all feeling a terrible sense of loss—and we were in denial. We didn't see what we didn't want to see. And until we faced up to the unthinkable truth—that we had a systemic problem—we couldn't act on the root cause."

AT&T ultimately dealt with its deficiencies and developed major quality improvement programs to try to win back its reputation for reliability. But its reputation may never be quite the same. "The public gave us the benefit of the doubt twice because we had a hundred-year record of reliability," Laurie said. "But now we know we have to prove it again every single day. Sadly, no stack of reliability statistics can bring back the automatic willingness to believe that was produced by our incredibly long history of consistent results."

COMMUNICATION LAPSES

For some companies, the shortcomings aren't in their actions. They walk the walk but don't talk the talk.

Failure to communicate creates a void. People tend to believe the company simply isn't doing anything. That's what James Kilts discovered when he met with Boston community leaders shortly after becoming CEO of Gillette. To his surprise, they didn't believe that Gillette was active enough in community affairs. The revelation signaled to the company that it lacked a strong reputation for corporate citizenship not only in its hometown of Boston, but in many parts of the United States and the world.

In fact, the razor and battery maker was already donating millions of dollars and thousands of cases of free products to a host of charities. Trouble was, the company was taking a quiet, shotgun approach without any common thread to its philanthropy policy. And nobody except the direct beneficiaries was noticing much. "When you're spreading out your giving in fifty-dollar to one-thousand-dollar increments, no one knows what you're doing," says Cathy Chizauskas, Gillette's director of civic affairs. "It doesn't make much of a splash."

Gillette is now communicating much more clearly its community support, which it has focused strategically on three primary areas: women's cancer centers, economic literacy, and housing and emergency shelter. Gillette executives have also become much more vocal in their speeches about Gillette's community involvement. And the company created a Web site, www.gillettecancerconnect.org, and promoted it in a tie-in with the television show *Dawson's Creek,* when the program dealt with a character's breast cancer. The TV plug tripled the number of hits on the site.

Sometimes companies are communicating—but without enough impact. FedEx, long known for its express delivery service by air, has made a major expansion into ground transportation, the traditional stronghold of rival United Parcel Service. Apparently, the message hasn't been getting through to many consumers, however.

FedEx's reputation with the general public is not as strong as the company would like. UPS outscored FedEx in Harris Interactive's 2002 study of how the general public rates corporate reputations, at least partly because FedEx has fallen short in its communications strategy. FedEx became a household name because of humorous advertising that featured the memorable slogans "Hello, Federal!" and "When it absolutely, positively has to be there overnight" and such characters as the zany fast-talking guy. FedEx is clearly not living up to its historical standards of advertising and needs to create more effective communications as it expands its repertoire of delivery services.

FedEx officials acknowledge the need to spread the word more effectively. But, says Bill Margaritis, FedEx's reputation chief, "This is a work in progress, and we are turning up the volume at the grassroots level. This doesn't happen overnight; it takes time in this fragmented media environment to achieve the desired awareness of our broader offering of services."

At least FedEx isn't one of the faceless corporate giants. Failure to communicate has robbed some companies of the potential to develop a strong reputation. To most people, for example, Unilever remains a mystery. It hides behind its many brands—from Ragú spaghetti sauce to Snuggle fabric softener—and doesn't communicate with the public through corporate advertising or public relations. Unilever's CEO has mused in interviews about increasing corporate communications and making Unilever an umbrella brand for its products. But by 2003, Unilever was still maintaining its silence—and its feeble public reputation.

A CLEAR-EYED CEO

DuPont, America's oldest industrial corporation, was also branded America's biggest polluter in the 1980s. The federal government's polluter ranking placed DuPont squarely at the top. The company became environmental enemy number one to activist groups, and the reputation damage proved severe.

Environmental activists wanted the world to know the truth about DuPont and draped a huge banner on one of its New Jersey factories, declaring "DuPont Number One Polluter." Fortunately for DuPont, the banner was partly concealed, and the word "polluter" couldn't be seen by many motorists. Nevertheless, it was a wake-up call. The company realized that despite its many innovative accomplishments over the past two centuries, a negative environmental image would obliterate its positive reputation.

Edgar Woolard knew this wasn't just a public relations problem. When he became DuPont's chairman in 1989, he recognized that the company must confront its chief shortcoming and overcome it. The company may have been in compliance with legal requirements, but it wasn't meeting public expectations.

"We have been too inclined to act as though public wishes and concerns matter less than the technical opinions of scientists and engineers," Woolard said in a speech a week after becoming chairman. "But in fact, public opinion must be dealt with regardless of the technical facts." He noted that DuPont had sought renewal of a government permit to dump waste in the Atlantic Ocean off the coast of New Jersey because technical data indicated that it wasn't harming marine life. The company had ignored the feelings of New Jersey residents, who oppose any ocean dumping because the shore is a valuable economic resource and recreational area.

Eventually, DuPont withdrew its renewal application. But, Woolard noted, "We could have spared ourselves a lot of negative publicity had we withdrawn our request earlier—or not reapplied in the first place."

It takes a forceful, forthright leader like Woolard to challenge the status quo and force a company to face up to its failures. He had to stand up to people at other industrial companies and within DuPont itself who argued that he shouldn't speak out so boldly on environmental issues. He found that his colleagues feared focusing "attention on DuPont's environmental performance at a time when we still have shortcomings and are formulating new directions."

Under Woolard, DuPont set out to reduce its "environmental footprint" by cutting pollution and reining in its energy consumption. The company also reached out to environmental groups such as the National Wildlife Federation to exchange ideas and try to resolve policy clashes.

DuPont has encountered bumps along the way, to be sure, in its at-

---

CLEANING UP

After CEO Edgar Woolard vowed to create a culture of "environmental stewardship" and reduce pollution, DuPont embarked on a long-term mission to cleanse its tarred reputation. The following data show DuPont's progress, and the improvement partly reflects the spinoff of its Conoco oil subsidiary in 1998.

DuPont's ENVIRONMENTAL IMPACT	2001	1995
Global air toxic emissions (millions of pounds)	17.2	32.0
Global air carcinogens (millions of pounds)	0.8	2.0
Global greenhouse gases (billions of pounds)	64.6	191.1
Global hazardous waste (billions of pounds)	1.46	2.28
Number of environmental fines	20	31

---

tempt to create a culture of environmental stewardship. Activists have accused the company at times of "greenwashing" by using marketing to create an environmentally friendly image. They especially jeered at a commercial for Conoco, a former DuPont subsidiary, that showed double-hulled oil tankers surrounded by applauding seals and other wildlife. DuPont also still faces regulatory investigations and litigation, especially over past instances of alleged pollution. Most recently, the Environmental Protection Agency stepped up its investigation of the potential health risks of chemicals used in DuPont's Teflon.

Even so, today DuPont can honestly declare that it is cleaning up its act. For example, its global greenhouse emissions have fallen by 68 percent since 1990, while its global hazardous waste production has dropped by 47 percent. Those data partly reflect the spin-off of the Conoco oil unit in 1998, but they are also a testament to DuPont's progress in overcoming its environmental failings. Of course, it still has a long way to go to reach its stated goal: zero waste and zero emissions.

'FESSING UP IN PUBLIC

Should a company make a public confession of its shortcomings? In most cases, most definitely. Publicly acknowledging a widely perceived problem goes a long way toward restoring confidence and beginning the reputation healing. But the company must be on the mend before highlighting its shortcomings in advertising.

Home Depot would have reassured customers more about its service improvements had it said in its advertising, "We heard you, and we've started fixing things." Instead, its commercials merely told consumers that they could once again receive expert assistance at its stores.

McDonald's has also avoided confronting its service and product quality deficiencies head-on. It could learn a lesson from fast-food rival Hardee's, which recently 'fessed up. To try to rebuild its credibility and return to profitability, the Hardee's unit of CKE Restaurants created an ad campaign that directly addresses its sins. In the commercials, Andrew Puzder, CKE's CEO, concedes that Hardee's hasn't satisfied its customers in recent years, with consumers complaining about shoddy service, bad food, and a confusing menu. The ads conclude with the slogan "It's how the last place you'd go for a burger will become the first."

Hardee's is making the confession to help promote its new menu, which includes "thickburgers," the behemoths of the fast-food industry at 451 grams and nearly 1,100 calories. Such self-deprecation may indeed attract sorely needed customers; at the very least, Hardee's executives are confident that the confessional campaign will be novel enough to grab people's attention.

General Motors took its sweet time to publicly declare its shortcomings in automotive quality. But better late than never. At least it is accepting responsibility in its latest corporate image advertising campaign for what many people have long known: that GM lost its way and learned some humbling lessons from its competitors. The company's fall from grace is certainly stunning: it holds a U.S. market share of about 27 percent today, compared with about 45 percent in 1980.

Now GM claims it is on the road to recovery—and, it hopes, redemption. A corporate ad shows the sun piercing through dark clouds over a desolate winding road, along with the headline "The longest road in the world is the road to redemption." The ad goes on to state, "Thirty years ago, GM quality was the best in the world. Twenty years ago, it wasn't," and it then describes the company's quality improvements over the past decade.

GM has alluded to quality problems in the past, but never as blatantly as in this campaign. The advertising is certainly gutsy—and risky.

It's far from certain that GM's belated acknowledgment will significantly improve its reputation and draw more people into its showrooms. One thing is certain, though: GM will have to deliver outstanding quality because consumers are sure to be highly skeptical about whether it deserves redemption—or rejection.

STAY VIGILANT TO EVER-PRESENT PERILS

It was a simple decision made by a low-ranking employee: when rescue workers from the nearby site of the September 11 terrorism attack on the World Trade Center sought a few cases of bottled water from a Starbucks coffee shop, the employee charged them. In a matter of hours, the Internet had picked up the story, and it began circulating globally through e-mails, water-cooler chat and other word-of-mouth channels. Suddenly Starbucks was the target of ill will, its carefully cultivated reputation instantly besmirched. The employee's blunder occurred in an atmosphere charged with grief. Any show of apparent insensitivity met with great indignation.

"I hate Starbucks," declares Christopher Johnston, a financial planner in New Orleans. "It's absurd that this big company would charge rescue workers for water when small shop owners were giving them food and anything else they needed." More than two years later, Mr. Johnston continues to boycott Starbucks.

The reputation damage was compounded by Starbucks management's tardy and defensive response to the public relations disaster. At corporate headquarters in Seattle, nearly 3,000 miles away from Ground Zero, the company didn't recognize the potential public relations nightmare and understand the urgency of apologizing to the world as fast as possible. The employee's lack of sensitivity was shocking enough, but the company's delayed response to the incident proved even more troubling.

An e-mail message quickly began circulating relating the story of how ambulance service workers had sought water for people in shock from the disaster and ended up being charged $130 for three cases at Starbucks. "Can you believe they actually charged for it?" the e-mail said. "I would think that in a crisis such as this, vendors in the area would be more than happy to lend a little help by donating water. Well, not Starbucks! As if this country hasn't given them enough money! Now, I love frappuccinos as much as anyone, but any company that would try to make a profit off of a crisis like this doesn't deserve the American public's hard-earned money." The e-mail concluded with a call for a boycott of Starbucks.

Starbucks eventually apologized and reimbursed the ambulance company the $130. But not until Robert Jamieson, a columnist at the *Seattle Post-Intelligencer* newspaper, challenged Starbucks in print did it issue public statements about the incident.

In a September 25 press release, a full two weeks after the terrorist attacks, Starbucks tried to protect its honor and called the newspaper column damaging to the morale of the many employees in New York who had volunteered their time and donated food and beverages at Ground Zero. The company appeared defensive and self-serving when it issued a press release the next day touting its donation of more than 14,000 gallons of coffee to the relief effort and quoting a Red Cross official's praise for Starbucks.

Then, on September 27, the company finally addressed the issue in its coffee shops by posting a letter from its CEO. "As president and CEO of Starbucks, I was dismayed to learn about this incident," Orin Smith stated in the letter to customers. "While it is unquestionable that the appropriate response should have been to donate the water, I cannot put myself in the place or state of mind of the young person who made this decision in the frightening and chaotic aftermath of this unimaginable tragedy. Regardless, the decision is not defensible and is totally inconsistent with what we stand for and would expect from a Starbucks partner [employee]."

But it was too little too late for people like Gina St. Denise, an executive assistant who lives in Redondo Beach, California. She was angrier with Starbucks' management than with the New York employee. "Mistakes do happen," she says, "but the lack of a quick, meaningful response to something that monumental is what really bothered me. The company was so defensive I couldn't believe it." She no longer patronizes Starbucks and urges her family and friends to follow her example.

It was indeed hard to believe that this was really Starbucks bungling such a serious challenge to its reputation. In its coffee shops, Starbucks promotes its ranking as one of America's best places to work and displays pamphlets describing its good deeds regarding such issues as children's literacy, humanitarian aid to coffee farmers, and environmental protection. It clearly perceives the importance of corporate citizenship to consumer goodwill and corporate reputation.

Starbucks' hiring materials stress the need to smile and be friendly, "provide excellent customer service," and "enjoy helping others." To motivate employees, the company offers them outstanding benefits and stock options. In short, Starbucks understands that its frontline coffee servers represent the corporate brand and affect its reputation as much as or more than the quality of its lattes and frappuccinos. "Our partners are an integral part of achieving our goal of becoming a great, enduring company with the most recognized and respected brand in the world, known for inspiring and nurturing the human spirit," the Starbucks Coffee Career Journey pamphlet states. "Partners help us maintain our uncompromising principles as we grow."

Yet despite all of its reputation-building achievements and activities, Starbucks stumbled badly in the immediate aftermath of America's most chilling catastrophe. The incident itself reflects weakness in Starbucks' employee communication and training procedures, especially in instilling its brand values. The employee's decision to charge rescue workers for the water showed that the company's highly touted values of customer satisfaction, respect for others, and a "good-neighbor" policy in local communities hadn't completely permeated its workplace. His actions reflected not only terrible judgment but also a lack of the social responsibility Starbucks espouses.

For its part, Starbucks says it wanted to get all of the facts straight before responding to the incident. Audrey Lincoff, director of public affairs and media relations, says the company believed it had put the matter to rest after reimbursing and apologizing to the ambulance company and asking that a posting about the issue be removed from an AOL bulletin board. "We were surprised to learn that people continued to share this [story] on the Internet since the matter had already been resolved," she continues. "It was not until a columnist from our local Seattle paper chose to write his column that we realized how widespread this had become. In other words, we thought we were being vigilant in responding to those who had raised concerns with us."

The reaction from corporate headquarters suggests both overconfidence in the strength of Starbucks' reputation and naiveté about the power of the Internet and word-of-mouth communication. Starbucks clearly didn't realize how delicate reputation is and how alert it must be to unexpected threats.

EVER VIGILANT

You can't be too vigilant. It's as simple as that. Whether through careless neglect or outright hubris, many companies are not nearly sensitive enough to the never-ending threats to their precious reputations.

Companies must be vigilant to both incidents like the Starbucks public relations gaffe and to gradual but steady reputation erosion. It doesn't take a crisis to ruin reputation. Trouble can come in the form of a slow, almost unnoticeable decline in reputation, prompted perhaps by a new competitor with a better product, such as the Japanese assault on the U.S. auto market. In fact, gradual reputation erosion, if it goes undetected, is often the most pernicious and hardest to correct.

Some companies feel invincible. But it's foolhardy to say that nothing can happen to damage your reputation, no matter how powerful it appears. Indeed, American companies with the strongest reputations, such as Coca-Cola, must be extra vigilant these days because of intense anti-American feelings in some foreign countries.

For large companies, the potential for damage is greater than ever in an age when information seems to travel at the speed of light and they can be so easily blindsided. "It's so different from ten years ago," says Eric Kraus, vice president of corporate communications at Gillette. "The thing that really hampers us now is that something very local quickly becomes a global pain in the ass because of the Internet and twenty-four-hour cable news channels." He says he checks various electronic news retrieval sources first thing every morning to try to keep pace with the information superhighway. Gillette also has created an elaborate system to monitor Internet chat rooms and other sites for dangerous misinformation about the company and its brands.

Ideally, companies are watchful enough to head off threats before they become problems. To accomplish that, it's critical to assign specific people responsibility for guarding reputation and, like Gillette, to develop strong monitoring and internal communication systems.

Of course, no system is foolproof. It isn't always possible to head off threats to your reputation before they become public knowledge. The next best thing, then, is to keep your ears cocked and detect dangers to your reputation before they get out of hand. To gain the advantage, develop a plan of action and respond to the issue both internally and externally. Don't dilly-dally, and don't be defensive. And be prepared to react to every imaginable situation.

BP, the energy giant formerly called British Petroleum, certainly never expected to clash with Native Americans over one of their most famous warriors and leaders. But that's exactly what happened when the company slipped up and named a new oil project Crazy Horse. Descendants of Crazy Horse were deeply offended and, together with the Interfaith Center on Corporate Responsibility, immediately protested the commercial use of such a sacred name.

It would have been far better had BP been more culturally sensitive, but at least the company recognized the potential reputation threat in the important U.S. market. BP reacted quickly and gracefully. It didn't let the controversy escalate and spark a courtroom battle. Not only did the company change the name of the project to Thunder Horse, but BP executives also met personally with Crazy Horse family members and tribal leaders to offer gifts and express their apologies.

The company told the Native Americans that it regretted the misuse of the Crazy Horse name, which a BP spokesman said he came to understand would have been like calling an oil discovery "the Virgin Mary number three." In the end, BP's strategy won positive press coverage and kudos from the Interfaith Center and other corporate responsibility groups for the company's sensitivity to Native American culture and values.

Unfortunately, it often takes a calamity to learn the importance of vigilance. Fast-food companies such as Burger King had to recall hazardous toys in their kids' meals and be sued before they took proper precautions. Only after children suffocated on some of their toys did they realize the need to be more watchful. Restaurant operators saw that

REPUTATION THREATS

In a survey of nearly six hundred corporate executives by Hill & Knowlton, criticism by the news media was named as the leading threat to reputation. It was an even greater concern than unethical behavior. Here is the percentage of respondents who said they are most concerned about these threats to corporate reputation.

Criticism of the company or its products in print or broadcast media: 49%

Unethical corporate behavior: 42%

A disaster that disrupts operations: 36%

Litigation or adverse court judgments: 35%

Allegations about product safety problems by a special-interest group or customers: 29%

Allegations about product or employee safety problems by government officials: 24%

Criticism of the company or its products on the Internet: 13%

they, not the toy makers alone, should test the giveaway trinkets for safety.

Cruise-ship lines have learned a lesson from the Norwalk virus, which caused stomach ailments among many of the ships' passengers, hurt their reputations for health and safety, and cut into bookings in 2002. By 2003, the cruise lines were being extremely cautious about severe acute respiratory syndrome (SARS) in order to prevent another blow to their image. They canceled or shifted itineraries in hard-hit Asian countries, while passengers from such cities as Hong Kong and Toronto either were banned from sailing or received a medical check at dockside. The cruise companies realized that prevention is the best medicine for an ailing reputation.

Sometimes even the most dedicated watchdogs aren't vigilant enough about their own reputation. The staff of *The New York Times* is very alert to the shortcomings and wrongdoing that hurt the reputations of corporations, but it allowed its own reputation for journalistic integrity to be seriously damaged in 2003. The newspaper disclosed that there had been "widespread fabrication and plagiarism" in the reporting of former staff member Jayson Blair, which the publisher, Arthur Ochs Sulzberger,

Jr., called "a huge black eye" for the *Times*. Realizing the potential harm to its image, the *Times* gave a full accounting of the known inaccuracies in the reporter's articles and vowed to prevent any further journalistic fraud. It even asked readers to report any additional falsehoods in Blair's work to a special e-mail address.

But clearly, the newspaper wasn't vigilant enough in recognizing the damage a dishonest reporter could inflict on its reputation. There were early warnings within the newspaper of problems with Blair's work and the *Times* said that it had reprimanded him and that he had taken a personal leave of absence. But after his return, the newspaper apparently didn't continue to monitor closely what was an obvious threat to its reputation.

At least companies should learn from such painful experiences and develop a system for detecting reputation threats. Howell Raines, executive editor of the *Times*, sent an e-mail message to employees, telling them a committee would be formed to address what had gone wrong. He also said that lack of communication among editors and news desks was a central issue and offered "a blueprint for corrective action."

But such moves weren't enough. To restore morale and confidence in the leadership of the *Times*, Raines and Gerald Boyd, the managing editor and number two newsroom executive, ultimately submitted their resignations.

BEWARE OF BOYCOTTERS

Nestlé botched its reputation badly in late 2002, first by making an insensitive move and then by trying to justify its decision rather than protect its good name. Its lack of vigilance led to calls for boycotting the company, one of the most forceful and increasingly common reputation perils.

It all started when news leaked out that Nestlé was seeking about $6 million from Ethiopia to compensate for assets nationalized by a military regime more than a quarter of a century earlier. Everyone from the antihunger group Oxfam International to individual citizens denounced Nestlé. How could a company with annual profits of more than $5 billion demand money from a famine-stricken nation?

Activists immediately latched on to a statement made by Nestlé CEO Peter Brabeck-Letmathe in a 1999 speech entitled "Beyond Corporate

Image: the Search for Trust." "A few years down the road, we are going to be asked not only if we have maximized short-term shareholder value," he said, "but also some other, more difficult questions. Among them will certainly be: What have you done to help fight hunger in developing countries?" His words had certainly come back to haunt Nestlé. "That is the question Oxfam is now asking," the group said, referring to the speech.

As people called for boycotts of Nestlé's products and fired off angry e-mails to corporate executives, the company tried to explain its stance on the Ethiopian issue but proved unconvincing. Nestlé argued that it was a matter of principle and that such compensation payments were necessary if Ethiopia expected to attract foreign investors in the future. Finally, after all the uproar, Nestlé officials backed down and announced that they would donate any money the company collected from Ethiopia to hunger relief programs.

The Ethiopia fiasco reveals Nestlé's lack of vigilance in anticipating and heading off the reputation threat of a major boycott. Nestlé's failure to sense the reputation damage is especially surprising because the Swiss company is no stranger to boycotts. It was the target of perhaps the most famous international boycott of the late twentieth century. For some ten years, activist groups promoted a boycott of Nestlé because of its aggressive marketing of its infant formula to breast-feeding mothers in poor developing nations. Eventually, in 1986, the boycotters and Nestlé reached a truce.

Boycotts pose one of the most worrisome threats to corporate reputation. Not only do boycotters shun companies themselves, but they also encourage other people to stop buying their products. A boycott can be an international campaign orchestrated by a group such as Oxfam or Greenpeace, a community protest, or an individual's personal crusade.

Companies may not like boycotts, but the worst thing they can do is ignore them. They should never shut off communication with the individuals or groups leading the campaign. Rather, they should make contact with the boycotters early on to begin a dialogue. While companies shouldn't bend easily to such pressure tactics, there's always a good chance of making peace. It may require a company to admit it erred and change its ways. But that just might make it look heroic and bolster its reputation.

In 1990, the StarKist tuna business bowed to demands from the Earth Island Institute, a San Francisco environmental group, that it stop

BOYCOTTING BEHAVIOR

In the 2002 Harris Interactive study of corporate reputation, 66 percent of respondents said they had done at least one thing in the following list of boycott activities.

Refused to purchase a company's products or services: 57%

Encouraged someone else not to purchase a company's products or services: 49%

Signed a petition: 18%

Encouraged someone else not to purchase a company's stock or to sell a company's stock: 18%

Sold a company's stock or a mutual fund containing the company's stock: 7%

Displayed an anticompany message at home, on clothing or on one's vehicle: 4%

Participated in a march or demonstration against a company: 1%

buying tuna caught with nets that kill dolphins. Although the boycott hadn't hurt its sales much, StarKist realized that its image was on the line—especially after it received letters from dolphin-loving school-children. StarKist couldn't afford to be branded a slaughterer of dolphins. It emerged looking like a caring company and played up its actions by plastering a "dolphin safe" logo on its cans of tuna.

Surprisingly, many companies seem to turn a blind eye to the risks of being boycotted. Executives at Harris Interactive find that their clients pay little attention to such information. They'd rather learn about what makes people recommend their products and invest in their stock.

Companies are mostly aware of big, ballyhooed boycotts, such as Kentucky Fried Chicken's being targeted by People for the Ethical Treatment of Animals (PETA) for alleged mistreatment of chickens or Exxon and Mobil gasoline stations' being boycotted by environmentalists who believe that Exxon Mobil executives are undermining efforts to reduce global warming. There was even a Boycott Brand America movement during the war in Iraq, urging people around the globe to shun all American-made products.

There also are millions of quiet individual boycotters. Remember: anyone can be a boycotter. Harris Interactive's surveys show that 66 percent of the general public has participated in some type of boycotting activity against a company. Harris also found that boycotters tend to be affluent and well educated. They don't fit the stereotype of liberal college students and fringe groups.

Personal boycotters are less visible than the media-savvy activist groups. They are the disgruntled customers who stop buying your products and services and bad-mouth you to their friends and neighbors. Although they're often hard to detect, you can be alert to complaint trends in your customer service department and negative comments on your corporate Web site and in chat rooms on other sites.

As if spontaneous boycotts weren't enough, Web sites have even sprung up publicizing boycotts against such companies and organizations as Diamond Walnut Company, The Gap, Neiman Marcus, and the World Bank, and encouraging more consumer activism, or "marketplace democracy in action." Visitors to one site can download a boycott organizers' guide with tips on researching companies, using the media, sponsoring rallies to raise awareness, blitzing the target company with e-mails, and even securing an endorsement from a celebrity or well-known organization. Clearly, companies can't afford to let their guard down.

WHO'S IN CHARGE?

Corporate reputation is so valuable and so vulnerable that it demands a full-time watchdog.

Many CEOs say they are ultimately responsible for their company's reputation. That's true, of course, just as they are ultimately accountable for the company's financial statements. But they also rely on their vice president of finance to oversee the corporate ledger.

Companies must assign the day-to-day caretaker duties for their reputations to a specific department or executive. It must be clear who is empowered to protect reputation, who bears the responsibility of being the company's radar.

Sometimes there's a split in reputation management responsibilities between the chief marketing officer and the chief communications officer. The marketing executive typically works on building reputation, while the communications manager puts out fires. The two functions may mesh well, but they can just as easily conflict.

A small but growing number of companies are anointing one person as the primary reputation manager. After all, there's the CFO (chief financial officer) and CMO (chief marketing officer). Why not a CRO (chief reputation officer)? GlaxoSmithKline comes close: it established the position of vice president of corporate image and reputation, which is held by Duncan Burke. "It can be daunting, but it's a great job," says Burke. "You need to have one executive actively managing reputation all the time and reminding people that when you're a large company in the spotlight, you're certain to come under attack. The challenge is to be prepared."

Sears, Roebuck & Company also recently beefed up its reputation management process because the company says it may face fifteen to twenty "minicrises" a day. The key is to determine which to focus on. Overnight customer surveys help Sears decide. The survey includes questions about whether consumers have heard anything about Sears in the news recently and whether their perception of the company is positive or negative. "We don't want to be Chicken Little saying the sky is falling over every negative story," says Ron Culp, who recently retired as senior vice president of public relations and government affairs. "We can look at the tracking data before we rush out with a press release and fan the flames of a potential controversy. People may feel they don't care about an issue as long as they get their washer delivered on time."

At FedEx, William Margaritis serves as reputation chief. In his job as corporate vice president of worldwide communications and investor relations, he commands a large crew, including vice presidents of corporate communications and investor relations, employee communications managers, and public relations managers for both domestic and international matters.

"Some of the best reputation battles are won before the fight ever begins," says Margaritis. "If you are a step ahead, if you have thought through all these potential issues and crises before they even occur, you are better prepared. For FedEx, this means involving the collective thinking of all its experts, a mix of people from around the company."

Nancy Daigler views herself as the reputation czar at Merck. The executive director of corporate communications, she tries to provide more focus and coordination, working closely with investor relations, the ethics office, and media relations, as well as public affairs managers outside the United States. She is kept very busy these days as pharmaceutical manufacturers face constant criticism and reputation damage from politicians and patients railing against the rising cost of drugs.

Daigler gets involved in communicating the company's side of the story when a newspaper headline announces, for example, that "Merck Is Accused of Inflating Price of Heartburn Drug" or "Merck Ads for Arthritis Drug Attract Regulatory Scrutiny." But she much prefers her other role of trying to publicize the company's positive actions, such as its decision to streamline patients' access to Merck's drug assistance program for the needy. Merck officials believe that until recently, they did a poor job of communicating their corporate social responsibility activities.

"Protecting reputation is really everyone's responsibility at Merck," Daigler says, "but my staff [of 15 people] and I guide our reputation management process. The reality is that there's no way to prevent issues from arising; it's how you manage through them in the end that matters."

Vigilance isn't only about dealing with controversies. Companies should be attentive to more than the sudden squall. They need to be alert to seemingly minor problems that can weaken their image in the long run. David Sylvia, director of corporate identity at Altria Group, has been placed in charge of establishing the new name and image for the company formerly known as Philip Morris. "In the past, we didn't proactively manage corporate reputation," he says. "Now we have a new identity and a bit of a fresh start with Altria."

Early on, he is focusing on how the Altria name is used by the news media and the public. For example, if radio and television reporters butcher the name, he sends them a recorded "sound bite" of the correct way to pronounce it: *Al*-tree-uh. There was also an "Altria Identity Challenge" quiz on the company's Web site to test people's knowledge of the new brand name. "If we don't get it right now," Sylvia says, "we're doomed."

He is pulling together a "brand council" to oversee Altria's image that will include representatives from many departments, such as human resources, legal, investor relations, government affairs, compliance and integrity, and public affairs. They will be Altria's brand cops. "I will drive home the importance of managing the corporate brand and reputation within their departments," Sylvia says. "It's as important as managing our Oreo cookie and Marlboro cigarette brands."

HUMMINGBIRDS AND HUFFING

Here's a close-up look at how one reputation watchdog does his job.

It was all in a week's work for Doug Zacker, Home Depot's reputation guardian. First, People for the Ethical Treatment of Animals (PETA) issued an "action alert" charging the retailer with cruelly using glue traps to capture and kill birds flying loose in its stores. Mr. Zacker informed PETA that Home Depot doesn't use glue traps and is working to solve the problem. Among the possible solutions: netting in its outdoor garden centers—sort of like a giant driving range for golfers—to prevent the birds from flying into the stores. "There is often a communications gap between what people think and what's really happening," says Zacker. "I have to bridge that gap. When PETA put up that action alert, we got tons of mail."

Next came a report on ABC-TV's *Good Morning, America* about the risky practice by some children of "huffing," or inhaling household products such as paint and paint thinner to get high. In an interview with Diane Sawyer, an attorney for a civil rights group said that retailers, including Home Depot, were violating the law in California and selling products to kids containing the potentially dangerous ingredient toluene. The California group had sued Home Depot and other companies for such alleged violations.

Home Depot certainly didn't like being criticized on national television. But Zacker waited and watched before responding. It turned out that the story didn't have legs. It wasn't picked up widely by other media and didn't spark a flood of e-mails and letters. So he didn't issue a press release. But internally, Home Depot was busy checking whether its California stores were indeed being lax in enforcing the company's stated policy of checking identification to avoid selling certain products to minors. "There apparently was a gap in this case between what we said we'd do and what we were actually doing in some stores," Zacker concedes.

As Home Depot's reputation guru, Zacker is feeling his way in a position that's very new to corporate America. But he's a perfect illustration of how the job of reputation manager is taking shape.

Zacker must constantly keep his antennae up and attuned to possible reputation threats. He considers his job much like that of a project manager. Most of his projects are potential headaches other people would rather avoid. "Everybody's responsible for reputation, but nobody wants to touch the hot-potato issues," he says. "The danger is that they will end up festering because everybody is just staring at them like fly balls in center field."

So when there's a letter to the CEO or a newspaper article that could pose reputation problems, it's up to Zacker to bring the right people at Home Depot together and to drive the reputation management process. He has a broad enough knowledge of the company to ask the right questions and also to be a sounding board for other managers. The next step is coordinating communication on the issue both inside the company and to different external stakeholder groups. "People want to know you're doing something about an issue," Zacker says. "It's all about meeting people's expectations."

He also works closely with Home Depot's investor relations department. For instance, he tries to help resolve proposed shareholder resolutions so they don't end up on the proxy statement for the company's annual meeting. One recent resolution called for Home Depot to adopt the environmental conduct principles of the Coalition for Environmentally Responsible Economies (CERES). "We know our corporate responsibility reports need to be more sophisticated, but we were able to temporarily appease the organization proposing the resolution," Zacker says. "We explained that we're seriously looking at different reporting standards."

Jonathan Roseman, who also oversees reputation issues at Home Depot, views himself and Zacker as "counselors" to the entire organization whenever and wherever issues arise. "We aren't just public relations people," he says. "We consult with the business units and take a proactive approach. We say, 'If you do this, here's what might happen.'" He prefers to think of his role as reputation management and not reputation repair. "The Home Depot brand is the promise, and reputation is how you deliver on that promise," he says. "Doug and I are the promise keepers."

LAW TEN

MAKE YOUR EMPLOYEES YOUR REPUTATION CHAMPIONS

Citizens Financial Group describes itself as "not your typical bank." It might be more fitting to change its slogan to "Your warm and cuddly bank."

The bank's new credo urges employees to "hug the customer. Smile. Say 'thank you.' Give customers a reason to say, 'Wow, I love these people.' In short, treat the customer the way you would love to be treated all the time." Sounds pretty mushy—and pretty unrealistic in this era of dismal customer service. But Citizens isn't kidding. It really does expect employees to make the customer feel loved.

How does Citizens motivate its employees to deliver on its credo? It all starts with Larry Fish, chairman and CEO of Providence, Rhode Island–based Citizens Financial Group, a subsidiary of the Royal Bank of Scotland Group. Every morning, as soon as he arrives at his office, his first order of business is sending kudos to a few of the bank's employees. He writes a note to thank them or congratulate them on a job well done. He wouldn't consider conveying his good wishes by e-mail because it lacks the personal touch of a handwritten message. "I spend more than half of my time on people, connecting with them emotionally," says Fish. "People work for more than their pocket; they also work for their heart."

No one can champion a company like its own employees. But to make employees effective reputation boosters, companies must create a culture that supports and motivates them. They, in turn, will feel a robust allegiance and go above and beyond the performance expected of them.

By stroking his employees, Fish reinforces the loyalty of his squad of Citizens cheerleaders. "I have to nourish our employees," he says. "You can't have a successful business without happy employees. Happy employees smile and return calls promptly."

His kind words do indeed seal many employees' commitment to Citizens. Terri Raymond, vice president and district sales director of in-store banking, feels as if she's part of a family and a very important contributor to Citizens. "I know I'm a small portion of a large organization, but I don't feel small," she says. When Fish calls her by name and sends her congratulatory notes about her performance, it's a great ego boost. "The sweetest song to anyone's ears is their own name," she says, citing Dale Carnegie's famous line. "I feel like I'm working directly for Larry. He makes me feel more committed to my job and eager to perform for the bank."

Larry Fish also serves as a role model for managers like Terri Raymond. With her own staff, she has started emulating his practice of acknowledging significant moments in employees' lives, such as a marriage or the death of a family member.

Citizens encourages employees to feel comfortable about expressing their concerns to supervisors or even top-level executives. Fish calls a few branch managers each day to get a status report and ask them what they need from him. They might ask for an additional teller, geraniums for the office planters, or a $100 donation to the neighborhood Little League team. Fish also meets about fifteen employees for lunch twice a month "to preach our values of doing right by the customer." He figures they return to their jobs and talk about the lunch with colleagues. "So I end up touching a total of a hundred and fifty people with one of my lunches," he says.

Fish supports employees when he believes customers are unfairly criticizing them or even abusing them. He recalls a woman who treated one of the tellers badly but was a valued customer with $172,000 deposited in the bank. Nonetheless, Fish called her and told her he understood there had been a problem and that it would be better if she closed her account with Citizens. Flabbergasted, she said, "You can't do that." To which, Fish replied, "Yes, I can," and arranged for a check to be mailed to her. "You send a message to employees with such an action," he says. "The customer isn't always right."

At the same time, Fish is demanding of employees. "I can call a thousand people in the company by their first names," he boasts, "and I expect that of people who work for me." When he interviews candidates for executive positions, he makes sure they understand the Citizens culture. He asks what they do to stay fit. "This is a vigorous environment that's fast-paced, not contemplative," he explains. He asks what they plan to do in the community because Citizens wants generous people who will give back. And he asks what their typical workday is like. "We start early," he says. "If your biological clock is more oriented toward evening, it might not work." Fish himself sets the tone at Citizens for showing a high energy level and taking on new challenges—both in the office and in his private life. He has swum the icy waters between San Francisco and Alcatraz and climbed Mount Kilimanjaro with his children.

Citizens' biggest challenge is to maintain employees' spirit as it continues to grow larger. Since the early 1990s, Citizens has acquired a string of banks and expanded from 1,500 employees to more than 15,000. "We have to make sure as we get bigger that we retain the culture and employees still feel it," says Theresa McLaughlin, executive vice president and director of marketing. "We must keep acting like a small bank for our employees and customers." It helps that the bank is decentralized with five regional divisions, each of which has its own president, public affairs director, and other officers. The addition of so many new employees also spurred Citizens to write the credo that clearly spells out its values.

Citizens' advertising campaign is aimed at employees as much as customers. Called "legendary service," the campaign highlights employees who have provided exemplary service. In one ad, the drive-through window equipment fails and a teller dashes out in the pouring rain to process a deposit at the customer's car. In another, a loan officer completes a home equity loan at the consumer's home. There's also the tale of the assistant branch manager in Massachusetts who delivered a teddy bear to the new home of a one-year-old boy. He had left the bear behind at the mortgage closing earlier that day.

"These actual incidents bring the Citizens brand to life and give it heart," says McLaughlin. "It makes people say these guys are really different, that it really is not your typical bank."

To help inspire such behavior, Citizens offers extensive employee benefits, including child care subsidies, financial aid when a tragedy strikes, home buyer assistance, and a generous military leave policy. Citizens also makes a point of frequently honoring and rewarding outstanding employee behavior. For Thanksgiving 2001, the bank awarded more than 5,000 employees below the level of vice president with "success bonuses" of $100 to $400 each because of the company's substantial growth. Every year, Citizens devotes a full week to employee appreciation events, with barbecues, miniature golf tournaments, Family Feud games, comedy shows, and costumed employees galore. (Top managers wear wizard hats.)

"It's so important for people to be proud of where they work," says Fish, one of the wizards. "I tell our people I'll never let them down on integrity. If you deliver on that promise, your employees will go to the cliff edge for you."

CORPORATE AMBASSADORS

Larry Fish is rare among CEOs in that he recognizes the value of employees to corporate reputation and makes them his goodwill ambassadors. It's the employees who are on the front lines working with customers, suppliers, shareholders, government officials, and other audiences. They must be your loyal allies because their effect on your reputation is immense. They can be your biggest fans or your worst enemies.

Employees, of course, have the greatest impact in their dealings with customers. As many companies know all too well, poor service does incredible damage to their reputations. But what many companies underestimate is the more subtle influence of employees—from the executive suite to the mailroom—on reputation. Employees' behavior and comments outside business hours can carry significant weight. They affect how their friends, neighbors, and relatives feel about the company. In many cases, people's only experience with a company is through its workers. Word-of-mouth impressions gleaned from employees can be quite positive if they're fiercely loyal to their companies—or deadly if they're miserable in their jobs.

Research by Towers, Perrin, a human resources consulting firm, has found a strong relationship between employee engagement and customer satisfaction, which in turn correlates closely with strong corporate

WORKPLACE WINNERS

In a 2002 Harris Interactive corporate reputation study, the public rated these companies highest for being good places to work and for having good employees.

BEST COMPANIES TO WORK FOR

1. UPS
2. Johnson & Johnson
3. Coca-Cola
4. Home Depot
5. Walt Disney
6. Eastman Kodak
7. Harley-Davidson
8. FedEx
9. Maytag
10. Southwest Airlines/Sony/Microsoft

COMPANIES WITH THE BEST EMPLOYEES

1. Johnson & Johnson
2. UPS
3. Dell
4. Home Depot
5. Harley-Davidson
6. Walt Disney
7. Southwest Airlines
8. FedEx
9. IBM
10. Coca-Cola/Maytag

reputation and financial performance. However, Towers found that few managers motivate employees successfully. A minority of employees in the Towers study said that their managers communicate effectively (28%), empower workers (24%), provide goals and directions (21%), and recognize and reward good performance (21%).

A 2001 workplace study also revealed a low level of loyalty and commitment among employees. Walker Information, an Indianapolis research firm that studies employee relationships with their companies, found that only 24 percent of survey respondents feel "true loyalty" or commitment and a desire to stay with their employers for at least two more years. While 64 percent of people said they feel proud to work at their companies, fewer have a strong attachment (45%) and believe their employers deserve their loyalty (43%).

Today employee loyalty at some companies is even lower. Employees are more cynical and less trusting because of all the recent cases of accounting abuse and executive greed. What's more, job insecurity, poor morale, and excessive workloads have eroded employees' commitment to companies.

"Companies have been slow to involve employees in reputation management," says James Fink, vice chairman of Opinion Research Corporation in Princeton, New Jersey. "Employees need to be aligned with the company's business strategy and the desired shape of its reputation. They need to understand how they can affect the strategy in their interaction with customers, suppliers, and the local community."

But more companies are beginning to recognize the significant role employees can play in the reputation management process. Sears, Roebuck & Company recently started tapping twenty managers it views as up-and-comers and placing them as board members or volunteers at local nonprofit organizations. "Our internal influencers program will raise Sears' profile in the Chicago community, where we have been less involved since we moved out to the suburbs," says Ron Culp, who recently retired as senior vice president of public relations and government affairs. "Their reputation as bright, energetic, committed people will prove to be a positive for Sears' reputation."

Sears also keeps in closer touch with all of its employees these days. The retailer conducts a monthly online survey to measure employee sentiment and detect concerns and problems early on. In addition, there's a regular online newsletter from the CEO to keep employees informed of the latest corporate developments.

Some companies have long understood the benefit of making employees their biggest boosters. S. C. Johnson & Son, the household products maker, states in its corporate philosophy, "We believe our fundamental strength lies in our people." It encourages employee commitment with many work-life balance programs, such as sabbaticals, including benefits and partial pay, to "recharge their batteries" and a "no meeting day" policy two Fridays a month. The meeting-free Fridays allow employees to be more productive so they don't have to take work home on the weekend.

Nearly a century ago, Goodyear Tire & Rubber Company recognized that employees heavily influenced its reputation. F. A. Seiberling, Goodyear's president, posted signs throughout Goodyear's offices and factories with the simple statement "Protect our good name." In an advertisement in the *Saturday Evening Post* in 1915, Seiberling wrote that the message "gives to us a motive that is bigger and broader and deeper than money. It makes thousands of men happier in their work and more faithful to it. It has made of this business a democracy of united thought, a democracy of common endeavor, a democracy of purpose and principle."

Personal recognition goes a long way toward making employees your biggest advocates. More companies are providing bonuses tied to performance. Continental Airlines, for example, rewards employees with small cash bonuses if it meets its monthly on-time flight arrivals goal.

Other companies reward employees with dinners and awards to recognize achievements that contribute to corporate reputation. The annual Good Citizens Recognition awards, for example, honor Johnson & Johnson divisions and their employees who were the top participants in blood drives, United Way campaigns, and savings bond purchases.

Each year, FedEx gives its humanitarian award to workers who "promote human welfare, particularly in life-threatening situations" and its Golden Falcon award to employees who demonstrate "exceptional performance or unselfish acts that enhance customer service." Winners have included a manager who expedited the delivery of donor organs and a technician who rescued a girl abducted by a stranger.

Because reputation building starts inside a company, internal communications and branding programs are essential. The goal is to turn every employee into a corporate brand manager. But first, employees must understand what the corporate brand means and how their jobs relate to it. It's also important to keep employees informed about philanthropy and other corporate citizenship activities, which can be very motivating.

In some ways, communicating with thousands of employees scattered around the globe is more challenging than reaching the public through media advertising. To be successful, internal communications must be much more than reference manuals, employee newsletters, and occasional e-mails. There's no substitute for personal contact. Employees should learn about corporate brand image, values, and goals at town hall–type meetings with the CEO where there's opportunity for discus-

PROTECT OUR GOOD NAME—GOODYEAR

Some companies have long recognized how integral employees are to shaping and protecting corporate reputation. Here is an excerpt from an advertisement that F. A. Seiberling, president of Goodyear Tire & Rubber Company, wrote for the *Saturday Evening Post* in 1915. It discusses the company's policy of posting signs throughout its offices and factories reminding employees to "protect our good name."

Stripped to the waist, his huge torso streaming with sweat, a workman swings the heavy iron core to an iron table, and wrenches off a tire, which has just come steaming from the heater. His eye falls on the legend over his head, and he smiles. Our good name is also his good name. The two are intertwined. He will protect the one, while he subserves the other. His thoughts are—as they should be—chiefly of himself, of his little home, and of his family. Their good name, his good name, our good name—his good work will stand guard over them all.

Two thousand miles away—in Seattle, we will say—the same thought, in the same simple words. An irritating moment has arrived—the temptation to speak sharply to a customer, to fling a slur at unworthy competition. The salesman, or the manager, or whosoever it may be, looks up, and the quiet admonition meets his eye: Protect our good name. In a twinkling it smooths the wrinkles out of his point of view. He is himself again—a man with a responsibility which he could not escape if he would; and would not, if he could.

Back two thousand miles again to the factories—this time to the experimental room. An alluring chance to save—to make more profit by skimping, by substitution. No one will ever know. But the silent monitor repeats its impressive admonition: Protect our good name. What chance to compromise with conscience in the presence of that vigilant guardian? Thousands of men striving to keep a name clean. And keeping their own names clean in the process.

We Americans, it is said, make a god out of business. Let the slur stand. Whether it be true or not—it is true that business is our very life. Shall it be a reproach to us that we try to make business as good as business can be made? Think of *this* business, please, in the light of its great animating thought: Protect our good name.

sion and debate. Honest and frequent communication from the CEO and other top executives is crucial. And it should be two-way communication that gives employees access to executives to raise questions and concerns.

Internal marketing may be viewed cynically if it simply amounts to a lot of boring jargon and cheerleading. To rally employees, the communications must be inspirational and ring true. Corporate executives must repeatedly reinforce the values and behavior that are needed to meet the brand promise until they become second nature. After all, the image employees project to customers is whatever they believe that image to be. In the end, employees should come away with a feeling of empowerment in and ownership of the company.

BMW of North America tries to forge a strong bond with new employees through a two-day orientation. They learn what the BMW brand stands for and the importance of consistently living up to that image of performance and driving excitement. "All employees are ambassadors of the company," says James McDowell, vice president of marketing. "We give them frequent opportunities to drive the cars, and they can lease them at special rates. It's important that they feel connected to the product and enthusiastic about it."

CULTURE CLUB

Corporate culture is the key to creating a corps of dedicated employees. The workplace environment must excite and engage employees if they are to give the peak performance that will bolster the company's reputation with customers and other stakeholders.

"One of the essential but often overlooked elements of a great corporate reputation is that aura of surprise and excitement employees feel when they come to work," says Ken Roberts, chairman and CEO of Lippincott Mercer, a brand identity consultancy. "It translates through the employees into a more satisfying experience for the customer and warmer feelings about the company."

Establishing such a culture is hard work that requires constant attention. No company understands that better than Ben & Jerry's, the ice cream maker that has become legendary for its commitment to corporate responsibility and enjoys a superb reputation. Community service and environmental protection are important elements of the Ben &

Jerry's culture, but it's also about having fun while making fabulous ice cream for consumers.

Ben & Jerry's culture wouldn't work at many companies. But every company should heed Ben & Jerry's attempts to nurture and strengthen its culture. After the company was acquired in 2000 by Unilever, it became crucial to reassure employees about Ben & Jerry's continuing commitment to "improving our planet" and being a fun place to work. That, in turn, would reinforce *their* commitment to the company and help maintain its positive reputation with the public.

The company decided to form a Culture Club, a team of fifteen people from various departments to assess Ben & Jerry's culture historically and at the present time. A Global People Survey measured workers' attitudes about the company, and employees met in focus groups to discuss corporate values.

"What I find very different here is the level of commitment and passion—and fun," says Yves Couette, a Unilever veteran and president and CEO of Ben & Jerry's. "It's been a real eye-opener for me." He did bring to Ben & Jerry's an innovative process management system from Unilever. "Ben & Jerry's was very creative," he says, "but messy."

Couette encourages employees to continue many of Ben & Jerry's ways—from wearing blue jeans and bringing their dogs to work to making the annual Take Your Child to Work Day a special celebration. Employees' children create their own ice cream flavors and design their own paper cartons in the Cookie Dough Room and take nature walks around the pond near the company's headquarters.

Couette quickly saw how playful and irreverent the culture is—and he has absolutely no intention of changing it. How many employees would feel comfortable entering a contest in which they draw funny pictures of the CEO? Well, at Ben & Jerry's, employees were invited to let their imaginations run wild in drawing pictures of Couette and then post their artwork in the cafeteria. The contest title: The Three Faces of Yves (with apologies to the book and film *The Three Faces of Eve*).

To welcome the Frenchman to Vermont, employees donned berets on his first day on the job, built an Eiffel Tower out of ice cream cartons, and piped Edith Piaf music through the intercom system. After Couette's arrival, some employees lobbied to dream up a new name for the stuffy-sounding OCEO (Office of the Chief Executive Officer). Employees suggested new titles and voted on the entries. The winner: MOM, Managers of the Mission. Now employees ask, "Did you get

MOM's approval?" (Inspired by "Old MacDonald Had a Farm," OC-EIEIO was another contender.)

The company's "Vision for Growth Brand Cone" describes Ben & Jerry's as "a company of genuine, caring people, creating adventurous super premium products." The brand essence is defined as, "joy for the belly and soul."

Ben & Jerry's employees clearly feel pride in the company. It isn't unusual for them to walk into a grocery store and reconfigure a display of Ben & Jerry's ice cream if it's mixed up.

When Chrystie Heimert travels by air, she says, people see her Ben & Jerry's bag and ask if she really works there and if it's a cool job. "It makes you feel so proud; people don't react the same way if you have an IBM briefcase," says Heimert, director of public relations. (In true Ben & Jerry's style, her business card identifies her as the director of public elations.)

The company's esprit de corps means low employee turnover. When Ben & Jerry's does have openings, the human resources department is swamped with résumés. People even ask to do unpaid internships to get their foot in the door.

With its employees so fired up, managers want to make consumers feel as enthusiastic about Ben & Jerry's, too. Ben & Jerry's recently created a "Get Connected" program to encourage employees to interact with and learn more about their customers.

They can answer customer letters, attend consumer focus groups, or visit stores with a sales representative or delivery person and pick shoppers' brains. Some people volunteer to lead factory tours or scoop ice cream at a Ben & Jerry's shop.

"When we travel, we'll call up a loyal consumer and invite them to lunch or breakfast," says Walt Freese, the company's marketing chief. That's really getting close to the customer!

Ben & Jerry's hopes to create a group of dedicated "consumer crusaders" in all of its departments. Employees who participate in several activities will reach the "110-volt" consumer connection level and advance to an all-expenses-paid "consumer safari" outside Vermont "to engage with consumers in their natural habitat."

ENEMIES WITHIN

Companies that fail to make their employees their reputation champions are taking a big risk. Employees can become their most angry adversaries and erode their reputation.

Disgruntled employees not only let their performance slip, but they also are likely to paint their company as a villain to the outside world. Although they may present a very jaundiced view, employees enjoy a high degree of credibility because they're insiders and have developed a relationship with consumers.

Avon Products understands well how much clout the Avon Ladies ringing America's doorbells possess. They mean everything to the cosmetic company's reputation. They go into women's homes and are largely responsible for the public's perception of Avon. Andrea Jung, Avon's chairman and CEO, knew that she couldn't afford to alienate them when she decided to move the brand into retail stores. If she didn't communicate the decision just right, she risked a mutiny by Avon's 450,000 U.S. door-to-door sales representatives. Clearly, some hand-holding and reassurance were in order.

More than a year before Avon's entry into J.C. Penney stores, Jung began what she calls a "hypercommunications plan." She and other top managers met with the top-selling sales representatives and detailed Avon's plan for a higher-priced cosmetics line at Penney's that wouldn't compete directly with what they were peddling directly to women. "Out top sellers have great credibility and backed up the messages we were sending out to the entire sales force," says Jung. "We made sure our reps were the first to know as we developed our plans. It required honest and constant communication." Avon also acted quickly to dispel erroneous rumors about the Penney's plan that surfaced on the Internet.

In the end, the retail venture with Penney's flopped and was discontinued. But Avon had nevertheless succeeded in testing a new distribution channel without damaging its relationship with its independent sales representatives. In fact, Jung says that internal satisfaction surveys show that morale has reached an all-time high.

Unfortunately, few companies manage to maintain such positive employee relationships. IBM offended many of its employees in a controversy that quickly went public in 1999. The company announced plans to convert workers from a defined-benefit pension program to a cash-balance plan, angering many older workers, who expected to lose out. Employees squawked loudly. How could the company treat its dedicated longtime employees so coldly? After several months of open revolt, IBM backed down a bit and agreed to allow some workers over forty years old to remain in the old plan. But the issue still simmered among some employees, who continued to speak out at IBM's annual meetings and on Web sites that accused IBM of "pension theft" and "undermining the retirement security of tens of thousands of its most devoted employees." Eventually, they won their legal case against IBM. A federal judge ruled in 2003 that the company had indeed discriminated against older workers.

Relationships with labor unions require special care. AMR and its American Airlines unit didn't disclose some executive perks and did serious damage to their relationship with employees in the spring of 2003. To avoid bankruptcy, the company had asked the employee unions to accept sizable pay cuts. But at the same time, the company failed to give the unions details of lucrative bonuses and pension protections for senior executives. When news of the executive perks leaked out, the company's credibility was shot. Donald Carty, chairman and CEO, resigned to try to restore trust, but it will surely take much more to regain employees' loyalty.

Labor strife hurts a company's reputation when union leaders and workers paint an image of corporate greed. Verizon Communications became the target of one of the most public campaigns ever mounted against a company by its own workers. Bitter Verizon employees appeared in hard-hitting television commercials and in an NBC-TV *Today* show interview attacking the company's plans to lay them off, along with several thousand other workers.

The commercials, featuring members of the Communications Workers of America and their families, played on viewers' emotions. The workers complained that layoffs are the thanks Verizon workers receive after their hard work to restore telecommunications service in New York after the September 11, 2001, terrorist attacks. The media campaign, which put a human face on the layoffs, appeared just before the Christmas holidays in 2002, increasing the sympathy factor.

During the NBC interview, Michael Ware, an installation technician, told Katie Couric that for Verizon, "it's basically about the bottom line that comes first before our families. And that's what I think is wrong about it." The nationally televised interview did immeasurable harm to

Verizon's reputation and showed just how dangerous alienated employees can be.

Surprisingly, Verizon fought back in the media. It ended up further worsening its reputation with many employees and customers by running full-page ads defending its layoffs and attacking the Communications Workers' expensive ad campaign.

DIVERSITY AND REPUTATION

Creating a hospitable environment for all employees, regardless of gender, color, ethnic background, or sexual orientation, can contribute mightily to corporate reputation. Companies need to diversify their ranks to attract minorities as customers, satisfy clients who want to do business with progressive employers, and make their stock appealing to socially responsible investors. If the workforce is a mosaic of people, companies also tend to be more successful in attracting top talent.

"More and more in corporate America, our clients want our teams of workers to mirror their diverse workforces," says Allen Boston, Ernst & Young's national director for minority recruitment and retention. "A reputation for diversity is definitely an asset for us." To fill the talent pipeline, the accounting firm supports a variety of minority programs in high schools and colleges that encourage students to pursue master's degrees in accounting and MBA degrees.

Some companies clearly recognize how powerful a positive reputation for diversity can be and tout it in both employee communications and corporate advertising. Companies especially like trumpeting their inclusion in the burgeoning number of media rankings of diverse workplaces. And if there's any list that companies compete hardest to make, it has to be the *Working Mother* magazine rating of the best workplaces for women with children.

IBM's reputation has certainly benefited from its commitment to diversity, which dates back many decades. IBM was a pioneer in promoting women (its first female vice president in 1943), equal employment opportunity (a policy letter in 1953), and supporting gay employees (sexual orientation protections in 1984). As a result, women and minorities have become advocates for the company and its diversity programs.

"A consistent heritage of diversity translates into a strong reputation

TOP COMPANIES FOR WORKING MOTHERS

Working Mother named these companies as the best for women with children. The magazine based the list on companies' responses to questions about their corporate culture, percentage of women employees, and policies on work-life balance and women's advancement. Here are the top ten companies in alphabetical order:

Abbott Laboratories
Booz Allen Hamilton
Bristol-Myers Squibb
Eli Lilly
Fannie Mae
General Mills
IBM
Prudential Financial
S.C. Johnson & Son
Wachovia

that helps us attract and keep talented employees," says Ted Childs, vice president for workforce diversity. "IBM did things long before they were required by law or public opinion. We were driven by our beliefs and sense of morality, not political correctness."

Employee diversity enhances companies' reputations with potential customers and suppliers. Mitchell Goldstone, president of 30 Minute Photos Etc., a retail photo center in Irvine, California, became an IBM customer specifically because of its reputation for diversity. "Our company chose IBM because it welcomes gay and lesbian professionals," he explains. "We can't applaud IBM's efforts loudly enough, and we encourage people to visit IBM.com to learn about its written policy on the importance of diversity. We liken IBM, its products, and [its] employees to favorite members of our family."

But diversity issues have become one of the slipperiest slopes for companies, too. From discrimination complaints to politically incorrect behavior, some companies have strained relations with their employees and, in doing so, damaged their reputations.

More major companies are being tarred by accusations of discrimination by women and members of minority groups. Employees who file bias lawsuits create a negative image of the company both within the organization and to outside stakeholders. Reports of discrimination and derogatory racial comments by employees at Texaco received widespread publicity in 1996. Even though the oil company responded promptly with apologies and plans for more diversity training, its reputation was soiled badly.

Discrimination suits filed by minority employees have marred the images of even some of the most admired companies such as Johnson & Johnson, Coca-Cola, and Wal-Mart. True-blue Wal-Mart employees may shout the Wal-Mart cheer and follow the ten-foot rule handed down by founder Sam Walton ("Whenever you come within ten feet of a customer, you will look him in the eye, greet him, and ask him if you can help him"). But some female workers don't see eye to eye with the company. They have sued Wal-Mart in a major lawsuit charging discrimination in pay and promotions.

Companies can also hurt their relationships with minority employees by making insensitive blunders. AT&T learned a painful lesson from an embarrassing mistake involving its employee magazine. AT&T's "monkey business" cost it dearly in terms of damage to employee morale and corporate reputation.

Like most corporate propaganda, the employee magazine was typically innocuous. But when it landed in employee mailboxes in September 1993, tempers flared immediately. Irate African-American employees demanded to know why an illustration of a map of the world depicted people in native costumes in all but one region—Africa. How, they asked, could AT&T have used a monkey to represent Africa?

AT&T blamed the fiasco on a freelance illustrator and its own sloppy internal editing process. But the controversy soon spread beyond its walls. Civil rights groups called for a boycott of AT&T's long-distance service and organized protest rallies at AT&T offices. The Southern Christian Leadership Conference requested a meeting with AT&T officials to discuss why more managers weren't African-American.

Corporate executives felt as if the company were on trial. To many people, AT&T's carelessness with its magazine reflected a broader insensitivity in the company. Whether or not that perception was fair, AT&T's reputation required serious attention. Beyond apologizing to its employees and the African-American community, AT&T officials discontinued the magazine, set up a special telephone line to field calls

TOP COMPANIES FOR DIVERSITY

DiversityInc.com selected these companies as the ten best for diversity. The company based its ranking on a questionnaire asking companies about the racial/ethnic breakdown of their employees and other diversity issues.

1. Ford
2. Fannie Mae
3. American Express
4. Verizon Communications
5. IBM
6. Safeco
7. Deloitte & Touche
8. Eastman Kodak
9. Bank of America
10. Xerox

from upset employees, and promoted an African-American man to be a vice president for corporate relations on diversity issues.

The unfortunate incident shows just how fragile reputation and trust are on the highly charged issue of racial insensitivity and bias. AT&T had long prided itself on its policies for minority recruitment and development programs. "But on deeply emotional issues, trust is so fragile that protecting it requires extraordinary vigilance," says Marilyn Laurie, who was head of public relations at AT&T during the "monkey crisis."

LAW ELEVEN

CONTROL THE INTERNET
BEFORE IT CONTROLS YOU

A person died after drinking a can of Coca-Cola because the top was encrusted with dried rat urine.

The Coke trademark, reversed and read from left to right, can be translated in Arabic as "No Muhammed, no Makkah."

Mixing Coke with the food ingredient MSG creates a powerful aphrodisiac.

Do you believe those three statements about Coca-Cola? Most people don't. The comments are ludicrous on their face. But all three, along with more than a dozen other efforts to impugn Coca-Cola Company's integrity and products, have been circulating widely on the Internet through Web sites, chat rooms, and e-mail. Coke has nurtured its name and iconic reputation for nearly 120 years. The company created the modern image of Santa Claus in its advertising, and it was the first soft drink consumed in outer space. Not surprisingly, then, Coke takes any threat to its reputation very seriously. But these days, the company is focusing special attention on the World Wide Web because it presents a unique danger: an unregulated global forum that anyone, for any reason, can use to launch an anonymous attack with the potential to wreck a reputation.

The destructive potential of the Internet became clear to Coca-Cola in the late 1990s. An e-mail started making the rounds, telling people if they passed it on to ten other Internet users they would receive free bottles of Coke. Soon disappointed consumers started calling the company to claim their free soft drinks, forcing Coke to send online news sites a press release denying the rumor.

In 1998, Coke hired an Internet monitoring firm to help it detect and respond to rumors. But by 2002, as its consumer relations department was receiving calls and e-mails about more and more spurious rumors, including the one about the dried rat urine, Coca-Cola executives decided to take more forceful action. Leading the charge was Kari Bjorhus, a Web maven and the company's first director of interactive communications. Her strategy: fight fire with fire. She wanted to publish the rumors right on Coca-Cola's own Web site. She was confident that such a bold move would help discredit the rumors and reassure customers. "You take away the rumor's power by hitting it head on," she says. "You can't quantify the effect of these rumors, but intuitively you know that anything that makes people question our policies or product safety hurts our reputation."

But some senior Coke executives weren't so sure that was a sound idea. Why, they argued, put all those rumors in front of thousands of people when the vast majority wouldn't even know the rumors existed otherwise?

Bjorhus persisted and believes that what finally sold Coke executives on her strategy was an especially fast moving e-mail message in 2002 linking Coke with possible terrorism. The "grateful stranger story" claimed that a generous grocery store shopper had given an Arab man a little money when he didn't have quite enough to pay the cashier. In return, he had warned her not to drink any Coke products after a certain date. Coke issued a statement guaranteeing the safety and quality of its products but also informed local law enforcement agencies and the Federal Bureau of Investigation about the rumor.

Today, consumers visiting www.coca-cola.com can click on the "Contact Us" button on Coke's home page, then select "Myths & Rumors" to get the skinny on that and other canards about Coke. Divided into three segments—Middle East Rumors, Products and Packaging, and Ingredients—Myths & Rumors offers clear, logical answers to a variety of questions. In addition, on the Middle East rumor pages, Coke points out its good deeds in that region, including a program to revive cedar forests in Lebanon. More than sixteen thousand people a month check out the latest Coke myths.

Bjorhus works closely with other Coke departments to answer the rumors. She called on the company's scientific and regulatory affairs office, for instance, to rebut claims that the caramel coloring in Coke causes cancer and that the aluminum in the cans contributes to the development of Alzheimer's disease.

Coke updates its list whenever a new rumor starts picking up momentum. Bjorhus quickly posted a denial to the rumor that Coke was donating part of its profits to Israel. It had spread very quickly, especially in the Middle East. "We never just blow off a rumor, no matter how absurd it seems," Bjorhus says. "We bring it to light, and our customers thank us because they have affection for the brand. Now they can tell Aunt Gladys, who saw the rumor, the truth. That keeps our reputation strong."

CAUTION: ENTERING HOSTILE TERRITORY

Most people think of the Web as an extraordinarily useful tool, a wondrous source of information, community, and commerce. But if you have any responsibility for your company's reputation—and who doesn't?—you must treat the Web as potentially dangerous turf. If you haven't already, "Google" your company's name, using the search engine's group-search capabilities. When Coca-Cola is the search term, a list of more than 300,000 sites pops up in a fraction of a second. On the second page of the list during one recent search, there was a site labeled "The Coca-Cola Song," a silly little ditty about how Coke rots teeth and eats through wood and steel. Not exactly a threat to Coke. But it also contained some disturbingly sick comments about Catholic nuns. The next site below the Coca-Cola song was one labeled "Coca-Cola Works with Death Squads in Colombia."

The third page of sites included one that discussed in length the soft drink's alleged corrosive properties. The site contained statements that "in many states the highway patrol carries two gallons of Coke in the truck to remove blood from the highway after a car accident" and "to carry Coca-Cola syrup (the concentrate) the commercial truck must use the 'Hazardous Material' place cards reserved for highly corrosive materials." There's no telling what kinds of sites mentioning Coca-Cola are on the fiftieth or one hundredth page of the Google list. Coke notes, by the way, that it isn't aware of highway patrolmen using Coke for anything but refreshment, adding that water would be just as effective—and cheaper—for cleaning pavement.

If you try doing a search for your own company's name, you're likely to come away with an entirely new view of the Internet. The World Wide Web has replaced the water cooler as gossip central. Its impact, however, is vastly different: The Web reaches an estimated 730 million people, a number expected to exceed one billion by 2006. But some things remain the same: just as they did in their old water cooler conversations, the gossips are usually dishing dirt. Some of the cybercritics are activists. Others are disgruntled employees and customers. Through e-mails, chat rooms, and consumer-complaint Web sites, corporate critics are having a field day sullying reputations. Sometimes it's legitimate criticism, and that's fine. There were several postings on Internet message boards back in 1998 and 1999 warning about "creative accounting" and "monkey business" at Enron. But more often it's outlandish rumor, information twisted way out of context, or malicious lies. You ignore it at your peril.

Here's a little sampling of what's being said in cyberland about companies whose names you know very well. Starbucks Corporation enjoys the accolades of a few fan sites, including one operated by an enthusiast whose goal is to visit every Starbucks shop in the world. But the coffee company is also contending with many more antagonistic sites, among them www.ihatestarbucks.com, where a former employee compares his experience to "working for the devil" and a former customer claims to get ill after drinking all Starbucks beverages—except the vanilla latte.

Employees in a chat room at the career site www.vault.com dumped on Robert Nardelli, chairman and CEO of Home Depot, calling him the Wizard of Oz because "once we look behind the curtain, we see a frail, balding man who really has no clue how to solve our problems," including sluggish sales and customer service complaints. Tomato pickers, dissatisfied with their wages and benefits, created a Web site urging a boycott of the Taco Bell fast-food chain, which they label "Taco Hell." And companies are being tarred and feathered regularly on such inelegantly named Web sites as www.allstateinsurancesucks.com ("Allstate Screws Another Little Old Lady From NY") and www.chasemanhattan-sucks.com (a cartoon character urinates on the Chase name).

"I wasn't expecting to get ripped off by Kodak," photogeek wrote on

SPINNING A BIGGER WEB

Companies had better take the Internet seriously because it's only going to draw an ever-increasing global audience. It is expected to attract roughly 100 million more users annually for the next few years. Here are International Data Corporation's estimates and projections of the number of Internet users throughout the world in millions:

2000: 394.7
2001: 500.2
2002: 615.4
2003: 730.6
2004: 836.6
2005: 941.2
2006: 1,053.2

the Eastman Kodak section of the gripe site called Sucks500.com. Grumbling about a $100 camera rebate offer, he claimed, "This smells like fraud to me and should be subject to a class-action suit. Anybody with me?" At FuckedCompany.com, an Internet scribe slammed American Express, calling people who pay a fee to carry its green card "lemmings" and victims of "the biggest scam in the world."

It is difficult to gauge the precise impact of Internet buzz, but it definitely can erode a reputation. PlanetFeedback, a site where visitors vent about companies, estimates that its most avid users discuss their experiences with at least eight other people. Many of them are affluent women who are highly opinionated and influence the majority of the purchases in their households. PlanetFeedback relays comments from its sounding board to companies and keeps its clients informed about broader trends it detects in the consumer messages, as well. A hot issue these days is the role of food manufacturers and fast-food restaurants in the obesity epidemic that is sweeping America. PlanetFeedback is sending nervous companies a growing collection of comments indicating that regulation, such as warning labels on McDonald's Happy Meals, might be needed.

"Progressive companies have to develop a more sensitized ear to everything being said about them on the Internet," says Pete Blackshaw, who founded PlanetFeedback in 1999 with a fellow marketing manager from Procter & Gamble. He first realized the Internet's power at P&G,

when he tried to squash the rumor that tampons contain asbestos. Now P&G includes a "myths and misconceptions" section on its Tampax Web site, denying the asbestos claim.

FOREVER VIGILANT!

How are you going to defend yourself if you don't even know you're being attacked?

It's a simple concept: post a guard to watch for the enemy. But it's astounding how few companies are making a sincere effort to monitor what's being said about them on the Internet. A 2002 survey sponsored by the public relations firm Hill & Knowlton and *Chief Executive* magazine found that only 16 percent of companies closely monitor the Internet and only 39 percent check it periodically. But 43 percent of all companies surveyed said they don't watch the Web at all. Who's in charge there? What are they thinking?

Knowledge is power in cyberspace. Companies should troll chat rooms, discussion boards, online news media, and Web sites run by their competitors and critics to detect rumblings that could end up making headlines if a reporter or financial analyst discovers them first. Companies can also gain information about popular rumors from such Web sites as www.Urbanlegends.com, www.TruthOrFiction.com, and www.snopes.com.

Prowling the Internet on a daily basis requires money and manpower. Companies often hire one of the new Internet monitoring firms that have sprung up in the past few years, such as eWatch, Cyveillance, and Netdetec, to search for specific references to the company. Costs can range from $5,000 to more than $50,000 a year, depending on the monitoring firm hired and the scope of the intelligence gathering. "It's like fire insurance," says Nancy Sells, vice president of eWatch. "We give people the peace of mind of knowing that if something bad strikes, they can deal with it before it spreads too far." Dreamed up by two brothers in their basement in Saint Paul, Minnesota, in 1995, eWatch has grown to include eight hundred clients and is now owned by PR Newswire.

Gillette Company is among the most vigilant. It has enlisted a monitoring firm to scan 8 million Web pages a day in search of references to Gillette or its razor, toothbrush, and battery brands. Like guided missiles, preprogrammed "spiders" crawl over the Web looking for spe-

WHO'S WATCHING THE WEB?

Many companies are doing little if any monitoring of the Web and how their reputations are being affected by cyberspace. Surprisingly, some of the industries most under attack on the Internet, such as financial services and consumer products and services, are among the least vigilant. Most watchful are large companies and those in the technology and telecommunications industries, according to a survey by Hill & Knowlton and *Chief Executive* magazine.

The percentage of companies in each industry and the degree to which they monitor the Internet for information about themselves:

Business services: 15% very closely, 37% periodically, 45% not
   at all
Consumer products/services: 20% very closely, 29% periodically,
   49% not at all
Energy/utilities: 5% very closely, 57% periodically, 38% not at all
Financial services: 13% very closely, 35% periodically, 52% not
   at all
Health care: 21% very closely, 55% periodically, 21% not at all
Manufacturing: 12% very closely, 43% periodically, 43% not at all
Technology/telecom: 35% very closely, 47% periodically, 18% not
   at all

The percentage of companies by revenue and the degree to which they monitor the Internet for information about themselves:

Less than $50 million of revenue: 13% very closely, 34% periodi-
   cally, 53% not at all
$50 million to $500 million: 17% very closely, 38% periodically,
   44% not at all
More than $500 million: 25% very closely, 58% periodically, 15%
   not at all

cific words and phrases. The sophisticated search system tracks keywords to avoid pulling back irrelevant mentions such as people named Gillette.

Then Gillette employees sift through the company and brand mentions to find any that touch a nerve. For every thousand they read, only a handful may merit more attention. But those few could pose serious risks for Gillette's reputation. Such patrolling has turned up Web sites selling cheap counterfeit batteries under Gillette's Duracell brand that don't come close to meeting its quality standards and could even explode, creating legal problems.

The corporate affairs staff takes the lead in Internet monitoring at Gillette, but it's a collaborative effort involving the information technology, legal, and brand management departments. There's no fixed formula for dealing with Internet misinformation. "Where there's erroneous information about Gillette, we have to make some judgments," says Paul Fox, director of Gillette's global external relations department. "How wrong is it? Should it be removed or corrected? Or is legal action the answer?"

Yet even such an elaborate radar system doesn't always produce the desired results. "It's much easier to put things on the Web than to take misinformation off," says Fox. Some animal rights Web sites, for instance, still list Gillette among their adversaries even though it hasn't tested consumer products and ingredients on laboratory animals since 1996.

INTERNET FOES ARE PROS

Disgruntled employees and customers who take out their frustrations on the Web can certainly be a worrisome threat to corporate reputations. But the real danger lies with the pros, the environmental and human rights activists who create some of the most sophisticated protest sites.

An organization called Behind the Label sent e-mails at Christmastime encouraging people to avoid buying gifts at Gap stores. The e-mails contained an attachment, a video commercial that looked as professional as anything on network television. The models and clothing resembled those in many Gap ads, but the dialogue was anything but Gap's message. "I helped push African women into slums. I was just shopping," one young woman said, while another added, "I paid starvation wages. It was just a pair of khakis."

Look-alike Web sites are especially troubling because of the likelihood of confusion about a company's true position on controversial issues. On the eighteenth anniversary of the deadly gas accident at the Union Carbide plant in Bhopal, India, a new Web site took shape with an uncanny resemblance to the official corporate site for Dow Chemical Company, now the owner of Union Carbide Corporation. The Web hoax in December 2002 was so expertly executed that it initially fooled even sophisticated people into believing it was the official Dow site.

Both sites featured the red diamond-shaped Dow logo, identical graphics, even the same lead headline, "Just for kicks." But reading the main story quickly revealed that one was the bona fide corporate site and the other, the work of an anti-Dow organization. The official site's story told about Dow's contributions to a playground for disabled children. The activists' look-alike site used a soccer team analogy and appeared to be giving Dow's rationalization for why it doesn't have to deal with the Bhopal mess even though Union Carbide is now its "teammate."

PLOT YOUR COUNTERATTACK

Talk to some of the military's best minds, and you quickly learn that the most basic strategy is to neutralize an enemy threat. What that means for you is that as soon as an Internet-based threat has been identified, you must react. That reaction might be something as simple as evaluating the nature of the threat and deciding that it really is harmless. But remember: online gossip travels at nearly the speed of light. Think of a Web-based threat to your company's reputation as a particularly dangerous virus that can spread to infect millions of people in a matter of minutes. The appropriate response has to be determined swiftly and implemented without delay.

You certainly don't want to answer every crank. One can protest too much, adding a patina of credibility to otherwise groundless gossip. Even worse, an overheated counterattack can generate dangerous publicity about a situation that would otherwise be ignored by the news media.

But companies must respond to legitimate threats to their reputations. Employees may try to resolve individual complaints about products and services by identifying themselves as corporate representatives and entering a chat room. More serious allegations about corporate conduct require a more thorough investigation and detailed response.

A rogue Web site is the most dangerous but also the most manageable reputation hazard. It can potentially reach millions more people than a bogus rumor contained in an e-mail message or a chat room posting. But the Web site can be handled more easily because its owner can be located. A false rumor, on the other hand, often has unknown origins and simply keeps ricocheting from one e-mail account to another. It multiplies fast because an Internet user can simply hit a button and relay it to all the people on his "buddy list."

Rumors and attack sites don't die easily, so it may be worth devoting a permanent section of the corporate Web site to rebutting them, as Coca-Cola has done. Some companies fear that such a tactic might help keep bogus tales alive, but Web rumors typically take on a life of their own and aren't easily squelched anyway.

That's what executives at Tommy Hilfiger Corporation figured when they decided to make a racist rumor about its namesake founder into an established part of the corporate Web site. Click on "Tommy rumor," and you will find statements from Hilfiger, Oprah Winfrey, and the Anti-Defamation League denying that the designer ever made negative statements on Winfrey's television show about African Americans or other minorities who wear his clothing.

Tommy Hilfiger created the special Web page after receiving e-mails from people suggesting that the rumor must be true because the company wasn't denying it. But Tommy Hilfiger didn't want to become too public and put its denial in a television commercial seen by 50 million people. It feared that some people would get confused and come away from the ad believing that the designer had actually made derogatory comments about minorities.

Still, the company has gone far beyond its Web site in fighting the rumor, which could have sullied Tommy Hilfiger's reputation in the very important African-American market. The designer has achieved the difficult feat of making his styles appealing to both the preppy country club set and the urban hip-hop generation.

Employees have been trained on how to respond to the rumor and have been armed with handbooks and videotapes of Oprah Winfrey declaring that Tommy Hilfiger has never appeared on her show. The designer even hired private investigators to track down some of the people spreading the bogus e-mails and implicated dozens of people, including a U.S. Labor Department employee and the senior vice president of another company. Tommy Hilfiger reported such people to the top executive, general counsel, and human resources director at their companies or organizations, which usually led to disciplinary action or firing. In addition, Tommy Hilfiger demanded that the gossips send new e-mails to everyone they had contacted, explaining that the rumor was false. But no one has ever figured out who cooked up the troublesome tale, which has haunted the company for an entire decade.

Kroll, the risk-consulting firm that worked on the Tommy rumor, has developed a "cyber investigations and computer forensics" division that is attracting a growing number of Internet victims. "The nature of the Internet is that lies and truth can look much alike," says Alan Brill, Kroll's senior managing director for technology services. Among his cases: a bank's chief lending officer accused on a Web bulletin board of "fronting for a drug mob" and a retail store stigmatized on a Web site as a favorite place for child molesters to hang out in. Brill traced the rumors back to the individuals who posted them but made little headway in persuading them to remove the messages. But he did succeed in pressuring the bulletin board operator to remove the drug mob posting and the Internet service provider to shut down the Web site targeting the retailer. Without such a quick resolution, however, the damage from both cases could have been enormous and probably would have resulted in law enforcement probes and sensational media publicity.

Some rumors, however, can also be extinguished without such sophisticated sleuthing. By posting denials in several discussion groups, Mrs. Fields' Original Cookies scotched the rumor that it had supplied free cookies to a celebration party following O. J. Simpson's acquittal on murder charges.

Several companies were victimized on the Internet shortly after the September 11 terrorist attacks but also have managed to put the rumors to rest and suffered little lasting reputation damage. But to effectively quell malicious gossip, you have to be prepared to spend considerable time and effort. Dunkin' Donuts didn't waste a minute investigating and responding to a very disturbing rumor that swept the Web on September 11. Designed to play on heightened patriotic fervor and some people's distrust of Arabs, the e-mail message claimed that clerks at various Dunkin' Donuts shops in New Jersey and New York had burned American flags, defaced them with Arabic writing, and cheered after hearing news of the World Trade Center destruction.

By September 12, the company was hearing about the rumor from all quarters—everyone from irate customers to its coffee supplier was alarmed. So the world's largest doughnut-shop chain and its crisis management firm moved into emergency response mode. They joined forces to interview police officers who had investigated the complaints, watch videotapes from the doughnut shops' security cameras, and talk with the shops' employees. After finding no evidence of the alleged behavior, Dunkin' Donuts drafted e-mail denials and sent them to all of the people it could track down who had received the malicious message.

Foreign car companies were another September 11 target. E-mails claimed that such companies as Honda Motor Company and BMW Group weren't contributing to the relief effort at Ground Zero in New York, when in fact they had donated both money and vehicles. The jingoistic hoax, which reached thousands of people on the Web, praised Ford, General Motors, and DaimlerChrysler for their contributions. Some newspapers even irresponsibly publicized the hoax without checking its accuracy.

The rumor built and peaked in the winter of 2001–2002, when the American International Auto Dealers Association sent out an e-mail and letter blasting the hoax and detailing the contributions made by all car manufacturers. Even so, the association didn't see a significant slowdown in the rumor until late summer 2002.

COURT AS THE LAST RESORT

A company that becomes the target of a caustic rumor or Web site can sometimes end the problem by using conciliatory tactics. If that doesn't work, a counterattack with facts and figures is an appropriate response. But sometimes the only avenue available may be the courts. The trouble is, litigation is often unsuccessful because of First Amendment rights of free speech. What's more, a prolonged battle can generate unwanted media publicity and turn the gadfly into a martyr.

Dunkin' Donuts considered legal action against David Felton, a Connecticut man who became angry when his local Dunkin' Donuts didn't have skim milk and proceeded to set up a complaint Web site with the domain name www.dunkindonuts.org. But the company managed to avoid a prolonged and nasty conflict. After negotiating with Felton, it ended up buying www.dunkindonuts.org and steering its audience to the corporate Web site, www.dunkindonuts.com. People still can make complaints on the main Dunkin' Donuts site, but it is primarily focused on selling the company's products.

"You need to treat complainers with respect and restraint," says Mike

Lawrence, executive vice president of Cone, a public relations and crisis management firm that advised Dunkin' Donuts. "You don't want to sue and end up making a hero out of the disgruntled customer."

Nevertheless, legal action against Internet hoaxes is sometimes necessary. Internet law is evolving, and so far companies have a mixed record in their lawsuits against activists, disgruntled consumers, and other cybercritics. Each case has a different wrinkle or two, so it's difficult to generalize. But the First Amendment often wins out—as long as the corporate antagonist makes it crystal clear to Internet users that its site is a forum for comment or a parody of a company-owned site.

If false information not only hurts the corporate reputation but also affects sales or the stock price, a lawsuit may be the only speedy remedy. Several companies, including Lucent Technologies and Emulex Corporation, have been the victims of phony press releases that temporarily depressed their stock prices. The perpetrators were all found and charged with securities fraud. In the Lucent case, a day trader in Houston was arrested for posting a phony press release claiming that the telecommunications company would miss its earnings target. The stock price fell by as much as 3.6 percent before recovering.

But be aware that court decisions have upheld the rights of stockholders to post negative comments about a company on the Internet. The Public Citizen Litigation Group successfully defended shareholders in California who had criticized Hollis-Eden Pharmaceuticals on message boards.

Sometimes there are conflicting decisions. For example, legal challenges to such sites as www.wallmartcanadasucks.com and www.lockheedmartinsucks.com failed, but an arbitration panel, in a divided decision, voted against the corporate critics and awarded the disputed domain name www.vivendiuniversalsucks.com to the company.

"It's a fast-moving area of the law, but there are still many complicating issues," says Diane Cabell, associate director of the Berkman Center for Internet and Society at Harvard Law School. "For example, since the Internet is global, what happens if a company sues in another country where the suffix 'sucks' doesn't have any meaning?"

Some companies have tried to head off a nemesis by registering domain names themselves using the company name along with such derogatory terms as "sucks" and "I hate," but don't expect that to stop people from finding alternative names, such as NorthWorstAir for an anti–Northwest Airlines site and the www.Untied.com site for blasting

United Airlines. Given the permutations of words like suck and its clos-est relative, that seems like a rather expensive and ultimately futile tactic.

Corporate critics are sometimes scared off simply by a letter threaten-ing legal action by deep-pocketed companies. But legal warnings may be less effective in the future because of a growing online database of legal analysis and commentary intended to protect individuals from corpo-rate bullying. The Electronic Frontier Foundation and law school clinics at Harvard University, Stanford University, the University of California at Berkeley, the University of San Francisco, and the University of Maine have created the Chilling Effects Clearinghouse (www.chilling effect.org) to help people distinguish between permissible freedom of expression and possible trademark infringement. The site promises to help nonlawyers understand the legalese in cease-and-desist letters.

A FRIEND IS A FRIEND IS A FRIEND

Let's say, for whatever reason, that over the years you've found a lot of uses for those ubiquitous cotton swabs called Q-tips. Eager to share your amazing discoveries with the world at large, you go to all the trou-ble to register and create a Web site called the "One and Only Q-tips Home Page." Here novices can learn just how valuable a piece of equip-ment a Q-tip can be. They make dandy emergency toothbrushes, for example, and when allergies fill your cat's eyes with gook, break out the Q-tip to swab them clean.

Many companies would fall all over themselves to get the author of this Web site some attention. The PR department would try to get arti-cles about the site into the "Style" or "Living" sections of newspapers all over the country. The advertising honchos would tell the agency to cook up a new campaign touting all the amazing uses of Q-tips. Somebody might even offer the Web site creator a post as a consultant.

So what did Unilever, the actual maker of Q-tips, do when it discov-ered this gentle, albeit somewhat wacky, Web site? The company threat-ened to sue, forcing the site to shut down. Now the site's creator has concocted a new home page that depicts a Q-tip and a coffin. "Alas, the little guy is once again crushed by the big corporate weenies," declares the new page, which helpfully lists the name and address of the Unilever lawyer responsible for the original site's demise. Faith Kaminsky, an attorney herself and the creator of the Q-tips page, now boycotts the brand. She also has made a legal end run around Unilever, creating "the one and only Cue-tips Homepage," featuring the same novel uses for Q-tips as the old site but showing drawings of pool cues rather than cotton swabs.

Now let's look at how another company—which happens to enjoy one of the world's best reputations—handled a similar situation. A nostalgic Johnson & Johnson customer has created an Internet site devoted to the history of the Band-Aid. It features photos of Band-Aid boxes through the years. What happened when J&J discovered the site? A J&J manager sent a friendly e-mail providing more product lore. The Band-Aid site acknowledges that Band-Aid is a J&J trademark and states clearly that the site isn't affiliated with the company. But for those who are interested, the site does provide a link directly to J&J's corporate Web site. A little common sense still counts for something.

WHERE DANGER LURKS, OPPORTUNITY ALSO RESIDES

Don't get the impression that the Internet is nothing more than a minefield for corporate reputations. The fact is, it also provides unprecedented opportunities for companies to burnish their reputations. Citizens of cyberspace tend to be above average in income and education, and many of them influence public opinion. They're what the public relations firm Burson-Marsteller has dubbed "e-fluentials." These politically active people were pioneer users of the Internet and number about 11 million. They are much more likely than the average person to pass on information—both pro and con—about companies via the Internet, but negative experiences travel farthest. Burson-Marsteller's research shows that e-fluentials pass on positive experiences to eleven people on average but relate negative news to seventeen.

Companies can reach out to key Internet users by registering visitors to their Web sites and by culling their internal databases for the e-mails of customers, suppliers, investors, government and regulatory officials, and members of the media.

The Internet enables companies to forge stronger bonds with stakeholders by keeping in touch on a regular basis through e-mail and thus controlling the information flow without the news media filtering their messages. The airlines have used e-mails, for instance, to communicate directly with frequent fliers about service cutbacks and their financial situation since September 11, 2001.

Companies also can strengthen their reputation by making their own Web sites more than a digitized collection of annual reports and press releases. A creative Web site can make the company less institutional by painting a friendlier, more human picture of the CEO. Dell, for example, includes many of CEO Michael Dell's speeches as well as a list of "Michael's Computers" and a section on "Michael in the Media."

"It's crucial for companies to build trust and value with influential visitors to their Web sites so they can neutralize the negatives and nurture the positives," says Leslie Gaines-Ross, chief knowledge and research officer at Burson-Marsteller. "Unfortunately, companies are really behind the curve about how their Web sites can enhance their reputations." She found in analyzing more than a hundred Web sites of leading companies that only 12 percent showcase their CEOs.

Companies also can use the Web to put issues and problems into perspective. Nike, long accused of contracting its athletic shoe manufacturing to Third World sweatshops, is using Internet technology to try to mend its reputation. Human rights activists have created Web sites that exhort consumers to "Just Stop It" and "Just Do It—Boycott Nike," contending that the workers who make Nike shoes in Asia and Latin America are overworked and live in poverty.

Now Nike is trying to give its side of the story by offering visitors to its Nikebiz Web site the chance to take a virtual tour of a Vietnamese factory that produces sneakers. While watching women sewing shoes and attending school programs in the factory, viewers hear about Nike's code of conduct, contract workers' wages and benefits, and the company's contribution to the Vietnamese economy.

More than eight thousand people have clicked into the factory and generally found it informative. But Nike acknowledges that some skeptics believe the company has simply produced slick, sanitized propaganda about factory working conditions.

Nike representatives also lodge responses to critics' comments in chat rooms and on Internet bulletin boards. The company is especially concerned about its reputation damage among teenagers and college students, big Internet users who are very interested in social justice issues and are its primary customers. "There's no such thing as a completely perfect supply chain with more than 850 factories in more than fifty countries," says Vada Manager, director of global issues management at

Nike. "But we keep making improvements, and the online tour and other information on our Web site have definitely improved our reputation and level of trust."

Even companies with the absolutely worst reputations can use the Web to show how they're trying to recover and to explain their situations. Some of the companies rocked by scandals and plummeting stock prices have tried to put matters into perspective. But with their credibility already shot, companies should be as clear and candid as possible and avoid superficial rhetoric.

Global Crossing, the telecommunications company plagued by financial woes and government investigations into its business practices, posted detailed information about its Chapter 11 filing on its Web page, including a glossary of bankruptcy terms. But its site wasn't all downbeat—there also was a list of the top ten reasons to still believe in the company. Hope springs eternal.

LAW TWELVE

SPEAK WITH A
SINGLE VOICE

When Lee Green became director of corporate identity and design at IBM in 1993, he knew the company's corporate brand was in "horrendous shape." He just didn't realize quite how horrendous.

When he asked people throughout IBM to send him examples of corporate and product logos, he expected to receive thirty, maybe even forty. His hunt actually netted more than eight hundred different logos. "The IBM logo had been bastardized in more ways than you can imagine," Green recalls, pointing to an old logo with the word "POW!" in a cartoon balloon above the IBM name and another showing Mickey Mouse and IBM as partners.

Maureen McGuire was equally surprised by what she found when she was promoted to director of worldwide product advertising and promotion in 1994. That year at Comdex, the big computer technology trade show, IBM employees manned twenty-seven different booths, each with its own logo promoting its own specific product brand. The booths looked like little fiefdoms. McGuire collected photographs of all the booths to make the point to her colleagues that "there was no real IBM corporate presence at Comdex."

What chaos!

The company that began life as a small manufacturer of meat scales, time clocks, and tabulating machines and evolved into a technological trailblazer had lost its way—and its powerful reputation. The company was tearing apart its own brand; it didn't need its competitors to do it.

Many people predicted the inevitable breakup of the once invincible computer industry titan. Believing that the IBM brand was no longer well regarded and the company would be dismantled, employees had taken to identifying themselves more with the names of divisions such as ISSC (Integrated Systems Solutions Corporation) and ESD (Entry Systems Division).

IBM's problems were myriad, but at the heart of the crisis was the fragmented corporate brand. "It was total disarray," says McGuire, who is now vice president, worldwide marketing management and integrated marketing communications. "There was absolutely no marketing coherence." IBM had decentralized, and product managers throughout the company were independent agents, hiring their own ad agencies and crafting their own messages. When Louis Gerstner joined IBM in 1993 to engineer its now-famous turnaround, the company did business with more than seventy agencies. To Gerstner, the challenge was clear: IBM needed to regain its focus and consistency to project a strong corporate image once again. It had to learn to speak with a single voice.

All communications and marketing messages must be working together to reinforce a corporate brand. Stakeholders can't feel very good about a company they don't understand. "When there's a fractured presentation of your identity or products, it sends the signal that there is confusion at the company," says Green. "It was especially important for IBM that its customers perceive a collective point of view because IBM is selling integrated solutions."

One of Gerstner's early moves was hiring Abby Kohnstamm, with whom he had worked at American Express, as IBM's first true corporate marketing executive. She went to work researching IBM's corporate brand image and analyzing its labyrinth of agencies. She found that the company still retained some goodwill with the public but that people were angry that the company had allowed itself to deteriorate and become irrelevant to many consumers.

Soon IBM shocked Madison Avenue by doing the unthinkable: consolidating all worldwide advertising under one roof, at the Ogilvy & Mather agency. Together, IBM and Ogilvy went to work creating a uniform look for the brand. They scrapped most of those 800 logos and developed advertising that communicated the same corporate image no matter which product or service was being promoted in which country of the world. They chose a traditional look for the official logo: The IBM name in horizontal stripes, a design that had been created in 1972 to signify "speed and dynamism." But the advertising had to be break-through.

Ogilvy's first campaign—"Solutions for a small planet"—included an international cast, from Czech nuns to Parisian senior citizens, speaking in their native languages with subtitles at the bottom. The advertising underscored IBM's global reach and told the world that it was a new company—more human, nimble, and innovative. It was the first time IBM advertising had generated any buzz since the humorous Little Tramp PC ads of the early 1980s. "We were pleased to no end," says McGuire, "when we heard that Bill Gates at Microsoft saw our ad with the nuns and said, 'This is IBM?'"

IBM also made a smart corporate branding decision as it moved more heavily into computer services. It coined the term "e-business" in the mid-1990s and has included it ever since as a unifying tagline in much of its advertising. IBM executives say the e-business strategy brought employees together and made them realize that the company was back on its feet and had a clear direction.

It isn't just the quality and consistency of a message that counts; quantity matters, too. IBM doubled its advertising and marketing budget, realizing that an ongoing ad campaign is critical to its corporate brand and reputation. Negative perceptions often develop in the vacuum created when companies aren't communicating regularly with their many constituencies.

Corporate branding extends beyond advertising and marketing materials, of course. At IBM, it includes product design, which has been centralized in a corporate design department to achieve a distinctive visual identity. Green, who oversees all design work, characterizes IBM's look as "pure, simple, elegant in form." Products are usually black, designed to blend into the customer's environment. In its research, IBM finds that people can pick out its products from the competition's even when there aren't any visible logos.

Now that IBM has regained a consistent corporate brand image, its marketing chiefs aren't about to lose control. They have developed detailed standards and guidelines for using the IBM brand. For the red "e" in its e-business logo alone, there are several pages of rules—"avoid placing on color tones that diminish the impact of the red color," never

LOONY LOGOS

By the 1990s, IBM's corporate brand image had fractured. Product managers had run wild, creating their own ads and logos. Today, IBM keeps some of the old logos in its "Hall of Shame" as a reminder of how brands can be sabotaged. Here are three of the logos in the Hall of Shame, as well as IBM's official logo, which dates back to 1972, when Paul Rand replaced solid letters with horizontal stripes to suggest "speed and dynamism."

THE HALL OF SHAME

THE OFFICIAL LOGO

incorporate into text or headlines, and avoid cute 3-D, glowing, or blurred versions.

An online Integrated Marketing Communications Solutions Center provides information about existing advertising campaigns and a library of IBM photos and images to use in ads and brochures, as well as "marketing intelligence" on advertising by competitors such as Microsoft, Dell, and Hewlett-Packard. The goal is to keep everyone in tune with IBM's brand vision.

IBM has also developed a "Little Blue Brand Book" and a "Managing the Brand" intranet for employees. Because the company is so large and far-flung, its marketing executives believe that all employees need guidance on using IBM's valuable brand and its trademarks. They realize that there's a tendency for people to make decisions without considering their collective impact.

The intranet site is comprehensive, with such features as a "brand school" to teach employees about the branding process, rules for cobranding with another company, and design guidelines for using trademarks on signs, stationery, and business cards. "People have a tendency to be too creative with our core brand assets," says Green, describing an "e-bert" cartoon character that an employee created using the red "e" from IBM's trademarked "e-business" logo. It made him wince. "That was the wrong thing to do," he adds, "because it trivializes a very critical element of our corporate brand."

Of course, there's no better teacher than past mistakes. To remind employees what happened when IBM lost control of its corporate brand, the company still displays some of those eight hundred logos from 1993 at its design center. IBM calls it the Hall of Shame.

CONSISTENCY AND CLARITY

As IBM understands all too well now, a good reputation requires consistent communication over many years. Sending out the same message—whether through the identical corporate logo, uniform customer service, or a consistent advertising theme—can do wonders for a company's reputation. The key is to keep your corporate brand image clear and consistent.

Unfortunately, it's all too easy to get sidetracked and start confusing people with multiple advertising campaigns and inconsistencies in the products and services you deliver. Over time, that muddies the corporate identity and weakens reputation. Consumers, employees, investors, and other key stakeholders no longer understand what you stand for. It's hard to admire a company that seems in disarray.

ITT Industries certainly lacked coherence. After ITT Corporation split off its insurance business and hotels and casinos, the remaining industrial products company ended up in a major identity crisis. Called ITT Industries, it was a branding mess with too many seemingly unconnected businesses. "They had overbranded and had too many branding levels with three different divisions and all of their products using the ITT prefix," says Hayes Roth, vice president, worldwide marketing and business development, at Landor Associates, the consulting firm that was retained to restore order.

ITT Industries considered a name change, but Landor advised against it because ITT still benefited from high international awareness—even if the public wasn't sure what it did anymore. In fact, when people were polled about what ITT Industries produced, everyone seemed to have a different answer. Many thought it made telephones, since ITT originally stood for International Telephone & Telegraph. Others guessed that it produced television sets. ITT Industries doesn't manufacture either. Its products are a bit more heavy-duty, things like sewage pumps, electronic connectors, and military hardware.

Instead of changing ITT's name, Landor fashioned a brand image based on the company's engineering process. The new slogan: "Engineered for life." The new logo: "engineered blocks" representing the letters in ITT. "To make the corporate brand stick," Roth says, "we put that logo on everything down to the pocket protectors engineers wear."

American Express didn't undergo a radical restructuring as ITT did. But it has strayed from its status image over the past decade and doesn't enjoy the same crystal-clear corporate identity that it did back in the 1970s and 1980s. There was the classic "Do you know me?" ads showing famous names but not-so-famous faces. By the 1980s, the company had expanded its card collection from green and gold to include the new superpremium platinum, and the marketing campaigns meshed well. The slogan "Membership has its privileges" and the series of classy celebrity photos shot by Annie Leibovitz set a very highbrow, artistic tone.

Today, however, the credit card and travel services company is offering a panoply of different credit cards—some 25 variations—and is scrapping with MasterCard, Visa, and Discover in a game of one-upmanship. Some consumers say the American Express card isn't special anymore and seems like all the other cards soliciting their business with low introductory interest rates, rebates, and bonus airline miles.

To bolster its reputation, American Express needs to create a strong corporate brand umbrella to enhance the individual cards and keep its image front and center. Recognizing that it had become too focused on promoting individual cards at the expense of the corporate brand, American Express did develop a broader ad campaign with the slogan "Make life rewarding" and even brought Leibovitz back to contribute her memorable photography. But it's still part of the rewards-driven marketing approach and lacks the wit and sophistication of past advertising.

Sometimes distinctly different parts of the same company have conflicting interests and don't speak as one, complicating the reputation management process. This is especially common after a merger that brings together two very different corporate cultures. DuPont, a staid chemical manufacturer in Delaware, acquired the big Texas oil producer

Conoco in 1981 and found itself the owner of a company with a risk-taking, maverick culture. DuPont officials remember that they and their colleagues at Conoco sometimes clashed over energy policies and didn't always present a unified front to government officials. The dissension became very public in 1995, when Conoco executives were negotiating a deal with Iran to develop oilfields. Some DuPont board members opposed doing business with Iran, as did members of the Clinton administration, who eventually killed the plan. Conoco was spun off from DuPont in 1998, making it much easier for both companies to project a consistent image and manage their reputations.

It's important for multinational corporations to remember that they must protect and manage their corporate brands and reputations globally. That means creating a common brand message for all global markets, with perhaps a little tweaking to make it resonate with different cultures. Avon Products invested nearly $100 million in its first-ever global advertising campaign in 2000. Called "Let's Talk," it focused on the relationship between women and Avon and its sales representatives. "One of our top priorities has been to reinvigorate the Avon brand," says Andrea Jung, chairman and CEO. "We understood women's similarities around the world and felt a global campaign would be much more powerful. We want to be more consistent, to unify the equity of the Avon brand."

Of course, consistency doesn't mean constancy. You sometimes need to freshen up a corporate brand. Just don't overdo it. United Parcel Service is a good model to follow. It recently took steps to update its corporate brand and reputation and convey that it is now much more than a package delivery service. The changes aren't jarring, however, and they retain the brand heritage. The company transformed the UPS logo into a sleeker-looking shield without the bow-tied package on top and began calling itself "Brown" in advertisements, a play on the chocolate brown color of its trucks and uniforms.

BATMAN VERSUS SPIDERMAN

It was the battle of two of the world's mightiest superheroes. The setting was Denmark. The fight was over who would be the next action-figure toy from Lego Group, the 72-year-old Danish maker of plastic-brick building sets. At stake: nothing less than Lego's corporate reputation.

The conflict was heated, but Batman proved to be no match for Spider-Man, his wall-scaling opponent. The Caped Crusader was simply "too dark and too adult," says Francesco Ciccolella, Lego's senior vice president for global branding. "But with Spiderman, we felt that the fight between good and evil is displayed in a positive way." Lego has long promoted imaginative, childlike play, and developing violent products would chip away at its consistent image. In addition to Spider-Man, Lego has deemed Star Wars and Harry Potter suitable subjects for its construction sets.

But it isn't easy for Lego to stay focused on its heritage and principles. As companies grow and as they react to competition, they must develop new products, acquire other businesses, and target new markets. It's tempting to compromise values and create a toy that ties in with the hottest movie or the latest news. While some companies were cranking out war toys for Christmas to capitalize on the conflict in Iraq, Lego resisted the commercial pressure to produce realistic battle weapons. It does create some products with a violent nature, such as its Bionicle line and Darth Vader of Star Wars, but it considers them acceptable because they're merely fantasy creatures.

Lego, a shortened combination of two Danish words meaning "play well," has largely succeeded in sticking to its corporate values. An iconic brand, Lego was named "toy of the century" by several magazines and trade associations in 1999. The company estimates that it has sold more than 320 billion of its trademark building bricks. Bricks alone, however, could no longer make Lego thrive.

The company had switched from its original wooden toys into plastic during the 1940s and needed to diversify in a big way once again. Lego had to strike a better balance between heritage and innovation. But as Lego and other companies expand, they also risk losing control. Their many divisions and brands may be allowed to grow wild—what marketing experts call badly managed "brand architecture."

That has indeed been Lego's major problem. It allowed its toy chest to bulge with new products but paid little attention to the corporate brand. Lego diversified way beyond its building bricks into theme parks, clothing, board games, books, backpacks, watches, video games, magazines, software, and computer-controlled robots. Along the way, it created a host of new brand names, including Mindstorms, Technic, and Spybotics. Not everything has succeeded. Some products even hurt Lego's image. The company has long prided itself on safety, but its entry into baby toys forced its first product recall: it recalled some 700,000 plastic toy rattles when it was discovered in 1998 that they were lodging in some babies' throats.

But the primary problem wasn't the stepped-up product development; it was how Lego managed all the new brands. Many of the new products were essential. The company had no choice but to try to keep pace with the competition and with children's changing lives and tastes. Belatedly, Lego had responded to shifts in childhood play habits. Children were growing up more quickly, abandoning traditional toys such as construction blocks sooner for cooler playthings such as video games, skateboards, and digital toys.

Lego finally realized its brand management lacked discipline. Solving the problem meant calling in a consultant with expertise in corporate branding and reputation management. Enter Majken Schultz, a professor at the Copenhagen Business School and a skilled brand architect. She became part of a brand strategy task force with Lego business unit managers and went to work helping them tame the unruly brands. Professor Schultz's major focus has been refining the meaning of the mother brand and bringing the burgeoning product brands under the corporate parent's wing.

Lego created Ciccolella's brand management position, consolidated its advertising and public relations with a few agencies, organized its products into four categories (Make and Create, Explore, Stories and Action, and Next), and redesigned its packaging. Its new boxes are more uniform in color, logo placement, and standardized pictures and graphics. The company had learned through market research that there were fewer global differences in the way children perceive play and the Lego brand than they had assumed.

Lego employees now attend Brand School, a three-day seminar where they discuss the company's values and image. "The key value for Lego is trust," says Ciccolella. "We talk about what that means for people in research and development or finance. How do values affect their daily work? How do they walk the talk?" The cultural changes haven't come without some dissension. Schultz notes that "turf issues" arose over employees' changing roles and responsibilities in the switch from a product brand management process to a corporate brand system.

Ciccolella vows to keep a close rein on the Lego corporate brand as it continues to expand. "We don't want to become a headless chicken," he says, "always following the latest consumer trends."

Lego's stated goal is "to become the world's strongest brand among

BUILDING BLOCKS OF THE LEGO BRAND

The key elements of Lego's corporate brand and its revamped brand management system are:

CORPORATE MISSION: To nurture the child in each of us. To release the learning and development potential in each of us.

CORPORATE BELIEFS: Children are our role models. They are curious, creative and imaginative. They embrace discovery and wonder. They are natural learners.

CORPORATE VALUES: Self-expression, endless ideas, playful learning, active fun, trusted.

BRAND PERSONALITY: Unexpected, charismatic, unconventional, adventurous, clever problem solver, humorous.

BRAND POSITIONING: The power to create. Play on.

BRAND MANAGEMENT AND ORGANIZATION: Creating a senior vice president for global branding, consolidating advertising and PR agencies, merging brand and product development into a single unit, and marketing on a more efficient global basis.

families with children in 2005." One of its latest forays is into the girls' market, which Lego has barely tapped, with crafts for making jewelry and other fashion items. The company also has its eye on expanding further into the adult market. Already, it is selling its colorful bricks under the brand Lego Serious Play to business managers and consultants who build structures as they plot strategy.

Lego was the leading company in a recent reputation study in Denmark, with its emotional appeal, product quality, and social responsibility its top attributes. Its weakest: financial performance and vision and leadership. But Ciccolella says that even if Lego improves its financial performance, it probably won't ever be a major element of its strong reputation. "We aren't seen as the most aggressive tycoon in town because of our long-term approach and the fact we're a private company," he explains. "We don't have the pressure from pension funds and other institutional shareholders to meet certain financial targets."

BRANDING THE CUSTOMER EXPERIENCE

Consistency is about more than communications. The customer experience is also part of the corporate brand and should be both positive and predictable. When Starbucks offers the same atmosphere and product quality at its coffee shops in New York, Seattle, and Barcelona, it reinforces its corporate brand and reputation.

But other companies, especially as they've grown large, haven't retained that consistency. Customer relationship management may be a popular buzzword these days, but it isn't in the vocabulary of many service businesses. Unreliable service and product quality have hurt the reputations of many industries, particularly restaurants and retailers. As most consumers can attest to, not all Burger King restaurants and Home Depot stores are created equal.

A notable exception is Harrah's Entertainment, which has cultivated arguably the strongest name in the casino industry by offering "a branded customer experience." The Harrah's brand represents leisure travelers and low-stakes gamblers more than high rollers. It's very much a middle-class, middle-American identity.

Harrah's has seen its reputation strengthen considerably as it made sure its loyal gamblers enjoyed virtually the same experience at all of its gambling properties from Atlantic City, New Jersey, to Joliet, Illinois, to Las Vegas. Its hotel rooms are virtually identical, and many properties have the same types of buffets, coffeehouses, and steak houses. Its casinos may have individual themes, such as Mardi Gras, but all of them offer essentially the same games in the same configuration.

"Most important is that customers are treated the same by our employees, no matter which casino they're at," says Philip Satre, chairman. "If you're a platinum or diamond customer in Atlantic City, you won't feel like a stranger if you come to our properties in Nevada. I received a letter from a woman in Plano, Texas, who primarily visited our Shreveport, Louisiana, casino, but she said she had visited five or six others and her goal is to visit all of our twenty-six casinos in thirteen states."

Harrah's has achieved its customer consistency in part through a sophisticated information technology system that tracks gamblers' habits and rewards them with various VIP perks. Gary Loveman, Harrah's president and CEO, came to the gambling industry through an unusual route—Harvard University. He was associate professor of business administration at Harvard Business School and brought service management expertise that helped the company develop and refine its customer loyalty program.

The company collects and analyzes data about its customers through its nationwide Total Rewards player cards and uses the gamblers' profiles for marketing and promotions. When gamblers use a gold, platinum, or top-of-the-line diamond card at the casinos, it also allows employees to quickly learn personal information about them. It isn't unusual for a slot machine attendant to wish a customer "Happy birthday" because the database can tell him the person's birth date. So far, Harrah's has amassed a database of more than 25 million players and regularly receives feedback from them.

"When I stayed at Harrah's Joliet, it was great to walk in and have them know my name even though it was my first visit," Robert Fulton, a Total Rewards diamond-level customer from San Francisco, told Harrah's officials. "It made me feel really comfortable, as if I had been there before."

THE YUPPIE STIGMA

Bayerische Motoren Werke, more familiarly known as BMW, let itself be seduced during the 1980s by a new breed of consumer called yuppies. Those were the "young, upwardly mobile professionals" who became America's trendsetters and most conspicuous consumers. They bought Rolex watches, Filofax organizers, and Brooks Brothers suspenders. Their vehicle of choice: a BMW, which was quickly nicknamed "the yuppiemobile." The link was so strong that a newspaper editor even penned the headline "Yuppie Disaster" for a story about a truck loaded with BMWs that had overturned on a Houston freeway.

It was one thing for yuppies to buy BMWs and boost the German company's sales and brand image in America. But BMW took a wrong turn in 1988, when it veered away from its single-minded brand image as a sporty, powerful car that makes driving fun. Suddenly "the ultimate driving machine" was the ultimate status symbol. It was more about prestige than performance.

BMW ads started looking more like the Ralph Lauren/Polo brand with their images of high society. They featured lush Cole Porter music and showed guests arriving for a dinner party at a fashionable town house and a preppy crowd attending a Thoroughbred horse auction. The change in marketing focus, which alienated longtime BMW fans, happened at an especially bad time. Japanese carmakers were making their first big assault on the luxury-car market with their Acura, Lexus, and Infiniti brands, depressing sales of BMW and other European models.

BMW is a perfect illustration of a company that allowed itself to get distracted by the cultural and consumer trends that were driving its business. It's very risky business to change a successful marketing strategy to fit what may prove to be just a fad. Who knows how long a trend will last? You may be eroding a solid corporate brand image with broad appeal for the sake of a small slice of the market.

The yuppie was, in fact, dead by the dawn of the 1990s. BMW realized the error of its ways and started working to get back on track. It learned a hard lesson from its brief obsession with status and isn't even thinking of tampering with the brand again. "The yuppie image became a stigma for us and even today, people still sometimes call us the yuppiemobile," says Robert Mitchell, manager of corporate communications. "Perceptions die slowly, but BMW is really for people who understand the joy of driving."

BMW now boasts perhaps the most consistent corporate brand image and reputation of any automaker and is outselling many of its competitors. Its advertising is once again all about power and performance. Here's a sampling of the prose in some recent BMW ads: "While others are content to simply move the needle, we're never happy until we've completely buried it" and "[the] dramatic 24-valve inline six-cylinder engine will move you while its road gripping sensation thrills your senses—take your seat and start the show."

Beyond the performance message, BMW also strives to convey its corporate image for automotive innovation through cutting edge marketing. Its latest sports cars were cast in several James Bond movies. Now it has moved on to creating its own minimovies, which are promoted like other films but shown on the BMW Web site. Directed by such well-known filmmakers as Ang Lee, Tony Scott, and John Frankenheimer, the films make the BMW car, not the action hero, the star. "We want people to view them as really good films, not as long commercials," says James McDowell, vice president of marketing at BMW of North America.

The BMW brand will require careful tending. McDowell's biggest test will be maintaining consistency without sacrificing creativity. "For BMW, consistency across time and across markets and a devotion to the essence of the brand are the obvious prerequisites," he says. "The challenge is to do that and not inhibit the creativity and risk taking that any leading brand needs in order to stay vibrant."

BEWARE THE DANGERS OF REPUTATION RUB-OFF

From the very beginning, they looked like the odd couple of retailing. When Sears, Roebuck & Company began selling a new line of Benetton apparel in 1999, people in the fashion and retailing worlds were bemused—and bewildered. How could the American retailer of Craftsman tools and Kenmore refrigerators ever hope to get along well with an Italian fashion company that specialized in shock advertising? It was Benetton Group, after all, that had created ads depicting a nun and priest kissing, a pastel collection of condoms, a black woman breast-feeding a white infant, and an AIDS patient on his deathbed.

Strategically, the partnership made sense. Sears ballyhooed the deal, expressing hope that Benetton would overcome Sears' dowdy image and attract more teenagers and young adults to its stores. For its part, Benetton wanted "new momentum" to rebuild its presence in the U.S. retail market after having closed hundreds of its own stores during the 1990s. Sears predicted that the Benetton USA line would be a "megabrand," generating sales of more than $100 million a year.

But culturally, the companies made a miserable match. Ron Culp, who recently retired as senior vice president of public relations and government affairs, warned his colleagues at Sears, but to no avail. "I said,

'These people at Benetton are mad hatters; they're so un-Sears,'" Culp recalls.

His instincts were correct. It didn't take long for the fireworks to start—and the divorce followed soon after. But in the process, Sears allowed its folksy 110-year-old reputation to be sullied by Benetton's edgy advertising. The mass merchandiser learned the hard way how one company's reputation problems can rub off on a business partner.

What forced the breakup after just six months was an ad campaign that sympathetically portrayed prisoners living on death row. Benetton officials said they wanted to spark a debate about the ethics of capital punishment. The debate turned out to be more of a protest against Benetton and, by extension, Sears. Before Sears knew what had hit it, victims' rights groups and the retailer's own employees were up in arms about the "We on Death Row" ads. The ads brought back painful memories to people who had lost loved ones to the convicted murderers. The campaign also didn't sit well with Sears' conservative, middle-American customers. It raised the question in some people's minds of whether Sears joined Benetton in questioning the death penalty.

Sears officials defensively—and naively—claimed they had expected people to distinguish between the marketing for its Benetton USA line and the controversial United Colors of Benetton corporate advertising. But let's face it, Benetton is Benetton to most people.

There's no question that Sears ignored clear warning signs in its desperation to attract younger customers. But at least it had the good sense to pull the Benetton clothing out of its stores soon after the controversy erupted. "I know we're in a pickle; the people who are upset are for the most part Sears customers," Culp told Arthur Martinez, who was then Sears' chairman and CEO. "The victims' rights groups are giving us fair warning that they're going after Benetton and that Sears is the weak link. We should remove the Benetton product from our stores right away."

Sears had invested millions of dollars in store design and advertising for its Benetton line and had never even realized the sales boost it had expected from attracting more of the free-spending teenagers roaming the shopping malls of America. But had Sears not bailed out, the reputation costs would have been considerably greater.

Culp says the Benetton mess inspired the company to focus more on reputation management in making strategic decisions. The heightened sensitivity to reputation seems to be working, at least in picking partners.

Sears has since teamed up with an apparel company that makes for a much better fit. In 2002, it acquired Lands' End, which may not be as youthful and trendy as Benetton but does attract more affluent and educated customers than Sears. Its marketing approach and traditional styles also are much more in sync with Sears' wholesome midwestern image.

GUILT BY ASSOCIATION

The company you keep certainly affects your personal reputation. It is no different with corporations, as Sears learned so well. The possibilities for reputation rub-off from business relationships are endless. Whether a supplier, a merger or joint-venture partner, an accountant, a licensee, or a celebrity endorser, business connections will most definitely influence corporate reputation.

The rub-off can be positive. Visa International has long capitalized successfully on its exclusive credit card arrangements with such big events as the Olympics and the Tony Awards. And Coca-Cola earned reputation points when it created a literacy promotion in conjunction with the blockbuster Harry Potter children's films.

But corporate connections often create reputation headaches. Coke's recent $1 million grant to the American Academy of Pediatric Dentistry was roundly booed as a blatant attempt to change consumers' negative perceptions of sugar-laced soft drinks and their link to tooth decay. Nike, The Gap, and other apparel and shoe companies have endured reputation damage for contracting their manufacturing to Third World factories with meager wages and sweatshop working conditions. And the Enron scandal hurt many companies that it touched. J. P. Morgan Chase, one of the most aggressive lenders to the energy-trading firm during its meteoric rise, suffered both financial and reputation loss.

A company can experience rub-off reputation damage just by being part of a maligned industry, such as oil, chemicals, pharmaceuticals, or accounting. Even supporting philanthropic causes that are controversial, whether Planned Parenthood (contraception and abortion issues) or the Boy Scouts of America (gay rights issues), can stir protests and hurt a company's reputation.

Much like marriage, a business partnership isn't something to enter into lightly. So lend your good name sparingly and choose your partners with care. Scrutinize their past behavior and try to detect whether there might be possible conflicts or embarrassing actions ahead that will sully your reputation. Is your potential partner on a sound financial footing? Are its corporate culture and value system compatible with yours? What do your employees and customers think of it?

No one can predict the future and what catastrophes might befall a potential partner. But keep in mind that new business associates always pose a risk. Do your homework thoroughly, and don't ignore any warning signs. Careful research—along with a skeptical attitude—can prevent some rocky marriages, between both people and corporations.

Sometimes it seems easier to stay in a risky relationship, but comfort isn't worth harm to your reputation. The most vigilant clients fled from Arthur Andersen after its role in the Enron accounting scandal was revealed. But because of the cost and disruption of changing auditors, many clients stuck with the accounting firm even after its document shredding came to light. Although the credibility of all of Andersen's auditing work suddenly became suspect, some companies didn't jump ship until a criminal indictment for obstruction of justice made Andersen's survival seem unlikely. Taking fast action in that case, however, would have been far better because a company's accounting firm is so closely tied to its reputation. People trust a company's financial statements based on their belief in its auditor's scrupulous integrity.

The unraveling of Arthur Andersen clearly damaged the reputations of many of its clients, at least temporarily. Their stock prices actually fell as the magnitude of Andersen's involvement in Enron's accounting shenanigans came to light.

That's the conclusion of Paul Chaney of Vanderbilt University and Kirk Philipich of Ohio State University. Their study, "Shredded Reputation: The Cost of Audit Failure" published in the *Journal of Accounting Research* in September 2002, shows the tangible effects of being associated with a scandalized company even if you yourself are squeaky clean.

The study found that during the three days following Andersen's admission that a significant number of Enron documents had been shredded, Andersen's other clients "experienced a statistically negative market reaction." The stock price declines suggest that investors downgraded the overall quality of all of Andersen's audits. Clients in Andersen's Houston office, which had shredded the Enron documents, suffered the biggest market declines. "We argue that this cost is due to loss of reputation," the accounting professors assert.

BREAKING UP IS HARD TO DO

Once they tie the knot, companies need to keep a close eye on their partners' behavior. And at the first sign of serious trouble, they must consider whether it's time to sever the connection. A fast breakup will usually minimize the reputation damage, as some of Arthur Andersen's clients realized.

It isn't easy to sever a longtime relationship, however. Delta Air Lines, for example, struggled with whether to dismiss Andersen even after the document shredding had been revealed. Joseph Berardino, Andersen's embattled CEO, flew to Atlanta and made a presentation to Delta's board in January 2002 to try to persuade Delta, one of the firm's largest clients, to stick with him. But Delta sensed Andersen's worsening crisis and began searching for a new auditor. By early March, about a week before the criminal indictment, Delta selected Deloitte & Touche to replace Andersen.

Delta also moved quickly to end a risky airline partnership in 1999. After a string of accidents, including a deadly crash, by Korean Air's planes, Delta suspended its marketing arrangement with the Asian airline to avoid any negative rub-off effects on its reputation for safety. Delta later restored its partnership after it felt satisfied with the operational improvements at Korean Air.

CIT Group was at risk for reputation damage as part of Tyco International, which has been buffeted by accounting scandals and charges of executive wrongdoing. One issue touched especially close to home for CIT, a commercial and consumer finance company. A former outside director of Tyco pleaded guilty to charges related to his receipt of an undisclosed $20 million fee for helping arrange Tyco's $9.5 billion acquisition of CIT. The Tyco link hurt CIT's credit rating and increased its borrowing costs.

But in July 2002, CIT was spun off in an initial public offering of stock and wasted little time trying to erase the Tyco connection. It created a touchy-feely corporate ad campaign depicting it as "a partner" helping a fashion designer, an aviation executive, and other businesspeople realize their dreams.

Some companies have made the mistake of tying themselves together through long-term contracts without an easy escape hatch. Today's promising partner may become tomorrow's ticking time bomb. Don't lock yourself into a relationship that may sour sooner than you could have ever expected. The world seems to be spinning faster than ever, and business and social trends come and go at lightning speed.

Walt Disney Company and McDonald's signed a ten-year agreement to promote exclusively Disney movies with McDonald's kids' meals. But some recent Disney movies flopped at the box office, and McDonald's couldn't link up with any of the hotter kid flicks. At the same time, Disney's reputation for cleanliness and customer service in its theme parks can't be benefiting from the connection to McDonald's reputation for messy restaurants, slow and surly employees, and unhealthy food.

Even without a binding contract, a company sometimes chooses to stay with a troubled partner. The potential reputation damage may be quite apparent. Yet ending a relationship may mean giving up a valuable supplier. DuPont stuck with Huntingdon Life Sciences even though it tested the toxicity of products through animal research because DuPont said that the company was "uniquely qualified." It was a bold, surprising decision for image-conscious DuPont because animal rights groups have vigorously and sometimes violently attacked Huntingdon and its customers, investors, insurance company, and accounting firm.

The Stop Huntingdon Animal Cruelty organization claims success in driving away some Huntingdon investors and customers, as well as its insurer. Among the group's tactics: sabotaging oil tanker trucks belonging to a Huntingdon customer, attacking the apartment and stealing the credit cards of an investment banker involved in funding Huntingdon, and damaging a golf course where an executive from Huntingdon's insurance company was playing in a tournament.

DuPont itself was criticized on the Stop Huntingdon Animal Cruelty Web site for the killing of twenty marmoset monkeys in Huntingdon toxicology studies. Animal rights activists also tried to overload and shut down DuPont's e-mail system and Internet site, and they protested outside its buildings, accusing it of "killing puppies for profit." While companies shouldn't give in easily to such blackmail, they must carefully weigh whether the reputation harm is worth their standing behind their business partners.

If you do decide to split up, try to dissolve the damaging relationship quietly and amicably. A messy fight can cause its own reputation harm. Some very public, nasty spats have resulted from partnerships gone sour in recent years. The public may enjoy all the mudslinging, but it ends up cheapening corporate reputations.

That was certainly the case with two recent courtroom catfights. A few years ago, Calvin Klein sued Warnaco Group, the maker of its jeans and underwear, arguing that Warnaco had driven its good name into the ground through overproduction and distribution through low-end warehouse clubs. Calvin Klein charged that Warnaco and Linda Wachner, then its CEO, had become "a cancer on the value and integrity" of the corporate brand. Warnaco countersued, claiming that Calvin Klein himself had hurt his reputation by going on CNN's *Larry King Live* program and disparaging the Warnaco-produced CK jeans and underwear as substandard products. After those remarks, Warnaco said, retailers had cut back on their orders. Eventually, the fashion designer and Wachner literally kissed and made up, but the dispute left the CK brand's reputation for quality in doubt.

Rosie O'Donnell and publisher Gruner & Jahr USA also battled long and hard in the media and the courts when she felt she had lost control of the editorial content of her namesake magazine, *Rosie*. Understandably, the actress and former talk-show host was concerned about how the magazine might affect her personal and business reputation. But in the end, it was the contentious fight with the publisher and the magazine's rapid demise that hurt her reputation. She and Gruner & Jahr would both have been much better off had they ended their alliance without so much drama.

MARKETING AND MEDIA MATCHES— AND MISMATCHES

The marketing arena is ripe with opportunities for reputation rub-off, both beneficial and destructive. Advertising pitchmen and the programs in which companies advertise can significantly affect people's perceptions. Just be sure to pick your marketing partners with care to match your corporate personality.

The payoff can be substantial with the right endorser. A touching image-building commercial for Johnson & Johnson featured Nobel Prize–winning novelist Toni Morrison telling how her parents had encouraged her to achieve and urging children to always try to do their best. The ad barely mentions J&J but is incredibly effective in reinforcing its image as the caring company that makes products for babies and children.

Hewlett-Packard is trying to polish its image after its bruising fight to acquire Compaq Corporation by linking its name with such well-regarded customers as DreamWorks, BMW, and FedEx. As long as those companies maintain their strong reputations, the rub-off effects could be quite positive.

Actor Paul Newman recently teamed up with McDonald's to sell his salad dressings at the fast-food chain. It seemed like a clear win for McDonald's, given Newman's charisma and recent Oscar nomination, as well as the fact that he donates after-tax profits from his food business to charity. But the fast-food chain's burgers and fries won't help—and might even hurt—Newman's Own's reputation for all-natural products.

Another gamble is chanteuse Celine Dion's linkup with Daimler-Chrysler. She is lending some of her magic to DaimlerChrysler's reputation in the hope of persuading consumers to give Chrysler cars a try. At least that's the halo effect the company is betting on with its multimillion-dollar endorsement deal. But for DaimlerChrysler's sake, let's just hope that Dion doesn't crash her Chrysler Town & Country minivan.

Such celebrity goofs can cancel out any positive rub-off and actually harm the company's reputation. All too often, famous pitchmen end up embarrassing the advertiser. Boxer Mike Tyson caused such advertisers as Eastman Kodak and PepsiCo to run for cover to escape the negative fallout from his stormy marriage to Robin Givens. Actress Cybill Shepherd said she avoided red meat at the same time she was promoting beef in commercials, while actor Don Johnson was photographed sipping a Diet Coke at the same time he was pitching for Pepsi. And most recently, Los Angeles Lakers star Kobe Bryant was charged with sexual assault at the height of his endorsement career with such marketers as Nike, McDonald's, and Coca-Cola. Bryant denied the charge, but the onslaught of sensational publicity made the basketball guard a potential liability for the companies.

The TV programs on which a company advertises are as important to reputation as pitchmen. Companies and their ad agencies need to buy media time judiciously. Otherwise they may well find themselves in the midst of a morality debate that can undermine their reputations. A Michigan housewife named Terry Rakolta set off one of the biggest advertising flaps of 1989. She turned her wrath about the raunchy TV show *Married with Children* on Coca-Cola and other red-faced companies that had advertised on the program. Recently, the Gay and Lesbian Alliance Against Defamation and the National Organization for Women went on the attack when MSNBC announced a new cable television talk show starring Michael Savage, whose tirades on his radio program had upset many listeners. In no time, such national advertisers as Procter & Gamble, Dell, and General Mills vowed to shun his show. Eventually, MSNBC canceled Savage's show because he made a hostile, antigay remark.

But even without such well-publicized pressure tactics, companies can harm their reputations by advertising on shows that don't fit their image. One problem is that the so-called family hour is rapidly disappearing and advertisers are struggling to find shows with wholesome content.

The best protection is greater programming control. Television production is certainly an expensive proposition, but it can become a valuable part of a company's reputation-building strategy. There's no better example of the benefits than Hallmark Cards. Since the opera *Amahl and the Night Visitors* was broadcast as the first Hallmark Hall of Fame production in 1951, the television specials have markedly enhanced the greeting card company's reputation. That's largely because of its control over the quality and content of the shows. Hallmark doesn't accept scripts from outsiders. It commissions all of the scripts and often requires rewrites or even the selection of a different screenwriter to ensure that they meet its standards. When the scripts are finished, Hallmark management reviews them before the start of production. One project was in the works for twelve years.

"The Hallmark Hall of Fame has tremendous impact on the company's reputation," says Brad Moore, president of Hallmark Hall of Fame Productions. "It's the biggest contributor to our public face beyond our retail stores. We want to equate the Hallmark name with quality, good taste, and enriching relationships through the programs." The company runs only Hallmark greeting card commercials during the shows to guarantee that the advertising medium is free of any outside influences.

Like Hallmark, other companies are taking matters into their own hands. Johnson & Johnson has begun to sponsor and develop programs itself because there are so few family-hour shows it considers suitable for advertising its brands. It joined with other major advertisers and formed the Family Friendly Programming Forum to fund the development of more wholesome shows. On its own, Johnson & Johnson has started creating original movies for the TNT cable network, such as the Emmy Award–winning *Door to Door*, and it was the sole corporate sponsor of a series about a Latino family on public television. "Our values and reputation play a major role in these decisions," says Andrea Alstrup, corporate vice president for advertising at J&J. "Over the years, it had become more and more difficult to find programming that families can watch together and that was appropriate for Johnson & Johnson's advertising."

TOXIC PARTNERS

You might call it poetic justice that Martha Stewart and Kmart are so closely entwined. She and the company seem to deserve each other, given how badly they botched their reputations on their own. Now their wounded reputations are rubbing off on each other.

First Martha Stewart and her company, Martha Stewart Living Omnimedia, were portrayed as the victim of Kmart's financial mess when the retailer filed for bankruptcy protection. Kmart sells a broad range of products, from sheets and towels to garden tools and Christmas ornaments, under the Martha Stewart Everyday brand.

Less than six months after the bankruptcy filing, however, Kmart was the least of Stewart's worries. Stewart looked like an even bigger liability to Kmart as federal investigators explored whether she had acted on inside information when she sold her stock in the biotechnology firm ImClone Systems shortly before it announced that the Food and Drug Administration had refused to review its promising cancer drug. Martha Stewart Living Omnimedia's results worsened as the months passed, with quarterly losses in 2002 and 2003 that the company blamed partly on the government stock-trading probe.

It's extremely rare that both business partners end up tainting each other so dramatically. And it's hard to tell who is hurting whom the most. "Kmart should dump Martha Stewart," declares Craig Baker, a Los Angeles resident who says his female friends have started shopping at Target and Wal-Mart to avoid buying her products. "It's ironic because she had been thinking of dumping Kmart. But there's not as much shame in filing for bankruptcy as in having the feds come down on you."

As the investigation into her stock sale dragged on, Kmart made Stewart's smiling face less prominent in its marketing and started pushing new brands such as Joe Boxer. The retailer also closed hundreds of stores, cutting into the sales of Martha Stewart products.

Finally, in June 2003, a federal grand jury indicted Stewart on five

PARTNER PERCEPTIONS

Respondents to a 2002 public opinion survey by Harris Interactive rated these related companies on a variety of corporate attributes. Here are the percentages of ratings that were considered positive (a 5, 6, or 7 on a 7-point scale) and the differences between the companies. Kmart and Martha Stewart bring different strengths and weaknesses to their partnership, but Ben & Jerry's handily outscores parent company Unilever on all of the measures.

KMART VERSUS MARTHA STEWART LIVING OMNIMEDIA

Corporate Attributes	% Positive Ratings		
	Kmart	Martha Stewart	Gap
Have a good feeling about the company	47	20	27
Trust the company	49	23	26
Admire and respect the company	45	19	26
Offers products and services that are a good value for the money	60	44	16
Offers high-quality products and services	39	50	-11
Has a strong record of profitability	15	35	-20
Develops innovative products and services	20	44	-24
Recognizes and takes advantage of market opportunities	20	55	-35

BEN & JERRY'S VERSUS UNILEVER

Corporate Attributes	% Positive Ratings		
	Ben & Jerry's	Unilever	Gap
Admire and respect the company	75	43	32
Is an environmentally responsible company	51	23	28
Looks like a good company to work for	62	35	27
Develops innovative products and services	70	44	26
Supports good causes	45	21	24
Offers high-quality products and services	80	57	23
Trust the company	75	53	22
Offers products and services that are a good value for the money	61	54	7

criminal counts of securities fraud, conspiracy, and making false statements to federal agents. Whatever the outcome of the case, some retailing experts believe that Kmart may eventually drop her name from the household products. "I was very concerned during the summer of 2002, when Martha was in the headlines every day," says James Adamson, the former chairman of Kmart, which emerged from Chapter 11 bankruptcy protection in May 2003. "But we've separated Martha the person from the brand, and I believe the marketplace has started to recognize the brand is going to outlive Martha. If the product quality is right, consumers will look beyond the person."

Could either party have predicted such a poisonous partnership? Stewart might have foreseen that Kmart would end up seeking bankruptcy protection, given its steadily deteriorating financial performance. On the other hand, Kmart would never have expected the doyenne of domestic perfection to commit such a colossal mistake—saving a relatively paltry sum by selling the ImClone stock before its price plunged and then losing much more when her own company's stock dropped on news of the investigation. Indeed, *Mad* magazine declared her the "dumbest" person of 2002.

FAMILY TIES

Corporate marriages are serious business. They are certain to have rub-off effects on reputation, with one of the companies usually on the losing end. Time Warner has been tarnished by its troubled merger with America Online, as have Mobil following its acquisition by Exxon and Kraft Foods after its purchase by Philip Morris. It was hoped that the merger of Daimler and Chrysler would lend some of the Mercedes prestige to Chrysler, but if anything, Chrysler's weak image has tainted DaimlerChrysler's corporate reputation.

Altria Group believes that advertising the Philip Morris–Kraft connection improved its corporate reputation and contends that Kraft hasn't suffered from the tobacco ties. Altria says that both it and Kraft have closely tracked the impact of the tobacco business and corporate advertising on Kraft and haven't detected any negative rub-off on the food company's image or its sales.

But the impact seemed quite clear in 2003, when the Philip Morris USA division faced a $12 billion court-ordered bond while appealing a jury's decision that it had deceived smokers about the health risks of so-called light cigarettes. Concerned that Altria might need to tap the funds of its majority-controlled Kraft subsidiary to post the bond, investors became spooked. Moody's Investors Service cut its debt ratings for both Altria and Kraft, and Kraft's bonds and stock price suffered.

Altria is also ignoring the fact that some people have found Kraft's products less appealing after learning of the tobacco taint and have begun boycotting the food brands. Caleb Shulman of Rochester, New York, loved Kraft macaroni and cheese, but after watching Philip Morris's corporate advertising campaign and learning that a tobacco maker owns Kraft, he lost his appetite for it. "Now I refuse to buy Kraft products," he says. "Whenever I saw the ads, I cringed. They're only running the ads to gain credibility because of all the smoking-related lawsuits." What's more, some college students have protested the presence of Kraft recruiters on campus, and INFACT, a corporate watchdog organization, has called for an international boycott of Kraft's brands as long as Kraft remains connected with tobacco. "As Philip Morris's stock value continued to sink, the corporation shifted its strategy," says Kathryn Mulvey, INFACT's executive director. "Philip Morris knows tobacco's bad reputation will harm Kraft's image, but the corporation is desperate."

That doesn't mean your company should never buy—or be acquired by—a company with a damaged reputation. But be sure it's well worth the risk and do your due diligence to prepare to deal with the baggage that will come with the acquisition. If there's ongoing litigation, can you resolve it quickly? Is there a stigma that will have to be confronted and removed over time?

Dow Chemical Company may have underestimated how many reputation problems still dogged one of its largest acquisitions. Dow, which has faced plenty of reputation troubles of its own dating back to protests over its production of napalm during the Vietnam War, took on even more problems when it bought Union Carbide Corporation in 2001. Dow is now saddled with the continued fallout from the deadly gas leak at a Union Carbide pesticide plant in Bhopal, India, in 1984, as well as ongoing asbestos litigation against Union Carbide.

Activist groups are demanding that Dow take responsibility for the remaining environmental damage and for deaths and injuries related to the gas leak that have occurred in the years since the incident. But Dow argues that Union Carbide reached a $470 million out-of-court settlement in 1989 covering all claims related to the incident. While Dow says it is considering support for humanitarian aid projects in Bhopal, it stresses that it will not accept responsibility for the gas leak. Whether or not it makes any significant monetary payouts because of the Bhopal catastrophe, Dow will have paid dearly through reputation damage.

In another big merger, Exxon's acquisition of Mobil has diminished Mobil's reputation. Not only is Mobil now linked to the infamous *Exxon Valdez* oil spill in Alaska, but Exxon also is dismantling some of the programs that contributed to Mobil's positive image. Gone is Mobil's domestic-partner benefits program, which appealed to the gay community and investment funds with a social responsibility and diversity focus. Exxon Mobil has also announced that it will halt the sponsorship of public television's acclaimed *Masterpiece Theatre* program. The founding sponsor of the show in 1971, Mobil had accrued tremendous goodwill for its support of *Masterpiece Theatre*.

CoreBrand, a consulting firm that tracks reputation, has continued to monitor Mobil's reputation ratings as if it were still independent. The results show that Mobil's rating by executives of large U.S. companies has headed in the wrong direction, slipping from 76.4 in 1998 before the merger to 73.9 in 2002. (The maximum possible rating is 100.) But it still exceeded the combined Exxon Mobil's rating of 65.9 and Exxon's stand-alone rating of 66 in 2002. "Mobil had a great communications system and managed its reputation well," says James Gregory, CEO of CoreBrand. "Exxon is incredibly arrogant and has been almost anticommunications ever since the *Valdez* accident."

COMPATIBLE COMPANIES

Not all corporate relationships are destined to damage reputations. There are indeed some very happy corporate marriages and partnerships. Sometimes companies manage to get along just fine, even when their cultures seem at odds. Savvy companies keep their distance and don't tamper with the reputations of their new family members. That has worked well for Unilever, the mammoth British-Dutch consumer products marketer. It found a successful business in selling Calvin Klein's fragrances even though the designer's sexy, quirky advertising doesn't quite mesh with the company's more pedestrian ads for Dove soap and Lipton tea.

It's a delicate balancing act, but so far, Unilever also seems to have handled its acquisition of Ben & Jerry's Homemade adroitly. Unilever hasn't let its stodgy reputation affect the gourmet ice cream company and its strong dedication to social and environmental causes.

When Unilever bought Ben & Jerry's in 2000, the ice cream maker's fans shuddered to think about how the company would change. Some angrily accused their heroes—founders Ben Cohen and Jerry Greenfield—of selling out to "the establishment." But the fears seem largely groundless. Unilever wisely realized that Ben & Jerry's success stemmed as much from its culture of social and environmental responsibility as from the quality of its products. Though it has taken advantage of cost-saving synergies, such as merging Ben & Jerry's grocery sales team with its other ice-cream sales groups, Unilever hasn't tampered much with the company's political agenda. As a result, Ben & Jerry's reputation for social activism and an entrepreneurial spirit remains quite healthy. Its "head of social mission" visited West Africa to investigate allegations of forced child labor in the chocolate industry. The new flavor One Sweet Whirled is part of the company's campaign against global warming. And with the looming prospect of war against Iraq, Ben & Jerry's revived its Peace Pops ice cream bars.

Even so, the skepticism hasn't disappeared entirely. Consumers still inquire about whether Unilever is putting its conglomerate stamp on Ben & Jerry's business. "We sort of have a 'don't ask, don't tell,' policy about Unilever," says Chrystie Heimert, Ben & Jerry's public relations director. "If people do ask, we tell about the acquisition but also point out that our social mission is still front and center."

Some people think Ben and Jerry still run the company that the childhood friends founded in 1978 in a renovated gas station in Burlington, Vermont. That isn't always a good thing. Unilever clearly doesn't want its reputation affected by everything the ice cream company's founders have to say these days. The Ben & Jerry's Web page contains a disclaimer pointing out that the two men speak for themselves now and not the company. The reason? Cohen and Greenfield voiced their vehement opposition to going to war against Iraq, much more of a political hot potato than global warming and child labor; Unilever made it clear that it wholeheartedly supported American troops during the war.

PART THREE

—————

Repairing a Damaged Reputation

The greater the difficulty, the more glory in surmounting it. Skillful pilots gain their reputation from storms and tempests.

—ATTRIBUTED TO THE GREEK PHILOSOPHER EPICURUS

MANAGE CRISES
WITH FINESSE

Paul Critchlow, counselor to the chairman of Merrill Lynch, calls them the "Big Three."

First came the internal e-mail messages from Merrill research analysts who privately derided stocks they were recommending as good buys to clients. The e-mails sparked an investigation by New York State Attorney General Eliot Spitzer over possible conflicts of interest between the research and investment banking departments at Merrill. He charged that Merrill was promoting stocks of certain companies to win their investment banking business. In spring 2002, Merrill paid $100 million to settle the probe.

Second—and soon after—congressional hearings into the Enron Corporation collapse shone a spotlight on Merrill's involvement in structuring partnerships and deals that Enron had used to conceal its true financial condition. Then, third, there was Martha Stewart, the taste maven who came under scrutiny for possible insider trading involving her Merrill broker and his assistant.

Can any company's reputation survive such a barrage of controversy? A brokerage firm thrives because of the investing public's confidence in it. But a 2002 Harris Interactive public opinion survey of corporate reputation found people incredibly cynical about Merrill. "In my opinion," one respondent said, "Merrill Lynch is ethically on a par with Las Vegas and the Mafia." Other survey respondents commented, "Stop robbing old people" and "Stop being such money-grubbing pigs."

Such seething comments proved dispiriting to the many honest employees of the financial services giant. But the company managed to weather the crisis and is starting to rebuild its battered image. "During a period like this, you do everything to control what is in your power to control," says Critchlow, who was like a ringmaster leading a three-ring circus during the series of crises. "But frankly," he adds, "there have been some very tough times when we felt powerless to defend ourselves."

Critchlow, who served as senior vice president for communications and public affairs before being named counselor to the chairman and vice chairman for public markets in July 2003, doesn't minimize the fact that Merrill's reputation suffered tremendously from those three consecutive blows. How could it not, given all of the uncertainty about possible criminal charges and a flood of civil litigation that could leave it bankrupt? At one point, Critchlow says, Merrill had lost more than $20 billion in market capitalization due in large part to the reputation damage from the crises.

The crises demonstrated a serious breakdown in Merrill's proud culture, which traces its origins to a predecessor investment firm founded in 1885. Some Merrill employees had lost sight of an oft-quoted dictum of former chairman William Schreyer: "No one's bottom line is more important than the reputation of the firm." The crises also violated Merrill's clearly stated principles, which are enumerated in various corporate publications and posted on office walls. The list of principles puts "client focus" first, stating, "In our increasingly competitive industry, success rests not on our ability to sell a certain product or service, but on the degree to which clients value Merrill Lynch as their trusted adviser."

Many clients hardly viewed Merrill's research as trustworthy after the embarrassing settlement with the New York State attorney general's office. Was anyone still bullish on Merrill Lynch? Merrill's research found that only 39 percent of its clients believed the company had "high integrity" by fall 2002, a sharp drop from 64 percent before the May 2002 settlement announcement. But that was still far superior to what nonclient investors thought: only 16 percent gave Merrill high marks for integrity.

Some companies might have been overwhelmed by the crisis atmosphere at Merrill, which couldn't have come at a worse time. The controversies all developed on the heels of the September 11, 2001, terrorist attack on the World Trade Center, which damaged Merrill's nearby headquarters and forced an evacuation of the offices. The attack also claimed the lives of three of Merrill's employees.

But Critchlow, an old hand at crisis management and a Vietnam War combat veteran, wasn't intimidated. He earned his stripes as press secretary to Pennsylvania Governor Dick Thornburgh during the accident at the Three Mile Island nuclear power plant in 1979. And in his nearly two decades at Merrill, he had helped guide the company through other crises, including the 1987 stock market crash and, in the mid-1990s, the Orange County, California, bankruptcy and the county's lawsuit against Merrill, its broker-dealer. But he concedes that none of those came close to the intensity of the three-pronged crisis that began unfolding in 2002.

Critchlow's performance shows the importance of treading in a careful but sure-footed manner through the minefield of a corporate crisis. He knows well that what defines you is how you perform when the going gets tough.

One of his key principles is to gather all of the facts first before commenting to the media. Making a mistake early on ruins credibility. Critchlow and his team also developed a playbook for quickly disseminating the company's response because they realize that in today's information-driven world, speed of response has become ever more urgent. With Critchlow's office strategically located next to the general counsel's and around the corner from the CEO's, the communications staff could quickly get up to speed on the latest developments.

Throughout the crises, Merrill's actions were mostly reactive but quite strategic. For example, when they had to select a representative to testify about Enron before a congressional committee, Merrill executives didn't have a knee-jerk reaction and send David Komansky, who was then CEO. Instead, they chose G. Kelly Martin, president of the international brokerage division, who was articulate and had investment banking experience. Merrill didn't want to send anyone too junior and insult the congressmen. At the same time, someone too senior would make the situation look more serious than Merrill felt was warranted. What's more, testimony by the CEO would almost certainly end up on the front page of every major newspaper.

During the crises, Merrill planned its advertising carefully, tending to do less than usual. With the negative news still unfolding, the company delayed a major corporate image campaign. It did run a few ads after the 2002 settlement with the New York State attorney general. One ad declared that the company had set "a new standard for investment research" and detailed the steps Merrill would take to achieve greater accountability, disclose more information to investors, and insulate research analysts' compensation from investment banking. The other— a double-page spread—showed Komansky and his heir apparent, Stanley O'Neal, and stated, "Leaders respond constructively to criticism; we've heard the criticism and are responding beyond what was asked."

"Those ads were aimed mostly at employees to let them know that one part of the controversy was over and to stay cool," says Critchlow. "It didn't make sense to keep pounding people with more advertising because there was more controversy to come. You look foolish if you run a big image campaign ahead of the curve of recovery. It all falls on deaf ears and just gives your adversaries something to seize on to." Instead of image polishing, most of Merrill's advertising focused on promoting specific financial products and services.

While its external advertising tended to be low-key, the company stepped up employee communication. Employees needed information to avoid becoming demoralized, as well as to understand the company's new culture of greater accountability and less maternalism. The company had been known as Mother Merrill for its way of taking care of its employees, but that was no longer to be.

"If the result is we harm the firm's reputation, it's not acceptable," O'Neal said in a "town hall meeting" with Merrill's legal group. Referring to Merrill's ties to Enron, he said that the company seemed guilty of stupidity, which he called unforgivable. "We have to be better at conducting our business," he continued. "We have to be smarter. And we can be and we will be because we cannot afford to have these kinds of issues damage, continually damage, our reputation."

Merrill was pleased that it had taken enough preventive steps to avoid losing any "serious business" during the crises. The company sent letters to keep major clients informed of the various controversies and armed employees with "talking points" to answer customers' questions. The main message: Your assets are safe and segregated from the firm's assets. If big clients expressed reservations, a "SWAT team" of top-level managers moved in quickly to reassure them that Merrill would be fine and recommend that they not believe everything they read and heard in the media. Sometimes Merrill employees would fly on short notice to visit government officials, state legislators, or pension fund managers. Such face-to-face meetings, handled in conjunction with Merrill's lawyers, were most effective in allaying people's worries.

Merrill didn't rely solely on its own expertise. The company hired outsiders to provide advice about its reputation strategy, including former New York City mayor Rudolph Giuliani's consulting firm. Because of his leadership reputation following the September 11, 2001, tragedy, Merrill considered enlisting Giuliani as a spokesman but ultimately decided against using outsiders to defend the firm publicly.

Merrill also hired market research firm Penn, Schoen & Berland Associates, which has experience in both corporate and political issues, because the crises were all so fraught with politics. Through Penn, Schoen & Berland's work and other research, Merrill monitored its reputation with different stakeholder groups continuously. The company's reputation reached a low point in summer 2002, when nearly 40 percent of nonclient investors gave it an unfavorable rating.

The hardest part for Critchlow and his public relations team was their inability to defend the firm more assertively. While Critchlow and other Merrill executives agreed that some employees certainly had been guilty of bad judgment and unethical behavior, they disagreed with regulators and critics that they had broken the law. At first Merrill came out swinging, but it soon reconsidered the approach. Merrill feared that a pugnacious defense during Eliot Spitzer's investigation might lead to criminal charges that in turn would ruin the firm just as a criminal indictment had been the undoing of the Arthur Andersen accounting firm.

"We were fighting not with one arm behind our back, but with two behind our back," says Critchlow. "We briefly made an effort to rebut because we felt some e-mails had been taken out of context, but we decided pretty quickly we couldn't make a case with the public and fight the investigation. The implied threat of criminal charges in today's media environment is potentially fatal, and so the least costly course of action is often to settle."

The Washington hearings on Enron also proved extremely frustrating. The political atmosphere heightened media coverage, with leaks to the press before Merrill's appearance at the hearing. "It was saturation bombing," Critchlow says. "It had taken on McCarthylike proportions and was emotionally devastating. We couldn't do anything about the besmirching of our reputation."

MERRILL LYNCH'S REPUTATION ROLLER COASTER

Merrill Lynch aspires to regularly achieve a 75 percent favorability rating with nonclient investors, who are a prime target for new business. But the recent wave of crises pushed it well below that level. Here is a chronology of its reputation rating's ups and downs between spring 2002 and summer 2003. The difference between the totals of the favorable and unfavorable scores and 100 percent is the percentage of people who didn't answer or said they were unsure.

In May 2002, just before the New York attorney general announced the $100 million settlement of his investigation of alleged conflicts-of-interest in Merrill Lynch's investment research: 70% favorable, 21% unfavorable

In June 2002, several weeks after the settlement was announced: 60% favorable, 30% unfavorable

In late July–early August 2002, during the congressional hearings over Merrill's role in the Enron scandal and early revelations about possible insider trading by Martha Stewart and her Merrill broker: 57% favorable, 37% unfavorable

In fall 2002, when Merrill was less in the spotlight: 60% favorable, 28% unfavorable

In summer 2003, after the $1.4 billion Wall Street settlement, federal judge Milton Pollack's ruling in an investor class action suit in favor of Merrill, and Merrill's strong second-quarter earnings report: 65% favorable, 25% unfavorable

What mattered most to Merrill was getting each crisis behind it as fast as it could. Severing its ties with the people entangled in the legal troubles had to be part of the strategy. Merrill officials detected inconsistencies in statements by Martha Stewart's stockbroker Peter Bacanovic and his assistant and moved quickly to suspend and eventually fire them. That earned Merrill some reputation points in the polls. Similarly, the company fired two of its executives when they refused to cooperate in the Enron investigation.

Merrill's strategy failed a few times, however. For example, the timing of an opinion-page piece in *The Wall Street Journal* written by Stanley

O'Neal, the new CEO, proved to be a significant misstep. O'Neal wrote about his concern that companies had become too averse to taking risks because of the corporate scandals, increased government regulation, and perceptions of business executives as "a bunch of capitalist outlaws." Publication was delayed a few weeks after the article was submitted, and it ended up running in April 2003, just a few days before a record $1.4 billion settlement with Wall Street firms was announced by federal and state regulatory officials.

The article's thesis didn't sit well with Attorney General Spitzer, who complained, "You see the Stan O'Neal op-ed piece, and you think they didn't get it. They make me wonder, have we really learned anything?" He added that what the government has alleged about Merrill is "that you committed fraud—that is not risk."

Merrill declined any comment to the media but quickly drafted a statement to all employees from O'Neal asserting, "I get it, and I believe all of us at Merrill Lynch get it." He added, "While we as a company strive to put our clients first, we did not always fully live up to our ideals during this period. We can do a better job, and we will do a better job." O'Neal didn't want to become the poster boy for the Wall Street "I don't get it" pack. The media duly reported on his message to employees, ending yet another chapter in Merrill's seemingly endless battle with Eliot Spitzer.

Summer 2003 proved to be the high point of the crises for Merrill and Critchlow. Now all of the big Wall Street settlements, which ended up costing Merrill a total of $200 million, were behind it. It had also made an $80 million payment in a separate settlement with the U.S. Securities and Exchange Commission to resolve a complaint about its dealings with Enron. Most important, there finally was some truly good news to relish.

First came federal Judge Milton Pollack's strongly worded decision in favor of Merrill in a class action suit against the firm and its former star Internet-stock analyst Henry Blodget. The judge ruled that the plaintiffs, whom he called "high-risk speculators," failed to show that they had been defrauded by Merrill's stock research. It was an unexpected ray of light for Merrill and its employees. They viewed it not as a vindication of the firm but rather as an acknowledgment that investors bore some responsibility for their stock market losses, not just the brokerage houses. Still, Merrill kept a low profile and let the judge's ruling speak for itself. It steered clear of appearing self-congratulatory.

A few weeks later, Merrill reported that its second-quarter earnings had jumped by 61 percent, to $1.02 billion, its second best quarterly profits ever. At the same time, research data showed its favorability ratings starting to climb, reaching about 65 percent with nonclient investors and 77 percent with clients.

But Merrill wasn't quite ready to uncork the bubbly. Its reputation scores with nonclient investors still lagged its goal of 70 percent to 75 percent favorable; in addition, another wave of negative publicity began in August after the ouster of Thomas Patrick, the number two executive at Merrill, and other management upheaval.

The controversies had much longer legs than Merrill had ever expected, and the company was aware that there were still feelings of anger among the investing public. "You have to have patience that you will outlast the controversy as long as you have taken the proper actions," says Critchlow. "You know that eventually the press and politicians will move on to someone else."

CRISES ARE INEVITABLE— REPUTATION DAMAGE ISN'T

Crises are a fact of life for both individuals and corporations. You can— and should—try to prevent them by managing your business and reputation well. But no matter how vigilant you are, crises arrive as certainly as death and taxes. How an individual or company reacts can be far more important than the circumstances of the crisis. It's the response that makes all the difference in minimizing its damage to corporate reputation—and possibly even enhancing the image. Weathering a crisis well can actually increase a company's appeal. There's nothing like a battle-scarred hero—both in the movies and in real life.

But too often, companies become complacent. They begin to feel almost invincible. Their financial performance is strong, and they fall into the trap of believing they have little to worry about. Then they're blindsided by a crisis and don't have a response plan in place. Flailing around and looking helpless aren't inspiring to your stakeholders.

All companies are vulnerable, just in different ways. There are many types of crises, but the most commonplace involve corporate misconduct, product failures, or disastrous accidents. Disasters often involve loss of life—whether because of a chemical plant explosion, contaminated beef, or an airplane crash—and such deadly events can do extensive damage to reputation.

Less dramatic but often more damaging is a crisis of corporate misconduct. Such crises have proliferated over the past two years with the many instances of accounting abuse and executive greed, plus the Wall Street research scandal. In recent times, more companies also have been charged with sexual and racial discrimination and have been judged quite harshly for tolerating an environment of prejudice and hate.

Crises have always afflicted companies, but events of the late 1970s and early 1980s gave birth to a new and quite profitable field for the public relations industry: crisis management. In quick succession companies had faced a series of high-profile crises: the nuclear plant accident at Three Mile Island, the link between tampons and toxic shock syndrome that affected Procter & Gamble, the walkway collapse at the Hyatt-Regency Hotel in Kansas City, Missouri, and the infamous Tylenol poisonings. Suddenly crisis management was a hot field. Even leading business schools added courses on how to cope with a corporate crisis.

Poorly handled crises can produce severe consequences. The silicon breast implant controversy drove Dow Corning into bankruptcy proceedings. Perrier water never regained its cachet after some bottles were contaminated with benzene and it was recalled from the marketplace. Then there are some crises that completely decimate reputations and the companies themselves: recall the junk-bond scandal and the now defunct Drexel Burnham Lambert. Of more recent vintage is Arthur Andersen, which couldn't survive the damage to its reputation and the defections of its clients after its criminal indictment for obstruction of justice.

Of course, most companies manage to emerge intact from crises with weakened but salvageable reputations. And the most adroit companies actually burnish their reputations through forthright and ethical behavior during a crisis. DuPont, for example, responded at once when a railroad car carrying its sulfuric acid ruptured in a train derailment in Tennessee in September 2002. Its team of experts flew to the site and helped with the cleanup, receiving credit in a local newspaper article headlined "Acid Spill Was Handled with Aplomb."

When a crisis befalls them, companies like DuPont start from a position of strength. Their reputations precede them, and the public is inclined to believe they will do the right thing. If your company doesn't wear such a halo, your first goal must be to establish a feeling of trust. Achieving that trust requires both skilled communication and a substantive plan to rectify the problem, whether through a product recall, corporate governance reform, or some other remedy. A company must be specific about how it will address the consequences of the crisis and the steps it is taking to prevent a recurrence. And it should project a sense of concern, and if appropriate, contrition.

A hostile response only exacerbates a crisis. When the NAACP called for a boycott of the Adam's Mark hotel chain a few years ago because of alleged discrimination toward black customers, the company didn't resolve the matter quickly. Instead, it only made matters worse by going to court to try to stop the boycotting of and picketing at its hotels. A lawsuit had accused the hotel of a variety of discriminatory acts, including subjecting black guests to police scrutiny and requiring them to wear orange wristbands as identification during a Black College Reunion event in Daytona, Florida.

In the end, Adam's Mark settled the suit, while still denying the accusations. But months of negative publicity and the boycott itself had hurt its reputation, especially with minorities. Today, in its continuing efforts to restore its reputation, the company has posted a list of "diversity initiatives" on its Web site, including information about its minority-owned suppliers and the scholarships it awards to minorities.

TIMING IS EVERYTHING

The first few days are the most critical in trying to limit reputation damage in a crisis. Crises aren't like fine wines; they don't improve with age.

A communications void is highly dangerous during a time of crisis. Silence gives critics time to gain the upper hand and reinforces the public's suspicions that the company must be guilty. Without information from the company, rumors and misinformation can proliferate fast. Corporate lawyers may advise against a public apology early on in a crisis, when the facts aren't all in, but a company should at least own up to the problem and express regret.

A long-standing, positive relationship with the media can pay off handsomely in getting the corporate message out during a crisis. The channels of communication are already open, and the media are more likely to trust what the company has to say.

The Internet has developed into a mixed blessing for companies facing a crisis. They can communicate information more quickly and more thoroughly within the company and to the outside world. They might even establish a special crisis Web site. But the Internet also allows other people, who have little or no information about the actual circumstances of the crisis, to begin spreading their version of the facts around the globe through e-mails and chat room comments.

While the corporate response must be rapid, it should never be rash. If all of the facts aren't available, a company should say so and tell the public it will provide more details as soon as an investigation is completed. A company must analyze the situation as carefully as possible under very stressful circumstances and be careful not to make promises it can't or won't keep. The public can be very unforgiving.

After his firm lost much of its workforce to the World Trade Center terrorist attack on September 11, 2001, Howard Lutnick, the CEO of Cantor Fitzgerald Securities, vowed during tearful television appearances that he would take care of the surviving families. Soon afterward, however, word leaked out that the company had quickly taken the deceased employees off the payroll, a move that seemed to conflict with Lutnick's public pledge. His statements appeared hypocritical and angered many of the employees' survivors. Lutnick later made amends with the families of the deceased, but the incident had marred both Cantor's and Lutnick's reputations.

Surprisingly, some major, well-respected companies continue to believe it's best to keep quiet and just hope bad news passes. After an eleven-year-old girl was sexually assaulted at one of its stores in West Virginia in July 2003, Target Corporation faced a serious threat to its reputation as a safe place to shop. Parents across the nation watched the developments on the nightly television news as police searched for and eventually arrested the alleged assailant. Many wondered about the security of Target and other retailers' stores.

Yet Target didn't issue any public statements to reassure shoppers. It left communications to employees at the store where the assault had occurred. But employees are not accustomed to dealing with the media, and the inexperience showed. "The safety of our guests and team members is our concern at all times," the West Virginia store manager told the media and then declined to make any further comments. When asked for comment by a *Wall Street Journal* reporter, Target merely issued a statement that said, "We are very pleased that the police have captured the suspect. Our thoughts continue to remain with the family. Our gratitude goes to the police and all those involved in helping bring quick resolution to the situation."

Not only did Target avoid dealing with potential damage to its reputation, it also passed up a splendid opportunity to improve its image by letting customers know it cares about safety and is taking steps to protect them. Target managers clearly hadn't learned any lessons from the textbook Tylenol case.

THE GOLD STANDARD

Any discussion of crisis management would be incomplete without describing Johnson & Johnson's coolheaded handling of the Tylenol poisonings of the 1980s. Although before the crisis many people didn't know that J&J made Tylenol—the McNeil Consumer Products subsidiary's name was printed on the bottles—the news media quickly made the link to J&J, and its stellar reputation was suddenly at great risk.

Ironically, a few weeks before the 1982 poisonings, J&J CEO James Burke had raised the possibility of damage to the Tylenol brand when he and other members of the executive committee had met for their annual strategic planning review. He was marveling at how lucky the company was to enjoy so many profitable brands and offhandedly said, "What if something happens to one of them, like Tylenol?"

When that something did happen, Burke and other J&J executives succeeded in protecting the corporate reputation by being honest, direct, and quick to respond. Within a few days of learning the awful news that seven people in the Chicago area had died from taking Tylenol capsules spiked with cyanide, J&J decided to recall Tylenol—some 30 million bottles with a retail value of more than $100 million. That decision remains the gold standard of crisis management to this day and continues to be the subject of business school case studies and corporate reputation conferences.

The Tylenol crisis remains fixed in the public's memory because, much like September 11, it robbed Americans of their sense of security. People could no longer feel safe buying packaged foods and medicines. In terms of its reputation, Johnson & Johnson became a true hero to many fearful people through its reassuring response to the crisis. "One advantage we had is that we were seen as the victim," says Roger Fine, vice president and general counsel. Indeed, surveys conducted soon after the poisonings showed that nearly 90 percent of the public realized that J&J hadn't been to blame for the deaths. That finding confirmed the effectiveness of J&J's crisis communications.

More than in any other crisis, J&J's response illustrates a company's ability to emerge from calamity with an even more robust reputation. J&J showed that it sincerely cared about its customers, which is the first sentence in the company's Credo statement of its business philosophy and values. In fact, J&J executives say it was the Credo that had guided them throughout the Tylenol tragedy and actually made the big decisions relatively easy.

The best evidence of J&J's strong reputation during the crisis was Tylenol's comeback in the marketplace. After the company relaunched the analgesic in tamper-resistant packaging with a big marketing campaign, it swiftly regained more than two thirds of its precrisis market share of 37 percent.

Unfortunately, that wasn't the end of J&J's travails with Tylenol. In 1986, a woman from Peekskill, New York, died after taking Tylenol capsules that again had been laced with cyanide. At that point, J&J decided it would have to stop making capsules. Consumers would have to buy either tablets or caplets, which the company had developed as an alternative to capsules.

While J&J's crisis strategy looked seamless to the public, the company actually faced uncertainties and disagreements. There was debate within the company and with federal regulatory agencies over whether a complete recall would cause a national panic and encourage copycats to tamper with other drugs and packaged products.

Company executives also clashed over some of the media exposure the company received. One of the earliest decisions was to cooperate fully with the news media to get the facts out to nervous consumers. But for a low-profile company like J&J, its extensive dealings with the media during the Tylenol crisis represented a new and unfamiliar approach. Lawrence Foster, then corporate vice president of public relations, was opposed to granting the *60 Minutes* television program an interview about six weeks after the 1982 Tylenol tampering. He argued that J&J had already gained public and media support and had more to lose than gain if the company worked with the producers at *60 Minutes* and they "poked a finger in our eye." But CEO James Burke saw the show's large

SURVIVING THE TYLENOL CRISIS

Johnson & Johnson said back in 1982 that the Tylenol story had sparked the widest domestic coverage of any single news event since the 1963 assassination of President John F. Kennedy. Queries from the media exceeded 2,500, and two news-clipping services generated more than 125,000 articles about the Tylenol poisonings. Johnson & Johnson weathered the ordeal through a series of quickly but carefully orchestrated maneuvers. Here are some of the many steps the company took in those dark days of October and November 1982.

- It established toll-free consumer hot lines in the first days of the crisis to respond to the more than 30,000 inquiries about the safety of Tylenol.
- It took out a full-page ad in major newspapers offering consumers the opportunity to exchange Tylenol capsules for tablets.
- It distributed two letters and four videotaped reports on the crisis to employees and retirees to keep them informed and thank them for their support.
- J&J's corporate relations staff visited more than 160 congressional offices in Washington to discuss a variety of issues, including support for federal legislation making product tampering a felony.
- J&J executives made personal appearances and were interviewed in such major media as *The Wall Street Journal, Fortune, The Donahue Show, 60 Minutes,* and *Nightline.*
- It created a sixty-second commercial introducing Tylenol's tamper-resistant packaging that reached an estimated 85 percent of television households an average of 2.5 times during the first week of airing.
- It made four-minute videos about the new packaging for television stations to use during newscasts. It also established a toll-free number for consumers to call to receive a $2.50 discount coupon for Tylenol.

audience as potential customers when J&J reintroduced Tylenol capsules in safety-sealed packaging. That ended the debate, and J&J did the show.

Although the company is proud of its performance during the Tylenol crisis, Bill Nielsen, Jeff Leebaw, and other members of the public relations staff were relieved that the recent twentieth anniversary of the tragedy passed relatively quietly with only a few anniversary stories. The way the company responded is still an inspiration for J&J employees, but the company hopes never to have to endure such a crisis again.

CRISES CAN BE MANAGED, NOT CONTROLLED

There may be no worse combination than a control freak and a crisis situation. You can try to manage a crisis, but you can never completely control it. Successful crisis resolution calls for humility and patience. You will only deepen a crisis if you arrogantly believe you can control everything by simply calling an end to the controversy or by ignoring it.

You must confront a crisis and deal with it openly and courageously. If you dig yourself into a hole by being high-handed, defensive, or, worst of all, deceptive, the damage to your reputation will take far longer to repair.

Intel Corporation, for example, miscalculated its customers' expectations and adopted a rigid, unfriendly posture when a flaw was uncovered in its Pentium chips in 1994. Intel felt it could dictate what its customers would accept and end the crisis on its terms. The company maintained that the bug in its microchips cropped up only once in every nine billion random mathematical calculations and refused to guarantee replacement chips for customers likely to be unaffected.

But Intel's customers, especially IBM, were much more in charge of the situation than Intel realized. IBM, a major buyer of Intel's microprocessors, fired a broadside, halting shipments of its computers containing the Pentium chip and insisting that Intel had underestimated the potential for errors. At last Intel announced a "no-questions-asked" return policy.

A chastened Andrew Grove, Intel's chairman, commented, "We got caught between our mind-set, which is a fact-based, analysis-based engineer's mind-set, and customers' mind-set, which is not so much emotional but accustomed to making their own choice. I think the kernel of the issue we missed was that we presumed to tell somebody what they should or shouldn't worry about, or should or shouldn't do."

Intel's attempt to play down the Pentium chip problem undermined its reputation after it had spent millions of dollars on its "Intel inside" marketing campaign to make the Pentium a well-known consumer product.

Martha Stewart, too, spent millions of dollars crafting the image of a woman in control of everything from her culinary creations to the corporate culture at the hugely successful Martha Stewart Living Omnimedia. What she couldn't control was the scandal over her sale of ImClone Systems stock just before the release of negative news about its anticancer drug in December 2001. The controversy engulfed her and her company, and instead of managing the crisis, she arrogantly tried her best to publicly avoid or minimize it. She allowed her enemies, federal investigators, and the media to keep the controversy percolating, while she went about making her salads. It was as if she believed she could will the crisis away by ignoring it.

"In some respects, I think if she were perceived as a humble, self-effacing person who's trying to do the right thing, who made a mistake, people would forgive her," says Jim O'Rourke, who teaches management and corporate communications at the University of Notre Dame's Mendoza College of Business. "Martha could have said, 'I'm terribly sorry. I didn't know that was inside information.' But instead, it was a cover-up in almost Nixonian fashion."

It wasn't until Stewart was charged with securities fraud, conspiracy, and making false statements to federal agents in June 2003 that she began to address the crisis seriously. That was a full year after the federal investigation into her trading activities had first surfaced publicly. After the indictment, Martha Stewart Living Omnimedia ran a full-page newspaper ad stating that in light of the legal developments, "we want to reaffirm our commitment to you, our valued consumers and business partners." The Web site www.marthatalks.com was also established to give Stewart a forum to declare her innocence and her plan to "fight to clear my name," as well as to post gushy e-mails from her supporters.

But the crisis response was almost laughably belated. At that point, only die-hard fans already in the domestic diva's camp were receptive to the blatant image-polishing efforts. The maneuvers did nothing to defuse the crisis clouding her personal image and her business. And her decision to step aside as chairman and CEO also had little impact. Stewart personifies the company, no matter that her official title was changed to chief creative officer. Her reputation and the company's are inextricably linked, and Martha Stewart can't undo that relationship any more than she can control the crisis.

BE PREPARED FOR THE WORST

Coca-Cola Company, the consummate marketer and American icon, is surely well prepared to handle any crisis that might strike. Right? Think again. In 1999, Coke received uniformly negative reviews for its response when some European consumers, primarily residents of Belgium, complained of an unpleasant taste and noxious odor and fell ill after drinking its carbonated beverages. In the wake of the Tylenol poisonings and the Perrier benzene episode, it seemed hard to believe that a packaged-goods company was not better prepared to address potential contamination problems.

Coke's biggest sin was its tardy response to the contamination, which was eventually blamed on a poor-quality batch of the carbon dioxide that produces the bubbles in soft drinks, and on a fungicide sprayed on wooden pallets holding its cans. At first, the company didn't recognize the European health scare as a full-blown crisis. Then it seemed paralyzed as reports of dizziness, headaches, and nausea increased, more children were hospitalized, and some European countries restricted sales of Coke products. Government officials, not Coke executives, were taking the lead to protect the public, an instance of incredibly poor judgment on Coke's part. Very late in the crisis, Coke lamely tried to fix its unraveling image by running ads in Belgian newspapers taking the blame for its faltering quality control system.

The European contamination controversy showed the hazards of being a global marketer unprepared to deal with a crisis far from its home office. The crisis tarnished Coke's reputation with both European consumers and regulatory officials. And it certainly played a role in CEO Douglas Ivester's sudden announcement that he was resigning in December 1999, after only two years in Coke's top job.

Coke and other companies should prepare for such crises through regular simulation exercises. Such role-playing is very authentic and helps corporate managers practice their parts for when a real crisis erupts. DuPont, for example, staged a mock kidnapping of the head of its French operations by activists opposed to biotechnology. And Altria Group hired actors to help create a similar scenario in which a Kraft Foods executive goes missing in Mexico. Her speech to a group of activists is disrupted by demonstrators at the same time that an explosion rocks a Kraft plant. To add to the realism, Altria employees see videotapes of a news announcer telling about the Mexican crisis.

Many companies have formulated crisis contingency plans and organized a crisis team of top executives, communications experts, lawyers, and information technology and operations representatives. Some companies also call in a crisis management specialist from a public relations or consulting firm.

It's also helpful to establish a crisis command center and put together a crisis management manual with various contingency plans; names, e-mail addresses, and telephone numbers of key personnel; media contact information; and alternative work locations for certain types of emergencies.

Every crisis also needs a designated leader, usually the CEO, and a chief communicator, usually the most senior corporate communications executive. Media training for the CEO is essential, of course, as he or she will become the public face of the company in a crisis. But for some companies, it may be preferable to send another, more personable executive to the front lines. CEO James Burke did a superb job in his television appearances at the time of the Tylenol crisis. But during the Ford Explorer/Firestone tire controversy, Jacques Nasser, then CEO of Ford Motor Company, wasn't very natural or telegenic and didn't connect well with TV viewers.

BUT YOU CAN NEVER BE FULLY PREPARED

Crises often come out of left field. Who could imagine there would be anything to worry about in a can of shaving cream? Gillette was indeed startled to find its shaving cream linked to mad-cow disease during the 1990s. It turned out that shaving cream and gel contain fatty acids and glycerin that provide moisture and lathering qualities and can be derived from animal sources. When Web sites about mad-cow disease started including shaving cream and other cosmetics and toiletries in a list of products containing bovine by-products, news reporters and anxious consumers began contacting Gillette.

Although taken aback, Gillette managed to quell that potential crisis fast. The company drafted a statement explaining that in the manufacturing process, chemical treatment and high temperatures break down the structure of the ingredients and would therefore destroy any potentially dangerous agents. "Gillette products meet all legal and regulatory standards for product safety," the company declared in its statement.

The mad-cow fears faded, but Gillette officials still keep "stand-by statements" in their files just in case shaving cream becomes suspect again.

A much more serious crisis took Bayer by storm in fall 2001, when anthrax bacteria suddenly began appearing in people's mail. Bayer, which produces the Cipro antibiotic for treating anthrax, suddenly faced a surge in demand but chose to keep a low profile because it said it didn't want to appear to be exploiting the terrorist acts to boost sales.

However, the company was too quiet and too unprepared to deal with such a highly sensitive and political crisis. It soon found itself caught up in a public debate over its ability to manufacture Cipro in sufficient quantities and possible government action to permit production of a generic version. Bayer tried to recover from the public relations damage with full-page newspaper ads stating that it was committed to meeting the bioterrorism threat by tripling its production of Cipro. But the anthrax scare shook people's confidence in Bayer, and the German company faces a skeptical public as it works to rebuild its reputation.

Paul Critchlow, the counselor to the chairman at Merrill Lynch, says that it was the September 11, 2001, attack on the World Trade Center that convinced him that a company is never really prepared for a crisis of such magnitude. Fortunately, Merrill had gone through an emergency drill just two months earlier based on the scenario of a hurricane hitting lower Manhattan. That provided a framework for establishing command center operations, alternative work locations, conference calls with key managers, and other elements of a crisis plan. Nevertheless, Critchlow says, until it happens, you can't imagine the communication disruptions such a disaster will create: no office phones, no e-mail, no intranet, cell phones that work intermittently if at all. "Be prepared to be unprepared," he advises. "Be prepared to improvise. You have to make it up as you go along, using every means available to you—and some that you never thought you would use."

Like many of the scores of companies directly affected by the World Trade Center catastrophe, Merrill proved resourceful and flexible. When corporate managers couldn't seek refuge at the company's data-processing center near Ground Zero because of the danger of a gas leak, they trooped a half mile farther, to Greenwich Village, and went to work in Critchlow's brownstone. "I opened the door," Critchlow recalls, "and said to my wife, 'Honey, I'm home—and I have a few friends with me.'" Nearly a hundred, to be exact. The Merrill executives ran the multinational firm using the five phone lines at the house, while Critchlow's children fetched food and drinks from a local deli. Later in the day on September 11, Critchlow did an interview outside his home with CBS News reporter Lesley Stahl, who was roaming the neighborhood. "Instinctively," he recalls, "I made it a point to be confident, to say that we were already working to, first, account for all of our employees and, second, to get our business functioning for the clients."

LET THE CRISIS RUN ITS COURSE

Crisis management involves a lot of explaining and defending. When is it time to go on the offensive and move more aggressively to heal the reputation wounds? Not too soon; a crisis must be ridden out.

A company in crisis should survey its stakeholders frequently to monitor its reputation and watch for an uptick. There's no point in proclaiming its virtues until it sees a steady rise in positive ratings. Most important, a company should be certain that the crisis is really behind it before it wastes millions of dollars on corporate image advertising and its executives start making speeches about moving on. There's nothing worse than running an ad that crows about the company's bright future on the same day that news of more litigation or regulatory action breaks.

A positive message is most credible if it follows several months of upbeat developments. Like Merrill Lynch, Lucent Technologies held off on an image-rebuilding campaign. "You need a drumbeat of good news before you make a big advertising hit," says Kathleen Fitzgerald, former senior vice president for public relations and advertising. "We need to get traction—win some big deals, meet our financial targets, and get all the legal issues behind us—before we raise our visibility with a major image campaign." Unfortunately for Lucent, that drumbeat is very slow in coming. Its promise that it would achieve sustained profitability in fiscal year 2003 proved wrong.

But some companies are going ahead and tooting their horns even as the crisis is still unfolding. United Airlines, still mired in bankruptcy proceedings, was premature with some of its advertising. The tone was much too sunny and lacked credibility. "Of all the things we're introducing, one thing is most unexpected in the airline industry: optimism," the United ad proclaimed in announcing more flights and touting its frequent-flier program.

Similarly, WorldCom (now called MCI) began running full-page ads in fall 2002 to counter its competitors' attempts to pick off its nervous customers. But the upbeat theme of the ads strained credibility, given the continuing stream of negative news about its accounting fraud and mismanagement. Declarations that "our customer loyalty is as high as ever" and "our financial progress is exceeding expectations" elicited many cynical comments. The company should have been a bit more low-key, limiting its progress reports to customer mailings, its Web site, and internal communications. Remember: During a corporate crisis, modesty is a virtue.

FIX IT RIGHT THE
FIRST TIME

Everybody knows Kmart. But does anybody know what Kmart stands for?

Here's a quiz to test your Kmart knowledge. Pick the best description of its corporate identity: low-price leader . . . superstore for the masses . . . retailer of exclusive "designer" brands . . . niche marketer to minority groups . . . other.

Unsure? Well, you could have named any or all of them and been correct. In fact, it's hard to keep track of all the strategies Kmart has been pursuing to try to revive its moribund reputation.

Kmart is an object lesson in how not to repair a reputation. Salvaging a reputation is certainly a major challenge, but doing the salvage job right the first time makes a huge difference. Kmart, however, hasn't gotten it right on any try.

One of the company's first big overhauls, in 1990, included a five-year, $3.5 billion new-store opening and modernization program and redesign of the corporate logo from a red "K" and turquoise "mart" to a large red "K" and white "mart." The new logo was supposed to signal a "commitment to change." Little did Kmart know how much change lay ahead.

Before finally sinking into bankruptcy in early 2002, the discount retailer tried many ploys to improve its reputation—from Kmart Super-centers with grocery sections to Martha Stewart household goods to its trademark blue light specials—but the changes were never enough to achieve a turnaround. For example, when Kmart turned to desperate price slashing with its "blue light always" marketing campaign in 2001, the promotion only encouraged competitors to undercut it and did absolutely nothing to establish a distinctive image and restore its reputation.

"We lost so much credibility with customers, employees, and investors by not delivering on our promises," says James Adamson, Kmart's former chairman. "For Kmart to get its reputation back now, the public's attitude is going to be 'Show me,' not 'tell me.'"

He's right, of course. Many lapsed customers say they have been disappointed too many times by dirty, dimly lit stores, merchandise advertised in newspaper circulars that is out of stock, and rude salesclerks. Respondents who rated Kmart in a reputation study were extremely harsh. One respondent suggested that Kmart "go ultralow discount and compete with the local Goodwill." Another respondent has given up on the retailer: "Kmart? They're done for," he said.

Not quite yet. With Wal-Mart as the low-price king and Target as the more upscale of the downscale retailers, Kmart is still searching for a distinct image in its postbankruptcy period. For starters, it has concocted a new logo and color scheme for its stores—lime green will replace firehouse red because it connotes growth and nature.

Kmart hopes to avoid fighting competitors on price alone by tailoring its product selections better to local neighborhoods and targeting its marketing programs to key demographic groups. Adamson says that in the past some Kmarts in Florida actually stocked ice-fishing equipment, while stores in Minnesota didn't carry any.

An important but uncertain tactic will be tapping America's growing population of minorities, who represent 36 percent of Kmart customers. The company's new multicultural marketing includes a weekly advertising circular in Spanish, a promotional newspaper supplement called Tea Life for Asian Americans in California, and an apparel collection named for Mexican singer Thalia. But even as it expands its niche marketing strategy to minorities, it is falling back on its low-price ways with a "savings are here to stay" promotion. Sounds like the same old store.

The open question is whether alienated shoppers will keep giving

ATTENTION, KMART SHOPPERS . . .

Here is a chronology of Kmart's milestones and repeated efforts to turn around its business and repair its reputation.

1977   S. S. Kresge Company changes its name to Kmart Corporation.

1981   The two-thousandth Kmart store opens.

1985   Kmart begins selling the Jaclyn Smith sportswear line as part of a strategy to create its own "designer" brands.

1987   Kmart retains Martha Stewart as "entertainment and lifestyle spokesperson and consultant."

1990   A five-year, $3.5 billion new-store opening and modernization program is announced, and the corporate logo is redesigned to signal "commitment to change."

1991   The first twenty-four-hour Kmart Supercenter selling both groceries and general merchandise opens in Medina, Ohio.

1996   Some stores—renamed Big Kmart—are remodeled to make them cleaner, brighter, and more convenient for shoppers.

1997   Kmart launches the new Martha Stewart Everyday line of paints and bed and bath products and increases its focus on children's clothing with a new Sesame Street line.

1999   Kmart creates Bluelight.com, an e-commerce company, with Softbank Venture Capital and Yahoo!

2001   The "blue light special" makes a comeback in stores, after a ten-year absence, as the company goes head-to-head with Wal-Mart on low prices. The retailer also signs a new long-term merchandising agreement with Martha Stewart Living Omnimedia, including new home decorating and storage product lines.

2002   Kmart files for reorganization under Chapter 11 of the U.S. Bankruptcy Code, and federal investigators explore whether Martha Stewart acted on inside information when she sold her stock in the biotechnology firm ImClone Systems.

2003   Kmart continues to close stores, bringing the total still open to about 1,500, and focuses on its new strategy of marketing to ethnic minority groups. The company emerges from bankruptcy protection in May, and in June a federal grand jury indicts Martha Stewart on five criminal counts of securities fraud, conspiracy, and making false statements to federal agents.

Kmart another try. During the retailer's bankruptcy, some employees and customers expressed their loyalty on a "Kmart Forever" Web site. The site sold Kmart Forever T-shirts, and people shared their feelings about Kmart. But most of the comments were fond reminiscences about the smell of submarine sandwiches and buying kites and Slinkys, not praise for the stores as they exist today.

Some of the online postings about store closings sounded downright mournful. "I remember going to Kmart as a kid with Mom," Paul Gleason wrote on the community bulletin board. "We would stop by the deli and get treats. It's sad that I can't take my kids in for the same experience now that our local Kmart is gone. Thanks for the memories." Henry Virgil, a former employee, said, "I always told people I was glad to be a Kmarter. Now that our store is closing, I tell people I am a Kmartyr. Sad sad sad!"

THREE STRIKES, YOU'RE OUT!

You don't get many chances to fix a reputation, so do it right the first time. That may seem only logical, but many companies switch strategies as often as teenagers change fashions. While everybody deserves a second chance, no company is entitled to unlimited attempts to salvage its reputation.

Unfulfilled promises of reform and rejuvenation quickly wear out the patience of consumers, investors, and other stakeholders. Consumer activist groups and state regulatory officials repeatedly accused Household International of taking advantage of poor and minority consumers with loans carrying high interest rates, unfair penalties, and other conditions. And Household repeatedly denied that it was a predatory lender. In early 2002, the company even boldly declared in ads, "For 124 years, we've set the standard for responsible lending. And now, we're doing it again." The ad went on to say that the consumer finance company was taking extra steps to make sure borrowers understood the terms of their loans and to offer better rewards to people who paid on time. It was yet another attempt by Household to overcome its persistent reputation for misleading consumers.

But just seven months after the ad touting itself as an advocate for responsible lending, Household agreed to pay a record fine of as much as $484 million to settle allegations that it had deceived borrowers about the true cost of loans. In the largest settlement ever over consumer lending practices, the company also agreed to change a slew of practices that state regulators said had misled borrowers but had been quite lucrative for Household. Clearly, the advertising claim had been premature, and Household's reputation sank again on the publicity about the huge fine. When HSBC Holdings acquired Household shortly after the settlement, skeptics warned that HSBC was "bottom-fishing" and putting its own reputation at risk.

Reputation improvement strategies misfire for many reasons, including weak leadership, lack of a coherent vision, stingy spending on marketing and new-product development, or simply blunders in execution. Whatever the cause, the longer a reputation remains in rehab, the harder it is to save. As time passes, the chances of ever regaining a robust reputation fade. The best hope becomes simply eliminating the negative feelings and settling for a neutral reputation—not an inspiring prospect.

Sears, Roebuck & Company seems to have settled into that rut. Many consumers confess to being puzzled about the retailer's identity, much as they are about Kmart's. Although its reputation is far stronger than Kmart's, Sears' corporate image has certainly bounced around. It has fluctuated from a hard-goods retailer to a seller of socks and stocks (through its acquisition and eventual spin-off of Dean Witter) to a marketer of big-brand appliances (not just its trusty Kenmore products) to a major clothing purveyor ("the softer side of Sears" ads). More recently, the company has sold its credit card business to Citigroup and overhauled its stores to try to make them more convenient for shoppers. Sears advertising also has been quite mercurial, ranging from humor to heartwarming heritage themes over the past few years.

"I find it hard to believe Sears is still in business," says Mark Allshouse of Baltimore, who keeps a Sears credit card strictly in case he needs to make an emergency appliance purchase. "They've futzed around with their identity so much that it seems they're remodeling their stores every three days. They've got to decide what kind of store they want to be."

At least Sears has survived its reputation weaknesses and is still trying to improve its image. Sometimes companies actually strike out. That's what happened to General Motors's Oldsmobile division. The century-old automaker has decided to halt production after several attempts to create a hipper image and improve the line's quality to compete with the luxury imports. Most memorable was the "It's not your father's

Oldsmobile" ad campaign in the late 1980s, featuring celebrities such as William (*Star Trek*) Shatner and Peter (*Mission Impossible*) Graves along with their children. But baby boomers, the target market, weren't convinced. Sales continued to slide. A few years later came a defensive ad campaign asserting that Oldsmobile wasn't "throwing in the towel" and urging consumers to "believe in the future." Then, in 1994, the upscale Aurora model was unveiled *without* the Oldsmobile moniker on the exterior. The Olds name was relegated to the dashboard.

The company continued to invest engineering resources and capital into new cars and new marketing. But by 2000, Oldsmobile finally decided the struggle was hopeless and began phasing out production. Rick Wagoner, GM's chairman and CEO, called the decision extremely painful. "Oldsmobile is the oldest automotive brand in America," he said, "and over the years it was one of the jewels in the General Motors crown." But in the end, it turned out to be your father's Oldsmobile after all.

A TALE OF TWO "REINVENTED" TECHNOLOGY COMPANIES

Many companies hope to repair their reputations by reinventing themselves. They aim to establish a fresh image by restructuring their business. Few succeed, at least on the first try. Two technology companies illustrate the different fates of such a strategy and show the importance of having a dynamic leader at the helm.

IBM succeeded in remaking itself in the 1990s, changing its primary image from a maker of mainframe computers to a services provider with a strong e-business and consulting focus. By the time that Louis Gerstner became IBM's CEO in 1993, the company had deteriorated and become unprofitable. The American icon seemed headed for extinction. People both inside and outside IBM widely expected it to be broken up into smaller, independent units, but Gerstner managed to keep it intact. Because of his remarkable leadership, he pulled off one of the most successful corporate resurrections ever. To be sure, there was also some luck involved: the fast growth of the Internet helped advance the company's e-business and services strategy.

"In the early nineties, we were seen as an arrogant hardware company that was no longer relevant to people thirty-five and younger; the people who still admired us were an older, dying generation," says Maureen McGuire, IBM's vice president for worldwide marketing management and integrated marketing communications. "But today, we're no longer considered the world leader in arrogance. We have a much broader portfolio of products and services, and we're actually admired by young people, who now see IBM as a dynamic company with a successful future ahead of us."

IBM executives certainly don't seem arrogant about their accomplishments. They stress that although the company's financial results and reputation have rebounded nicely since the early 1990s, they are still on a journey. "We were a great company once," says Nicholas Donofrio, senior vice president for technology and manufacturing, "and we will be a great company again."

At about the same time IBM began its painful transformation, Wang Laboratories tried to pull off a similar feat. Once one of the world's major minicomputer makers, Wang had failed to adapt to the personal computer revolution of the 1980s and ended up seeking Chapter 11 bankruptcy protection in 1992.

The company emerged as a much smaller organization a year later, ready to establish a new reputation as a major player in computer services. But hard as it tried, it couldn't accomplish what its initial post-bankruptcy advertising campaign promised in 1993. Wang's television commercial showed one of its office buildings being blown up and a single flash of light remaining in the rubble. The light became a video monitor listing Wang's new businesses: software and network integration. "A new Wang sparked to life," the ad says. "True innovators never die. They just reinvent themselves." Print ads trumpeted Wang's "power of imagination."

But Wang's imagination wasn't powerful enough to restore its reputation for technological prowess. The company made a string of acquisitions, but its services business was dwarfed by companies such as IBM. Prospective customers didn't perceive Wang to be a technology leader any longer.

It then looked for growth overseas and changed its name to Wang Global to convey an international image. But its stock price languished even during the boom in technology stocks in the 1990s. Finally in 1999, Wang was swallowed up by Getronics, a Dutch information technology services company.

Wang lacked the size and resources of IBM, of course. It also didn't have a take-charge leader like Louis Gerstner and IBM's history and legendary reputation to build on. Even in its darkest days, McGuire says, IBM's research found that there was still a halo over the company. "People always saw IBM as trustworthy," she says, "and they still believed IBM had global capability and felt customer service was important."

COSMETIC MAKEOVERS

Like the boy who cried wolf, companies sacrifice their credibility with each failed attempt to fix their reputations. That's certainly the case with Revlon. The cosmetics company has been undergoing the world's longest makeover but looks about as lackluster as ever.

Once the biggest name in mass-market cosmetics, Revlon has been talking about making itself over for the past twenty years. Repeatedly, it has struggled to become a more formidable competitor against the likes of L'Oréal, Procter & Gamble, and Avon Products. But its efforts to burnish its reputation have always proven to be more cosmetic than convincing.

Companies like Revlon make the mistake of overpromising and creating unrealistic expectations. Revlon has reported a long string of quarterly losses, and its new-product development and marketing have lagged behind those of its chief rivals, disappointing investors, financial analysts, retailers, consumers, and its own employees. Known for its brassy lipsticks and nail polishes, it has fallen out of touch with changing women's styles. Indeed, it still considers the 1970s-era drugstore perfume Charlie as one of its leading brands.

Marketing and image mean everything in the beauty products business. Charles Revson, one of Revlon's founders, made the famous pronouncement that he wasn't just marketing cosmetics, he was selling "hope in a bottle." He understood his industry quite well, but in more recent years, Revlon just hasn't been able to get the marketing formula right. First, the company abandoned glamour by dropping model Cindy Crawford as its spokeswoman and ending its longtime advertising on the annual Academy Awards telecast. Instead, ads in 2001 proclaimed, "It's fabulous being a woman" and featured unknown models on a stock exchange trading floor, in a supermarket, and in a public restroom. Revlon hailed the new approach as a way to shake things up because the company had been "stuck in the 1980s."

Then, less than a year later, the company dropped the campaign, blaming its failure on, of all things, the impact of the September 11, 2001, terrorist attacks in New York and Washington, D.C. Revlon said that pushing "fabulousness" had turned out to be the wrong message for the post–September 11 mood in America. The company did a complete turnabout and returned to using celebrities such as Julianne Moore and Halle Berry. The new ads announced "a new Revlon." But they used a tired tagline, "Be unforgettable," a reworking of the 1980s slogan "The most unforgettable women in the world wear Revlon." Stuck again in the 1980s.

Revlon, which is controlled by New York financier Ronald Perelman, clearly hasn't brought enough vision, creativity, and consistency to its makeovers, not to mention financial investment. It takes pizzazz and money to make an impression in the beauty business after you've lost your magic.

Revlon developed some gimmicky promotions in 2002, becoming part of the storyline on the ABC soap opera *All My Children* and creating a line of makeup linked to the James Bond movie *Die Another Day.* But in 2002 its loss increased to $286.5 million from $153.7 million in 2001. By late 2002, the company seemed headed for a bankruptcy filing—until Mr. Perelman bailed it out. He announced plans for an infusion of as much as $150 million from a loan and stock offering to give the company's latest CEO, Jack Stahl, formerly president of Coca-Cola, a chance to try his hand at, yes, one more makeover.

FROZEN IMAGE

Some companies fail time after time to improve their reputations because they haven't kept pace with the times and just can't catch up. What's more, their old image may have been so strong that people have trouble refocusing their perceptions.

Polaroid Corporation, for one, has been pigeonholed that way. People still admire it as the innovator that developed instant photography. But that reputation isn't terribly relevant in an era of one-hour photo processing and digital photos that can be e-mailed around the world in seconds. It's as if Polaroid's image were frozen in time.

Polaroid has tried numerous times to change its reputation, but it hasn't been innovative and radical enough in its new-product development and marketing to make a comeback. It has always counted on the next great product to rescue the company, and the savior has never come.

Polaroid actually became a leading marketer of low-end digital cameras at mass-merchandise stores during the late 1990s, but it certainly never achieved the technological cachet of companies such as Sony and Olympus. Facing the reality that most of its customers were closer to the grave than the cradle, it made a play for the youth market. But many of its inexpensive products seemed gimmicky. For example, the i-Zone pocket camera produced miniature sticker photos for kids to put on their school notebooks. A Barbie pocket camera came with a built-in compact, mirror, and picture holder. Such toylike cameras certainly weren't the kind of product concept to rebuild a business around.

Polaroid once enjoyed a near-flawless reputation. It was back in 1947 that Edwin Land, a Harvard University dropout and the founder of Polaroid, introduced instant photography at a meeting of the Optical Society of America in New York. Priced at $89.50, the Polaroid Land Camera delivered prints in one minute. It was a technological marvel that delighted consumers the next year when a Polaroid marketing crew demonstrated the camera at the Jordan Marsh department store in downtown Boston. People clamored to buy all fifty-six cameras in the store that day. Polaroid's reputation grew, and renowned photographer Ansel Adams soon signed on as a consultant. In 1972, Land and his new SX-70 model graced the cover of *Life* magazine alongside the headline "A Genius and His Magic Camera." Polaroid was in its heyday; even the actor Sir Laurence Olivier promoted its cameras in ads.

A half century later, Polaroid was caught in a life-and-death struggle. Polaroid's fall was largely due to its failure to adapt to the growth of digital technology and one-hour film developing. But it was also weighed down by a big debt burden after its battle against a hostile takeover attempt in 1988 by Shamrock Holdings, an investor group led by Walt Disney's nephew, Roy E. Disney.

In 2001, Polaroid filed for bankruptcy protection, which further tarnished its reputation with many of its stakeholders. "We obviously lost face on Wall Street and with retirees and charities we couldn't support as much," says Skip Colcord, director of corporate communications.

In 2002, Bank One Corporation's OEP Imaging Corporation unit purchased the bulk of Polaroid's assets. The challenge now is to restore financial health and develop a long-term business strategy that can cre-

POLAROID'S PROGNOSIS

To try to understand the effect of its financial problems on consumer perceptions, Polaroid conducted a survey of one thousand Americans in 2002. The study included two other companies for comparison: Walt Disney Company, which enjoys a stronger reputation, and General Motors Corporation's Oldsmobile division, whose reputation is so weak it is going out of business. Based on these responses, however, many people clearly weren't aware that Oldsmobile's days are numbered.

The percentage of people who agreed with the following statements:

Will Be Around for a Long Time
  Disney: 96%
  Polaroid: 74%
  Oldsmobile: 65%

Is Strong Enough to Weather the Current Economic Downturn
  Disney: 91%
  Polaroid: 67%
  Oldsmobile: 60%

Would Recommend Their Products to a Friend
  Disney: 82%
  Polaroid: 76%
  Oldsmobile: 54%

Offers Products That Fit Your Lifestyle
  Disney: 65%
  Polaroid: 70%
  Oldsmobile: 55%

ate a fresh corporate image. Polaroid's research shows that the percentage of people rating it favorably dropped to 62 percent in 2002 from 75 percent in 1996. But the company does have some things working in its favor as it tries to reshape its reputation: Only 19 percent of people it surveyed were aware of the company's bankruptcy, and 70 percent said its products "fit their lifestyle." That's no guarantee they'll buy Polaroid cameras, but at least they haven't ruled them out. "Some people still love Polaroid," says Bernice Cramer, divisional vice president for corporate marketing and product development. "They're what we call sharers, who take a picture and give it to someone as a bonding experience."

To help restore its reputation, Polaroid has recruited a new management team: Jacques Nasser as chairman after his ouster as CEO of Ford Motor Company, and J. Michael Pocock as president and CEO, from Compaq Computer, where he was vice president of corporate strategy before the merger with Hewlett-Packard. But financial analysts question the choice of Nasser as a turnaround agent, given his rocky tenure at Ford.

So far, Polaroid seems to be up to the same old tricks: its pitch to kids is a cheap instant camera that changes colors when you touch it, and it has developed yet another instant camera that is simply a more compact version of its OneStep model. Looking more to the future, it hopes to capitalize on the growth of digital imaging with a new self-service kiosk in stores, where consumers can print photos from their digital cameras. Polaroid is also licensing its name for digital cameras and other consumer electronics products to make the corporate brand more visible.

"Our job is to extend our reputation beyond instant photography," says Cramer. "We also need to reach opinion leaders at technology and arts events to let them know we're not dead and we ain't giving up yet."

LAW SIXTEEN

NEVER UNDERESTIMATE THE PUBLIC'S CYNICISM

Adolph Coors Company seems the model of a gay-friendly company. It forbids discrimination against homosexuals, offers domestic-partner benefits to gay couples, and supports an array of gay organizations from the Human Rights Campaign political advocacy group to the Colorado Climax ice hockey team.

It values the gay community and its purchasing power so much that it has appointed special "ambassadors" to forge stronger ties. First, there was Mary Cheney, who is a lesbian and the daughter of Vice President Richard Cheney. More recently, Scott Coors has played corporate cheerleader. He's the openly gay son of William Coors, the company's former chairman, and great-grandson of founder Adolph Coors.

Why, then, do so many gays and lesbians refuse to drink Coors beer? Call it consumer cynicism. Bad reputations always die hard, and Coors's never ending struggle to win over the gay community demonstrates the difficulty of regaining trust once it's lost.

Coors may be truly sincere about its workplace equality and philanthropy, but many people still view the company's progay moves as hypocrisy. To them, the company's motivation is pure and simple: to sell more beer to one of the industry's key target markets.

Dig deeper, and you will see why the gay boycott has continued for more than a quarter century. The Coors family, through its donations and membership in conservative organizations, has been in league with groups the gay community considers its foes. Joseph Coors, a former president of the company, helped found the right-wing Heritage Foundation, and family-controlled foundations continue to fund it and other conservative groups. The company tries to distance itself from the foundations, but activists argue that much of the foundations' largesse is derived from the family's success in selling the Rocky Mountain brew.

"The foundations are just a smoke screen," argues Rob Petitpas, chairman of the National Lawyers Guild's Lesbian Gay Bisexual Transgender Committee. "Coors's efforts to have a presence in our community is only a way to increase their profits, which the family then uses to fund organizations that want to roll back gay rights."

The gay protest against Coors was part of a broader labor-union-led boycott that began in the late 1970s when Coors employees voted against union representation. But there also was perceived employment discrimination against gays. The company tried to resolve the discrimination concerns early on by adding an antibias provision covering sexual orientation in 1978. But the family's connection to homophobic organizations continued.

Years of mistrust create a very stubborn, pervasive cynicism. The boycott dates back so far that some young gays and lesbians aren't necessarily sure why they aren't supposed to order a Coors. But many still feel gay solidarity and boycott the beer.

How strong is the acrimony toward Coors today? There are no definitive measures, but gays appear to be split on the issue. *The Advocate,* a major gay magazine, conducted an online poll in fall 2001 and found that 48 percent of the people responding observe the Coors boycott, 44 percent do not, and 8 percent are undecided. One respondent likened gays drinking Coors to "Jews buying beer from Hitler," while another said, "The Coors family and corporation have gotten past this—why can't the gay community? Let it go!"

To be sure, Coors's reputation is slowly improving. It runs ads touting its positive employment polices in gay publications and has made headway in selling its brews in more gay and lesbian bars, even in New York and California, the bastions of the beer boycott. But many of the biggest, most popular gay bars still sell only Budweiser, Miller, and imported brands.

"It's a heavy burden Coors carries around," says Robert Witeck, a gay public relations executive who has done consulting work for Coors. "But people at the company need to accept the reality that they're never going to get everyone in the gay community to like them and drink their beer." He has advised the company to be more open about family members and the foundations, but he says, "Being transparent is the hardest thing for Coors."

This is no time to resist "transparency," one of the hottest post-Enron buzzwords. People are demanding complete transparency and reformed behavior before they'll even think of giving a company the benefit of the doubt.

Coors declined to comment on the continued boycott and backlash. But a few years ago, when she was still the company's gay and lesbian liaison, Mary Cheney discussed the problem and Coors's response. "The gay community tends to be more politically aware and more loyal to brands it considers supportive of gay issues than other niche markets," she said. "That creates a big challenge for Coors."

On the positive side, she said, Coors donates money to such organizations as Parents, Families and Friends of Lesbians and Gays and the Gay and Lesbian Alliance Against Defamation and sponsors local gay softball teams and bowling leagues. But Coors's funding of such groups has created enmity within the gay community itself. Activists accuse the groups of selling out and have gone so far as to create posters calling the antidefamation group "Coors's whore."

It just might take the death of an entire generation for Coors to completely cleanse the stain from its reputation. Even Cheney acknowledged, "Some people will be in favor of the boycott until the day they die."

A CYNICAL NEW CENTURY

How does a vilified company mend its frayed reputation? Not easily. As we advance into the new century, it's clear that we live in an increasingly cynical age. People just naturally expect to get spin, not sincerity, from companies, politicians, even their churches. Cynicism was percolating through the American populace long before most people had ever heard of Enron. But the scandals of the last two years have certainly made the cynics feel vindicated and given birth to many new pessimists.

Cynicism can be born from a pattern of behavior—or sometimes it simply stems from the basic nature of a business. Some industries, such as oil, liquor, chemicals, tobacco, and HMOs, have long been scorned and viewed with skepticism. Now add Enron, Tyco International, MCI, the accounting industry, and Wall Street to the list of corporate bad boys that will face cynicism and outright hostility for years to come. Accounting fraud, executive greed, and mismanagement have outraged the general public, robbed many people of their retirement investments, and cost thousands of employees their livelihood. There's a new show-me attitude, but you can't be sure people will believe you even if you tell the truth. A Gallup Poll in 2002 found that only car dealers are trusted less than HMO managers, CEOs of large companies, and stockbrokers. Surprisingly, accountants earned the trust of half the respondents even after Arthur Andersen's disgrace and accounting abuses.

But many companies aren't heeding such survey results. Instead, they seem to be only reinforcing the public's misanthropic views. Despite the bear market in 2002 and thousands of layoffs in the securities industry, many Wall Street CEOs had the gall to pocket paychecks topping $10 million.

The pharmaceutical industry also keeps fueling the cynicism and may soon join tobacco among the most hated businesses. By rights, drugmakers should boast one of the best reputations because they develop products that save people's lives. But the high cost of medicine and aggressive, even illegal marketing practices are turning the pharmaceutical industry into a pariah.

The reputation damage grows daily. Headlines shout, "Investigators Find Repeated Deception in Ads for Drugs" . . . "Bayer Stock Falls as Drug Lawsuits Frighten Investors" . . . "Bristol-Myers Squibb Settles Charges of Patent-Law Abuse" . . . "Schering-Plough Faces SEC Case on Private Chats." Senior citizen groups run ads proclaiming, "Glaxo is taking away your right to affordable prescription drugs," to protest GlaxoSmithKline's decision to cut off sales to Canadian pharmacies that sell cheap prescription drugs to Americans. When Roche announced that its new AIDS drug would be priced at a whopping $20,000 for a year's supply, far out of many people's reach, demonstrators descended on the company's Nutley, New Jersey, plant. They erected a graveyard at the plant's gates with dozens of tombstones bearing the epitaph DIED OF AIDS, KILLED BY ROCHE'S GREED.

The cynicism is touching even Johnson & Johnson, which had long avoided the pharmaceutical industry stigma. J&J is shielded somewhat

HOW TRUSTWORTHY ARE THEY?

The percentage of respondents surveyed by the Gallup Organization in 2002 who said that most people in the following groups can be trusted:

Teachers: 84%
People who run small businesses: 75%
Military officers: 73%
Police officers: 71%
Coaches of youth sports: 68%
Protestant ministers: 66%
Doctors: 66%
Accountants: 51%
Professional athletes: 48%
Catholic priests: 45%
Journalists: 38%
Government officials: 26%
Lawyers: 25%
Stockbrokers: 23%
CEOs of large companies: 23%
HMO managers: 20%
Car dealers: 15%

by its reputation for making gentle products for babies, but that may not be enough protection these days. William Weldon, J&J's chairman and CEO, recalls being startled when a man told him he believed that pharmaceutical companies aren't seriously seeking cures for disease because that would eliminate their drug sales. "The loss of confidence in the business community has really turned the tables," says Weldon. "Now it's almost like you're guilty until proven innocent."

When cynicism becomes deeply ingrained, it's extremely difficult for some companies and industries to budge their negative reputations. Liquor companies such as Seagram Company and Anheuser-Busch met with skepticism when they created ads warning people not to drink and drive. Hard as they try, it seems that some companies just can't redeem themselves.

That's certainly the case with Microsoft, which seems to have as many enemies as fans. To its supporters, Microsoft is an aggressive competitor that produces innovative products and services. Other people view the software company as a manipulative bully that tries to stifle competition and force consumers to use its products.

Microsoft has tried to polish its reputation by playing up its philanthropy, but skeptics see the large charitable donations by Microsoft and its chairman, Bill Gates, as mere attempts to offset negative publicity. In the midst of the government's antitrust case against Microsoft, the Bill & Melinda Gates Foundation was established, giving critics more, not less, ammunition. The foundation says its endowment totals $25 billion, but even that could never be enough for Gates's die-hard critics.

"When I hear about Microsoft's donations, I think here's this giant company just trying to look good after all the bad press it got," says Greg Roland of Mount Prospect, Illinois. "I also think they donate far less than they could, given Bill Gates's billions." Microsoft is familiar with such cynics but considers them ill informed. "People don't realize that Microsoft has a long history of giving going back to before the company went public and before our recent public relations challenges," says Bruce Brooks, Microsoft's director of community affairs. "We're responding to community needs, not to public-relations concerns."

AS GOOD AS IT GETS?

Despite the deep-seated cynicism Microsoft and other companies face, it's far from impossible to change attitudes. No matter how much people despise a company, it can usually soften the feelings over time. What's important to realize is that a company will never convert each and every cynic. But it can make progress if it's patient.

It's better to meet with critics than let cynicism fester. The critics will never be good friends, but the level of animosity can be reduced and misperceptions corrected. Communications must be improved in order to defuse the adversarial relationship. A company may succeed in swaying some cynics to be more open-minded and less fixated on its past sins.

It must be remembered, also, that things can always get worse. Without any response to soften the cynicism, it can deepen and spread. The worst thing to do is take a defeatist attitude and sit out the debate. That's what Mark Goodin, a consultant to the American Association of

Health Plans, concluded. "You should run toward the negatives, not away from them," he says. "Negatives are like diseases; if you don't manage them, then they'll only get worse."

Health maintenance organizations and other managed care companies face incredibly deep-seated resentment. Politicians in Washington and movie producers in Hollywood keep hatred of HMOs simmering with a steady stream of rhetoric and films about patients denied proper care. Employees of managed care companies cringed when they attended the movie *As Good as It Gets* a few years ago. Across the United States, theater audiences burst into applause and cheers after actress Helen Hunt's rant against an HMO that wouldn't cover the costs of her son's asthma treatment. Goodin calls that movie "a seminal moment" for the managed care industry. "I knew the reputation of HMOs was bad," he says, "but I really didn't know it was that bad."

It's also hard to fight those gut-wrenching patient stories in the media and on the Internet. The Web site of the Foundation for Taxpayer and Consumer Rights includes a litany of such tragedies: HMO fails bone cancer patient, HMO denies quadriplegic child vital therapy and chance to walk, HMO tells family to transport stroke victim themselves.

When the media began retelling such horror stories over and over, Goodin and the health plans association investigated them and found that some weren't completely factual. They proceeded to put together a case file called Anatomy of a Horror Story and distribute it to reporters. Soon the questionable stories stopped showing up in newspapers and on television.

Also aware that Hollywood continues to be fascinated with storylines about heartless HMOs, Mr. Goodin and the association retained the William Morris talent agency. They hoped to develop an early-warning system for television and movie projects in the works dealing with managed care. Ideally, the health insurance association could try to insert its perspective into the movie or TV show. And at the very least, it would be prepared to react to a negative portrayal of HMOs.

When the movie *John Q,* starring Denzel Washington, was released in 2002, the association didn't attack its depiction of a desperate, gun-wielding man who takes over a hospital when his health plan won't cover his son's heart transplant operation. Instead, it criticized lawmakers, not filmmakers, in an advertisement that declared, "*John Q.* It's not just a movie. It's a crisis for 40 million people who can't afford health care." The ad went on to blame the government for failing to help the uninsured and the underinsured like the fictional character John Q.

"Instead of criticizing the inaccuracies and unfairness, we embraced the movie and said we were glad Hollywood raised the issue," says Goodin. "As a result of taking an unexpected approach, we got a lot of media coverage, and, more important, we didn't come across as inhumane by trying to defend the indefensible."

A SEAT AT THE TABLE

HMOs are working together to reduce the cynicism, but in some cases, a company may have to break ranks with the rest of its industry and stand apart from its peers. Your industry colleagues will probably become disgruntled, but critics will perceive you as conciliatory and courageous. Even in a reviled or hated industry, you can elevate yourself above your competitors. BP and Royal Dutch/Shell, for example, have forged stronger images of environmental responsibility than most other oil companies.

Altria Group has also stepped away from the tobacco industry and become less combative. It no longer wants to be considered part of "Big Tobacco" and is willing to upset its industry "friends" who prefer a united front. Slow but steady progress has become the reputation management strategy for Philip Morris.

Perhaps no company has taken more abuse than Altria's tobacco business. People delight in skewering the tobacco company. Not long ago, comedian Jay Leno turned his cynical humor on a Philip Morris promotion before it had even arrived on many people's doorsteps. The newspaper insert was a guide to the company's Web site, showing the many subjects covered—from the serious health effects of smoking to kicking the habit.

In his opening monologue on NBC's *Tonight* show, Leno dutifully noted the actual contents on the cover of the insert. "The people who make cigarettes want to help us," he deadpanned. "Now, if you can't quit smoking, open it up . . ." Printed inside the mock insert were tips on choosing a funeral home, writing your epitaph, and deciding on a tombstone.

Many people also scoffed at the lavish Philip Morris ad campaign touting its good deeds. One ad told how Doris left an abusive marriage and, thanks to Philip Morris's support of Chicago's Community Kitchens program, learned professional food preparation and landed a job as a "salad specialist" for a community hospital. Another described how Philip Morris works with minority-owned businessmen like George Hill, whose company makes glue to seal product packaging.

But critics believe that the company should have spent its $250 million "corporate outreach" ad budget on more philanthropy rather than more publicity. Some also view it as a ploy to divert attention from the cigarette business. "It's understandable that we've gotten so cynical when a company like Philip Morris tries to weasel around and make us believe it's a good guy just because it donates water to flood victims or helps the hungry," says John Hyde, a retiree in Placerville, California.

Clearly, Altria faces an uphill battle. But at least the company believes it's headed in the right direction. Long a very defensive, secretive company, in the mid-1990s Altria decided to abandon its bunker mentality and seek "a seat at the table." "We recognized we had to drop this 'us versus them' mentality and fundamentally change the way we do business," says Steven Parrish, Altria's senior vice president for corporate affairs. One of the company's directors had made the observation at a board retreat that the company was in danger of "losing permission to exist from society."

Previously, the company had taken an arrogant, confrontational approach to many of its opponents and to the news media. But Philip Morris learned that its repeated "no comments" had been more powerful than it realized. "People assumed we were guilty of everything," says Parrish. "Truth be told, we have no one to blame but ourselves for that."

The company's outreach to politicians, regulatory officials, the health care industry, and antismoking groups hasn't been easy. Opponents naturally remain wary of Philip Morris's motives. Parrish has met with people privately in their hotel rooms because they feared that being seen with him in public would hurt their credibility. Gradually, he has persuaded his critics that he's not trying to exploit them, just open a dialogue. As a sign of progress, he proudly notes that he appeared on a panel about legal addiction with David Kessler, a former commissioner of the Food and Drug Administration and one of the tobacco industry's most dogged foes. Kessler has even made positive comments about Parrish since Parrish endorsed some form of government regulation of tobacco products. Philip Morris has also received credit for establishing

CORPORATE CREDIBILITY GAP

The public gave these twenty companies the lowest scores for "corporate sincerity" in Harris Interactive's 2002 study of corporate reputation. Many of the companies' reputations have been hurt by recent financial scandals. But the list also includes Philip Morris (now Altria Group), Time Warner, Sprint, Exxon Mobil, AT&T, Microsoft, and Nike, which have long been viewed cynically.

1. Enron
2. Global Crossing
3. WorldCom (now named MCI)
4. Andersen Worldwide
5. Adelphia Communications
6. Philip Morris (now named Altria Group)
7. Qwest Communications
8. Bridgestone/Firestone
9. Time Warner
10. Sprint
11. Exxon Mobil
12. AT&T
13. Chevron Texaco
14. Citigroup
15. SBC Communications
16. Merrill Lynch
17. Microsoft
18. Ford
19. Kmart
20. Nike

a stand-alone Youth Smoking Prevention Department with an annual budget of $100 million.

"We never ever want to fall out of step again," Parrish says. "We saw how bad it is when you lose your reputation and seat at the table. It's very difficult to have a voice in the discussion about taxes, free trade, and regulation without that seat."

It takes great fortitude to endure the barbs day after day. Parrish recalls that his wife sometimes said he came home looking "shell-shocked." The animosity had gotten so bad that some Philip Morris executives actually felt afraid sitting behind the glass window at focus group meetings and listening to people's venomous comments.

Altria still has far to go in its crusade for a respected reputation. The tobacco industry's $206 billion settlement with forty-six states in 1998 put some litigation to rest. But individual smokers' lawsuits are still coming to trial, and the U.S. Justice Department has proposed in a civil suit that tobacco companies should forfeit $289 billion that they have earned since 1971 from the 33 million people who became addicted to cigarettes as teenagers. Altria's PR staff should be gainfully employed for many years to come.

"We still have to keep proving we're sincere and not just trying to reduce the amount of punitive damages in lawsuits brought by cigarette smokers," Parrish says, "I know we're out of the bunker. But people are still shooting at us."

DON'T SHOOT YOURSELF

If you're on America's most-hated list, the last thing you can afford is embarrassing publicity. Hypocrisy, insincerity, and condescension—or even just the perception of them—will be enough to undermine any effort to repair your reputation. You have virtually no reservoir of goodwill to offset any screw-ups.

But companies of ill repute often end up playing into their critics' hands by making some mortifying gaffes. Nothing could make cynics happier than slipups that validate their negative attitudes.

Altria's Philip Morris business seems especially prone to shooting itself in the foot. Just consider the infamous study "Public Finance Balance of Smoking in the Czech Republic." The company hoped to prevent big excise tax increases with the economic analysis, which concluded that the Czech government saves money on health care, pensions, and housing for the elderly when smokers die prematurely. Because of those factors and cigarette-related taxes, the study said, the Czech Republic had realized a net gain of $147 million in 1999. News of the study sparked a publicity nightmare for Philip Morris from the pages of *The Wall Street Journal* to ABC's *Politically Incorrect* program. The company came across as cold-blooded and calculating.

Philip Morris tried to do damage control. Similar studies in other Eastern European countries were canceled. The company publicly apologized, noting that the report had been prepared without the knowledge of headquarters officials in New York. "We understand that this was not only a terrible mistake, but that it was wrong," Steven Parrish said at the time. "To say it's totally inappropriate is an understatement." The forceful apology certainly helped, but the company's reputation still suffered a major setback.

CYNICAL ABOUT THE CYNICS

Some companies take an arrogant attitude toward public cynicism. They are financially successful and don't recognize the long-term value of forging a more positive reputation. There's no better example of such thinking than Exxon Mobil Corporation, which can be remarkably uncommunicative. If Exxon Mobil causes another environmental disaster, it won't have stored up enough "reputation capital" to win much public support.

The company has become the target of environmentalists and consumers for everything from the war in Iraq to its notorious Alaskan oil spill to its opposition to the Kyoto Protocol to combat global warming. People especially haven't forgiven Exxon Mobil for the 1989 *Exxon Valdez* accident, which spilled some 11 million gallons of crude oil into the unspoiled waters of Prince William Sound, Alaska. It's almost as if the spill happened yesterday, not fifteen years ago.

"I think it's going to take another generation for Exxon Mobil to recover," says Jeane Vinson of Kona, Hawaii. "I can't get the image of dead birds out of my mind." The anger is deep-seated. Declaring that Exxon Mobil hasn't "done anything that showed me they're trying to change their ways and be more responsible," Kristen Patscott of Richmond, Vermont, says she won't let her boyfriend stop at an Exxon Mobil gas station "even for a pack of gum or to use the restroom."

Such comments frustrate Exxon Mobil officials, but the company usually doesn't respond to them. The company is, in essence, cynical about the cynics. Tom Cirigliano, an Exxon Mobil spokesman, says that the company fears that any advertising campaign publicizing its positive environmental actions would be written off as propaganda. "The road we've chosen to take," Cirigliano says, "is one of example rather than PR." The trouble is, most people don't see the examples.

Cirigliano does make a valid point, however. The company would have to convey a very consistent, credible message to make any headway with its critics. Exxon Mobil has developed an ad campaign about technological advances in oil and gas exploration, and it has pledged $100 million over ten years to a global energy and climate research project at Stanford University. But the company's actions were greeted with— yes—more cynicism. Environmentalists counter that Exxon Mobil expects to spend much more—$100 billion—over the next decade on exploration for and production of oil and gas, the major causes of global warming in the first place.

LAW SEVENTEEN

REMEMBER—BEING
DEFENSIVE IS OFFENSIVE

Jon Harmon, global communications manager at Ford Motor Company, wishes he could redo the Ford Explorer–Firestone tire recall debacle. He would gather executives of Ford and Bridgestone Corporation's Firestone business in a conference room and not let them out until they had reached agreement on how to resolve the crisis quickly and to the public's complete satisfaction. "We shouldn't have come out until we made a decision that put customers first," he says. "That way, there wouldn't have been any finger-pointing."

But he isn't kicking himself. Although he and officials at Ford and Bridgestone/Firestone certainly learned some reputation management lessons, he believes that business school professors and crisis consultants were too strident in their Monday-morning quarterbacking of the companies' missteps. "We had to handle things in real time with phones and beepers going off all the time," Harmon says. "Information developed over time, and the more data that came in, the more we understood the tire problem."

That said, Ford and Bridgestone/Firestone provide one of the most instructive examples of how being defensive offends the public and jeopardizes corporate reputation. Even worse than simply being defensive is trying to shift the blame. The Explorer accidents alone hurt the companies' image, but deflecting blame only exacerbated the damage. Publicly bashing each other made both companies big losers in the public's mind.

Few would have guessed that Henry Ford and Harvey Firestone had formed a century-long business partnership and close friendship. Their families were even united when their grandchildren William Clay Ford and Martha Parke Firestone wed. But romance and camaraderie were hardly in evidence when Ford and Bridgestone/Firestone were linked to serious accidents involving Ford's Explorer sport-utility vehicle and Firestone's tires that left people dead or seriously injured.

Ford and Bridgestone/Firestone turned their finger-pointing into a public spectacle. Many people were appalled to see two of America's oldest industrial companies behaving like children trying to blame the other guy. Resolving the crisis was complicated because two companies were involved. Jon Harmon says that Ford believed it was best to tell the public as much as possible and get the recall behind it, but Bridgestone/Firestone preferred being more reticent, partly because it hoped to deflect lawsuits.

The acrimony peaked in May 2001, about nine months after Bridgestone/Firestone had announced the first recall of 6.5 million tires. On May 21, Bridgestone/Firestone said it would end its nearly century-old business relationship with Ford, complaining that Ford refused to acknowledge safety concerns about its Explorers. "Business relationships, like personal ones, are built upon trust and mutual respect," John Lampe, chairman and CEO of Bridgestone/Firestone, said. "We have come to the conclusion that we can no longer supply tires to Ford since the basic foundation of our relationship has been seriously eroded."

Ford then announced plans to replace all Firestone Wilderness AT tires on its vehicles, a total of 10 million to 13 million at a cost of as much as $3 billion. The move made Ford look safety-conscious and shifted the focus back to the Firestone tires. "We are deeply disappointed that upon hearing and seeing (the most recent) analysis of Firestone Wilderness AT tires, Firestone decided not to work together for the safety of our shared customers, which is the only issue that matters," Jacques Nasser, then president and CEO of Ford, said.

Next it was Bridgestone/Firestone's turn to fire back: "No one cares more about the safety of the people who travel on our tires than we do," Lampe responded. "The real issue here is the safety of the Explorer." He then asked the National Highway Traffic Safety Administration to begin an investigation into the safety of some Explorer models.

Firestone continued to hold to its defensive position. It resisted a second recall of as many as 3.5 million more tires but eventually caved in to government pressure in October 2001, ending the seventeen-month federal investigation of its tires.

The public remains sour on both companies. Ford was the lowest-ranked auto company in the 2002 Harris Interactive reputation study, which rates sixty companies from best to worst. Bridgestone/Firestone had owned last place for two years in a row until Enron Corporation supplanted it in 2002. Bridgestone/Firestone then moved to fifty-fifth place (out of sixty), not exactly an enviable position.

Still, both companies believe they are on the road to recovery. Ford did move up nine places in the 2002 Harris survey to the forty-third spot, partly because there were so many scandal-tarred companies such as Enron, WorldCom (now named MCI), and Global Crossing at the bottom of the ranking.

Despite Bridgestone/Firestone's continued weak showing in reputation studies, the company says its Firestone brand sales are rebounding. Firestone's public relations managers are less willing than Ford's executives to concede that the recall crisis was handled poorly. "Perhaps we could have been more assertive in our communications," says Christine Karbowiak, vice president of public affairs at Bridgestone Americas Holdings. "But I think we responded quickly, especially given that we weren't sure what was causing the increased rate of tread separation claims."

Some people predicted the Firestone brand's death during the recall. Karbowiak dismisses those crepe hangers and contends that Firestone is still "an American icon." The brand will continue, she says, because of the company's loyal dealer network and the "Making It Right the Bridgestone Way" program to improve quality assurance procedures and the tire manufacturing process. Firestone may well survive, but its reputation still has miles to go to recover.

THE STRAIGHT STORY

Defensiveness is clearly offensive. Yet too often, companies arrogantly put their corporate pride and legal defenses first. You watch companies like Ford and Bridgestone/Firestone and wonder why they didn't take a more forthright, conciliatory approach from the start. Defensive tactics are almost always damaging. It's far better to be apologetic and willing to accept responsibility. Companies should take action that convinces the public that a problem is being fixed as swiftly as possible. How much more respect Ford and Bridgestone/Firestone would have earned had they cooperated and shared responsibility for the accidents early on.

But they're hardly alone in their defensiveness. Lawrence Rawl, who was chairman and CEO of Exxon Corporation in 1989, took nearly a week to make any public comment after the disastrous *Exxon Valdez* oil spill in Alaska. When he finally spoke, he complained that the company was getting "a bad rap."

Beech-Nut Nutrition Corporation, the baby food maker, saw its sales and reputation plummet after it was charged with selling flavored sugar water instead of real apple juice. The Nestlé subsidiary and its executives initially denied the charges in 1986. Only after a full year of damaging publicity did Beech-Nut plead guilty and agree to pay a $2 million fine. But it took three years for the former president of Beech-Nut to admit that he had knowingly misled the public. The reputation damage from the apple juice scandal was immeasurable. Nestlé wasted little time in selling the damaged brand to Ralston Purina Company. Today, Beech-Nut is owned by Milnot Holding Corporation, a small company that also sells canned milk and chili.

The public wants to see a company take full responsibility for its actions and to show contrition. Your golden rule should be to tell it straight. Rather than trying to minimize a problem or duck responsibility, it's much more sensible to say, "We screwed up, we're sorry, and here's how we're going to fix things and make amends." You may even end up creating goodwill and fortifying your reputation.

General Motors's Saturn subsidiary faced several problems with its cars in its early days of production that could have destroyed its nascent reputation. But it moved quickly to recall the affected cars and actually enhanced its image. When a coolant problem surfaced, the company decided in May 1991 not just to repair but to replace all 1,836 cars that had been shipped with bad antifreeze. Even a recall of some 350,000 cars two years later won customer compliments. The electrical system defect that had caused some car fires didn't disillusion consumers because they believed that Saturn had put their interests first and acted in a timely fashion. Some Saturn dealers not only made the repair, but they also provided free gasoline, car washes, and coffee to the waiting owners.

Often a company reacts defensively by turning silent, clearly in the hope that the problem will go away by itself. It won't. Details will likely leak out, as the news media become even more aggressive in trying to ferret out the truth. Rumors will circulate on the Internet, employees will start gossiping and worrying about what's actually happening at their company, and activist groups may stage protests at offices and factories.

Many companies are tempted to blame the media in times of trouble. But even if you feel the media have blown your problems out of proportion, attacking the messenger only looks as if you're trying to shirk responsibility.

Gerber Products Company once fell into that trap. Like its competitor Beech-Nut, Gerber faced a grave reputation problem in the 1980s that it didn't handle very well either. When consumers began complaining that they had found glass inside jars of Gerber baby food, the company took an extremely tough, defensive stance. It contended that a recall was pointless and that the media had fueled a panic. The company said it felt like the victim of "a lynch mob." That attitude cost the company fourteen market share points.

Robert Johnston, a Gerber executive, later acknowledged how the company's defensiveness had hurt its reputation. "Not pulling our baby food off the shelf gave the appearance," he said, "that we aren't a caring company."

Once you have the facts straight, you should speak to the news media. "No comment" makes people think the worst. The company must be hiding something, they figure. But more important, being open with the media will show that you're dealing responsibly with a problem and providing as much information as you can to the public.

Lucent Technologies, already beset by serious financial troubles and thousands of employee layoffs, announced in fall 2002 that it had yet more bad news. The telecommunications company said that J. Hendrik Schon, a rising star at its renowned Bell Labs research division, had fabricated and falsified research results related to new types of semiconductors and transistors. Schon denied any wrongdoing, but he was fired after a panel concluded that he falsified the data. Lucent clearly didn't need more negative press, but it also realized that defensiveness would only prolong the scandal over the physicist's work, which had appeared in such prestigious journals as *Science*.

Some scientists questioned whether Lucent's supervision of its researchers was too lax, but the company simply stuck to the facts of the case at hand. "Our strategy was to handle the scientist's dismissal swiftly and without being defensive," says Kathleen Fitzgerald, former senior vice president for public relations and advertising. Lucent knew "there wasn't a systemic problem." Media coverage of the fraudulent research died out within a few weeks.

THE POWER OF CONTRITION

Apologies are good for the corporate soul—and reputation. There's no better way to defuse a business problem or crisis. That doesn't mean there might not still be reputation damage, but, if handled properly, an apology should minimize the negative impact and may even burnish your image.

To be effective, the apology should be made reasonably fast. Of course, the tone must be sincere. And don't mince words. If an apology is too stilted and looks like the work of a lawyer intent on reducing legal damages, it could hurt your cause. Let the CEO or another high-ranking executive deliver the apology.

Make an honest act of corporate contrition, and the public just may forgive you. That's the belief of James Adamson, who took charge of the restaurant company that owned the Denny's chain when it was accused of discriminating against black customers. He maintains that the company should have apologized right away instead of taking a defensive stand against charges of widespread racism. "If management had told African Americans that they were sorry and employees would either be fired or receive diversity training, the company could have avoided a U.S. Justice Department investigation," Adamson says. "Sometimes you have to say you're sorry and risk litigation to stand tall and protect your bonds with your customers. But instead, it took a $54 million class action settlement and many years of hard work to see the tide turn with the African-American community."

Of course, lawyers and public relations advisers must be involved in any decision about whether to make an apology and how to word it. There may well be conflict between the people who understand the value of reputation and corporate lawyers, who generally take a more limited view. Lawyers often discourage apologies because they could prove to be damaging evidence if lawsuits are filed. But the cost of regaining public confidence can easily outweigh possible legal expenses.

"The plaintiffs bar makes it very hard to act in a human way," says Roger Fine, vice president and general counsel at Johnson & Johnson. "There's tremendous pressure to defend yourself rather than apologize."

Johnson & Johnson stopped short of making an apology after a woman died in 1997 during a routine surgical procedure at Beth Israel Hospital in New York. One of the company's medical devices had been used during the surgery, and one of its sales representatives had been present during the operation. J&J did issue a statement expressing its condolences to the thirty-year-old woman's family—but not until a year after her death. The company also settled a lawsuit filed by her husband but didn't disclose its terms. The state fined the hospital, stating that it had allowed the salesman to help doctors operate the medical instrument, but in the end, a state board determined that he had played no role in the woman's death.

Companies may be too wary of apologies. Lamar Reinsch, a management and communications professor at Georgetown University, argues that an apology generally doesn't constitute evidence of guilt and may go a long way toward mollifying people and minimizing legal costs. People may be more inclined to reach a reasonable settlement of personal injury claims if they believe the company is truly repentant. "With an effective apology," Reinsch says, "a defendant may be protected from having to pay punitive damages."

True apologies are quite rare. Companies seldom say they're sorry and accept blame. But a company can minimize the damage to its reputation by at least expressing its regret and sadness without actually admitting to any wrongdoing. Statements of sympathy play well with the public. "The public loves to see you show remorse and be contrite," says Fine. "Saying we made a mistake—how can that not engender trust?"

A company's actions must match its words, however, in order to make an apology or gesture of sympathy effective. Exxon, for example, never did fully apologize for the 1989 Alaskan oil spill. It did express its regret in an ad, stating that it was sorry that the accident had occurred. It also hastened to point out in its own defense that it had "moved swiftly and competently to minimize the effect the oil will have on the

CORPORATE MEA CULPAS

Here is a sampling of some corporate statements ranging from expressions of sympathy and regret to full apologies.

"Most importantly, I want to tell you how sorry I am that this accident took place. We at Exxon are especially sympathetic to the residents of Valdez and the people of the State of Alaska. We cannot, of course, undo what has been done. But I can assure that since March 24, the accident has been receiving our full attention and will continue to do so."—Print advertisement signed by Lawrence Rawl, then chairman of Exxon Corporation, in response to the *Exxon Valdez* oil spill in Alaska, April 1989.

"I want to offer an apology to our fellow employees who were rightly offended by these statements; to men and women of all races, creeds and religions in this country; and to people throughout America and elsewhere around the world. I am sorry for this incident. I pledge to you that we will do everything in our power to heal the painful wounds that the reckless behavior of those involved have inflicted on all of us."—Peter Bijur, then chairman and CEO of Texaco, in response to allegations that some employees had made derogatory racial and religious comments about fellow workers, November 6, 1996.

"The death of Lisa Smart following what should have been a routine surgical procedure last year at Beth Israel Hospital in New York is a tragedy beyond what anyone can imagine for her husband, her family and all those who knew and loved her. She was the victim of a procedure that went terribly wrong and everyone involved has a right to know what happened. We are deeply saddened over the loss the Smart family has suffered and we share in their grief."—Johnson & Johnson statement in response to Lisa Smart's death in an operating room where the company's equipment was used and one of its salesmen was present, November 17, 1998.

"This summer, thousands of people had their travel plans disrupted while flying United Airlines. If you were one of them, I want to apologize personally on behalf of United."—James Goodwin, then chairman and CEO of UAL Corporation, United Airlines' parent company, in a television commercial, August 2000.

"Because it is our policy to communicate to customers, we regret if customers felt that the information we provided was not complete enough to meet their needs. If there was confusion, we apologize."—McDonald's Corporation statement posted on its Web site in response to litigation and complaints from people who said the company hadn't disclosed that it used beef flavoring in its French fries, May 2001.

"The e-mails that have come to light are very distressing and disappointing to us. They fall far short of our professional standards, and some are inconsistent with our policies. We regret that, and we further regret that the perception of our research integrity has clearly been affected. We have failed to live up to the high standards that are our tradition, and I want to take this opportunity to publicly apologize to our clients, our shareholders and our employees."—David Komansky, then chairman and CEO of Merrill Lynch & Company, in response to internal e-mails that were part of New York State's investigation of Wall Street conflicts of interest, April 26, 2002.

environment, fish and other wildlife." But the statement seems shallow, especially given how vigorously the company has battled in later years to limit its financial responsibility in Alaska.

Believe it or not, the *Exxon Valdez* litigation lives on fifteen years later—and so does the anger. In 2002, the energy company succeeded in winning a reduction in punitive damages to $4 billion from $5 billion, but Exxon Mobil, as the company is known today, is seeking a further reduction.

The reputation damage won't go away so easily. Defensiveness doesn't let old wounds heal. In a recent public opinion survey, one respondent accused Exxon Mobil of spending "millions of dollars in court trying to diminish your financial responsibility for the Alaskan oil spill. Forget the public relations spinmeisters. Paying up would be the first step in convincing me that you actually care about the environment."

Apologies have become a major issue for companies touched by the accounting and Wall Street scandals of the past two years. At the Merrill Lynch 2002 annual meeting, David Komansky, then chairman and CEO, apologized for the content of some e-mails from the firm's research analysts that had been part of New York State Attorney General Eliot Spitzer's investigation into conflicts of interest at Wall Street firms. Spitzer had earlier released dozens of embarrassing internal e-mails in which some Merrill analysts had privately derided stocks that he said the firm had been recommending in hopes of reaping investment banking fees.

But Paul Critchlow, counselor to the chairman of Merrill Lynch, says the media read more into Komansky's words and misinterpreted it as an apology for wrongdoing. "If you apologize for wrongdoing, you can put your firm in jeopardy," says Critchlow. "So it's in the interest of your shareholders to be cautious about an apology." A few weeks after the annual meeting, Merrill reached a $100 million settlement with the state without admitting any wrongdoing or liability.

After its massive accounting fraud, WorldCom (now named MCI) tried to restore its reputation through ads that expressed "regret that the actions of a few have affected so many." But the public expects a much stronger mea culpa. Joel Carico, for one, wasn't impressed by the ads. "All upper management at WorldCom should sign an open letter to the nation containing apologies for the corrupt business practices of the past and the widespread financial problems caused by the company," says Mr. Carico, an architect in Orange County, California. "It has to be

"I'M REALLY SORRY . . . BUT THAT'S NOT AN APOLOGY!"

The contentious Firestone tire recalls show just how cautious companies are about saying they're sorry when litigation is involved. They also illustrate how much people's definition of an apology can vary. The *American Heritage Dictionary* defines an apology as "an acknowledgment expressing regret or asking pardon for a fault or offense."

Given that meaning, it seems that Ford Motor Company and Bridgestone/Firestone may have actually apologized. They indicated regret for the accidents involving the Ford Explorer and Firestone tires even though they didn't seek pardon.

But Ford officials stress that they never made an outright apology in the long-running Firestone–Ford Explorer drama. "I think you apologize if you did something on purpose or cut a corner," says Jon Harmon, Ford's global communications manager. "But that wasn't the case. We always put safety first."

Indeed, in January 2001, attorneys for Ford visited Donna Bailey, a Texas woman who had been paralyzed in an accident in her Ford Explorer, after a legal settlement had been reached with her. But Ford quickly puts its spin on the meeting. In a statement, the company said, "Ford was not ordered to apologize to Mrs. Bailey as part of the settlement terms. Ford representatives requested the opportunity to meet with Mrs. Bailey to offer condolences to her on a personal level out of respect."

One Bridgestone/Firestone official seemed to backtrack in a court deposition in October 2000. Masatoshi Ono, CEO at the time, said that his earlier apologetic testimony before Congress had been meant to express his sympathy to people who lost loved ones in accidents, not to admit fault. The month before, he had told a congressional panel, "I come before you to apologize to you, the American people, and especially to the families who have lost loved ones in these terrible rollover accidents. I also come to accept full and personal responsibility on behalf of Bridgestone/Firestone for the events that led to this hearing." Shortly after the deposition, John Lampe replaced Ono as CEO.

a heartfelt apology, or else it's just seen as a way to get out of a tough spot."

Apologies aren't enough for some people. They want to see a just punishment when companies are dishonest and don't own up to their sins. "A little exemplary punishment might bring more corporate honesty," says Warren Jones, a high school teacher in Bakersfield, California. He recommends that "the culprits be publicly hanged, drawn, and quartered."

Frank McLaughlin, a real estate investor in Mystic, Connecticut, is of a like mind. "Those scoundrels at Arthur Andersen should be hung by their testicles," he says. "They're the worst offenders because they're the people who were supposed to keep companies honest. They don't even seem sorry." While the sentiment is a bit extreme, the accounting firm is now out of business.

KNOW WHEN TO SURRENDER GRACEFULLY

A company must never underestimate the opposition, and it has to know when it's time to concede defeat. Those are lessons lost on many companies, which become emotional and obstinate during a crisis or controversy. If they are put on the defensive quickly and unexpectedly, they dig in their heels and have a hard time giving up the fight.

Walt Disney Company became defensive in 1993 and 1994 during a protracted conflict over its development plans for the Virginia countryside near Washington, D.C. Disney hoped to build a theme park based on American history near a Civil War battlefield and wound up in a most uncivil war of its own. It became known as "the third battle of Bull Run."

Disney was caught off guard by the power and determination of its opponents. Rather than reading the situation correctly and surrendering gracefully, Disney resisted and allowed its reputation to be sullied.

The saga began in 1993, when the company announced plans to build a Disney's America theme park about five miles from Manassas National Battlefield Park. The company envisioned steam trains, a Lewis and Clark river raft expedition, Civil War battle re-enactments, a roller-coaster ride through a factory town, and a family farm with a barn dance and cow-milking lessons.

Historians and journalists were aghast, certain that Disney would concoct a simplistic version of history. The plan conjured up images of Mickey Mouse in George Washington garb cutting down a cherry tree and Donald Duck in powdered wig quacking the Declaration of Independence. How, critics wondered, could Disney be allowed to put its sugarcoated spin on momentous issues and events such as slavery and the Great Depression?

Wealthy local landowners, prominent historians, prizewinning authors, and environmentalists banded together to fight Disney and proved quite adept at lobbying influential government officials and generating media coverage favorable to their side.

Some three thousand protesters marched to the Capitol in Washington, chanting "Hey, hey, ho, ho, Disney's got to go." At the premiere of Disney's movie *The Lion King,* CEO Michael Eisner encountered protesters shrieking "Lying king!" And a shareholder in McLean, Virginia, filed a resolution for Disney's next annual meeting, opposing the theme park site and questioning why management had chosen "this unfortunate location when the company has so little to gain and so much to lose, namely its well-established reputation and role as a good corporate citizen."

Emotions often run high and cause companies to become stubborn and defensive. In the case of Disney's America, Eisner and other Disney officials felt strongly about both the park's commercial potential and its ability to increase young people's understanding and appreciation of history.

But Eisner's defensiveness played right into the hands of his opponents. In a testy interview with editors and reporters at *The Washington Post,* whose coverage of the issue had upset him, he said, "If the people think we will back off, they are mistaken." He added that he was shocked by the opposition and had "expected to be taken around on people's shoulders" for the decision to develop the park. He saved his most bitter comments for historians battling his project: "I sat through many history classes where I read some of their stuff, and I didn't learn anything. It was pretty boring."

He came off as both arrogant and defensive in the June 1994 interview. Disney soldiered on but realized that its reputation was clearly suffering. More and more people believed the company was trying to desecrate a sacred battlefield and distort American history. Three months later, the company finally surrendered.

TAKE THE OFFENSIVE

The best way to avoid a defensive posture is to take the offensive. That isn't possible with unforeseen crises and problems that strike suddenly. But alert companies can smell trouble coming and take actions that will not only prevent a crisis but will also make them look sensitive and far-sighted.

Disney at least learned from its disastrous failure in Virginia. The company realized it might never have been put on the defensive had it consulted historians and politicians long before announcing Disney's America. For its next theme park—Animal Kingdom at Disney World in Orlando—Disney executives sought advice and support from zoological and conservation experts very early on.

PepsiCo is wisely taking the offensive on another more controversial front. At a time when fatty food is fast becoming the new tobacco, PepsiCo is creating an image as a company that cares about good nutrition. Burger chains, packaged food companies, and soft drink marketers all face growing criticism for their role in America's obesity epidemic.

Already, McDonald's has been sued for allegedly causing young people to become obese and develop diabetes, heart disease, and other health problems. The suit claimed that the plaintiffs hadn't been aware of how damaging a steady diet of Big Macs and other fattening fare could be. Federal Judge Robert Sweet dismissed the case twice, but that doesn't mean the public relations problem or the lawyers are going to go away. Even the judge, in his opinion, referred to the fast-food chain's high-fat Chicken McNuggets as "a McFrankenstein creation of various elements not utilized by the home cook."

PepsiCo, in contrast, seems well on its way to keeping its strong reputation and maybe even fortifying it. Sure, PepsiCo sells sugar-laden soft drinks and unhealthy snack foods, but it has also assembled a varied product portfolio that includes Quaker oatmeal and Tropicana juices. Rather than getting defensive about its "bad for you" foods, PepsiCo calls them its "fun, indulgence" snacks. On a more positive note, its Web site includes a section on its "health and wellness philosophy." PepsiCo sponsors such fitness activities as the Marathon Kids running and walking program in Texas. The company also has retained some high-profile helpers, including Kenneth Cooper, the fitness expert, and Dean Ornish, the low-fat guru. And it's cooking up new products in its R &

D labs that are more nutritious, if not exactly yummy—potato chips with flecks of broccoli, anyone?

But archrival Coca-Cola Company appears much more defensive in its approach to the nutrition and obesity issue. Its Web site tries to make a case for the relative harmlessness of sugar and blames obesity mainly on people's sedentary habits. Certainly, lack of physical activity is part of the problem, but trying to absolve the sweeteners in its products seems unnecessarily defensive. It would be far better to simply suggest moderation in consuming soft drinks and point out the virtues of its Minute Maid juices.

It seems as if Coke is trying to avoid any responsibility for America's chubby kids. "Sugar consumption has not been shown to cause obesity," the company states. "The amount of sugar and calories in soft drinks is about the same as in many fruit juices." But what about the nutritional differences? Rather than selling more Coke, such comments are likely to alienate many nutritionists and parents even further.

LAW EIGHTEEN

IF ALL ELSE FAILS,
CHANGE YOUR NAME

ValuJet seemed like the perfect name when the no-frills airline took to the skies in 1993. It promised bargain fares but was no fly-by-night operator of puny turboprops. The Atlanta-based carrier had grander ambitions with a small but growing fleet of jets and plans to expand well beyond the southeastern United States. The name ValuJet said it all.

As ValuJet added new routes, it established itself as a fun, friendly carrier with the public. And as its revenues and profits soared, it became a high-flying stock, the darling of Wall Street.

Then suddenly, on Mother's Day weekend 1996, its reputation crashed along with one of its DC-9 jets in the Florida Everglades. The tragedy claimed all 110 passengers and crew members and made people question the safety not only of ValuJet but also of other low-fare airlines. Were they skimping on maintenance and other safety measures in order to offer those cheap tickets? In an instant, the ValuJet name had become a huge liability. A new name, it seemed, might be necessary to repair the airline's reputation.

But airline executives believed that ValuJet could recover and still retain its name once the negative media coverage abated. An investigation ultimately concluded that the plane had crashed because oxygen generators had caused a fire in the cargo hold. Although a maintenance contractor was held to be mostly at fault, federal investigators also blamed Valu-Jet and the Federal Aviation Administration for the accident.

After its fleet was grounded for three months, ValuJet flew again in September 1996—but with many more empty seats than before the crash. Fliers were too skittish to board a plane emblazoned with the ValuJet name. Who could blame them?

The company's financial results worsened, and its stock price dropped even further. There were rumblings about whether ValuJet could survive. Even so, employees still felt an emotional connection to the corporate name. ValuJet executives were proud of the company they had founded and didn't want to walk away from the name they had christened it with. They looked for lessons by studying other crises after which the corporate and brand names had survived, including the Tylenol poisoning cases and the crash of a Midwest Express DC-9 jetliner in 1985.

ValuJet's marketing department tried everything, including direct-mail and e-mail promotions offering free tickets. But the airline couldn't even give its seats away. Finally, in September 1997, the ValuJet name became another casualty of the Everglades disaster.

The solution had come in the form of a merger in July 1997. ValuJet merged with AirTran Airways, moved its headquarters to Orlando, Fla., and adopted the AirTran name. The company and its advertising and public relations agency, Cramer-Krasselt in Chicago, orchestrated extensive media coverage of the change, owning up to the fact that Air-Tran was the former ValuJet. "If we had tried to fool people by acting like AirTran came out of nowhere, they would have assumed we were trying to hide more bad things," says Peter Krivkovich, president of Cramer-Krasselt. "The point was that we had nothing to hide with our new name."

A name change alone, however, can't turn a company around and restore its reputation. ValuJet realized that. Before changing names, it brought in a new management team, added a business-class section to its planes, began giving passengers assigned seats, and ordered new Boeing 717 planes. AirTran's ads reflected the overhaul, declaring that "When ValuJet became AirTran, we decided to change everything."

Today, AirTran is growing even as many of its competitors are caught in financial turbulence. The reborn airline expanded into five new markets in 2002, took delivery of its fiftieth new Boeing 717, and posted a net profit of $10.7 million on revenue of $733.4 million.

"We succeeded in changing perceptions with a new name and new management," says Tad Hutcheson, AirTran's marketing director, "even though people sometimes were boarding the very same ValuJet planes. We haven't wanted any connection with ValuJet for a while now, but I think the day will come when we'll be proud to talk about the ValuJet name and its role in the airline industry again." Perhaps, but AirTran may be better off leaving ValuJet for the history books.

IT'S ALL IN THE NAME

Sometime a name change is the only way to shed a negative reputation, as the happy ending to the ValuJet–AirTran saga demonstrates. Still, you shouldn't be fooled into thinking that a new name is always a panacea. At first blush, a new name seems like an easy fix, a way to obliterate a rotten reputation and start fresh. But don't be too hasty; a new name should always be your last resort.

A company sometimes changes name with too little planning and too many grand expectations and sometimes even ends up reverting back to its old name—but only after considerable confusion and expense. Indeed, don't underestimate the financial expense of a name change. It can cost many millions of dollars to make a new name stick.

Just consider the poor judgment of Borland International, a maker of software development tools. It had hoped in 1998 that a new name, along with new products and services, would help revive its floundering business and its reputation, which had suffered after an unsuccessful attempt to compete with software giant Microsoft. But the uninspiring name Inprise Corporation didn't do the trick. Company executives soon realized how much corporate brand equity they had given up. Research revealed that Borland still enjoyed high awareness and a reputation for superior technology with software developers. So in early 2001, Inprise disappeared and the Borland name was resurrected as Borland Software Corporation.

Borland learned an expensive lesson: the core of a company is its name. Changing a name isn't like creating a new advertising campaign. The corporate name is incredibly powerful, conjuring up a wealth of images drawn from personal experiences with the company's products and services, advertising campaigns through the years, news media coverage, and myriad other influences. While some of those images may well be negative, what about the high awareness of the old name and recollections of what the company was like in better days?

A company must weigh that legacy and goodwill against a name's negative connotations. Heritage and familiarity are a lot to lose. The question becomes whether the negative perceptions are so intense and deeply wedded to your name that they overwhelm the positive associations. Dow Chemical Company considered changing its century-old name in the late 1980s because of the chemical industry's reputation for creating pollution and toxic waste. But word of the potential change sparked an outpouring of support for Dow Chemical from chemistry professors, and in the end the company decided to retain the word "chemical." So think long and hard—and do research with your many different stakeholders—before embarking on an identity makeover.

Some very damaged names have survived and even thrived. Although it isn't a corporate name, Tylenol was considered doomed in 1982, when seven people died in Chicago after swallowing capsules that had been spiked with cyanide. Even marketing experts declared that they didn't believe Johnson & Johnson could ever sell another product under the Tylenol name. But the pessimists were clearly wrong.

The Thiokol name also has proven to be extremely resilient. Morton Thiokol suffered serious reputation damage because it made the solid-fuel rocket motors that were blamed for the horrific explosion of the *Challenger* space shuttle seventy-three seconds after liftoff on January 28, 1986. Morton Thiokol, previously known to most people only for its Morton salt shakers, quickly became synonymous with the *Challenger* tragedy, which claimed the lives of all seven crew members.

Morton Thiokol weathered the adverse publicity, but with its stock price and profits suffering, the company decided that a split was necessary. So in 1989, it was divided into Thiokol Corporation for aerospace operations and Morton International for salt and specialty chemicals.

"We were deeply saddened by the *Challenger* accident and our role and NASA's role in it, but we never, ever would have tried to hide by changing the name," says Gil Moore, who was a public relations official at Morton Thiokol at the time of the *Challenger* accident. "Thiokol had a strong corporate identity with customers in the rocket field. Why would you throw that name away?"

In 1998, Thiokol did change the corporate name to Cordant Technologies to reflect its product diversification but kept Thiokol for its rocket business. Since then, Thiokol has had two more owners—Alcoa and Alliant Techsystems—but lives on today as ATK Thiokol Propulsion.

Some companies get carried away and change their names far too often. They create confusion and often never resolve all of their deep-seated reputation problems. For example, it has been a challenge to keep track of the restaurant chain Denny's, which went through three different name changes between 1987 and 2002. First, it became part of TW Services, then Flagstar, followed by Advantica Restaurant Group. Finally, Denny's was restored as the corporate name in 2002.

The changes related partly to the widely publicized charges in the early 1990s that some Denny's employees had discriminated against African-American customers by refusing to serve them or making them prepay for their meals when they ordered. The discrimination complaints, which even involved some black Secret Service agents, took a heavy toll on Denny's reputation and resulted in a $54 million settlement of two class action suits.

After several years of hard work, Denny's did succeed in creating a strong culture of diversity that has been recognized by such organizations as the NAACP. Once it had significantly improved its reputation with minority groups and undergone a financial restructuring, the company made the switch in 1998 from Flagstar to Advantica (a combination of the words "advantage" and "America"). But Advantica was one of those meaningless words that have a hard time catching on. So in the end, with the racism charges an ugly but distant memory, Denny's Corporation seemed the best bet.

Still, however, the company has much reputation rebuilding ahead of it with both investors and customers. The number of people eating at Denny's declined in 2002, and its stock price in mid-2003—about 60 cents a share—wasn't enough to buy a sandwich at one of its restaurants. The company acknowledges that it is now suffering from a reputation for poor customer service and needs to upgrade both its service and its food quality.

Sometimes a company must make a name change simply to get people's attention. It may make major strategic decisions that it expects to improve its reputation but finds that people's perceptions are incredibly stubborn. Even some companies that have sold off businesses that hurt their reputations have failed to improve their image.

Case in point: American Brands. After selling its American Tobacco subsidiary and such cigarette brands as Lucky Strike and Pall Mall,

American Brands couldn't shake the connection with the U.S. cigarette industry no matter how hard it tried. American Brands' only remaining tobacco interest was a British cigarette company, but investors and the media continued to lump it with the beleaguered U.S. tobacco industry. Whenever bad news hit the industry, such as a legal victory by an ex-smoker, American Brands' stock price suffered along with Philip Morris's and R. J. Reynolds'.

"They were stuck," says James Gregory, CEO of CoreBrand, a consultant to American Brands. "Their stock was going nowhere." So Gregory finally persuaded the maker of Titleist golf balls, Moen faucets, and Jim Beam bourbon that it was time to consider a new name. But first it needed to get out of tobacco completely. In 1997, the British tobacco business was spun off into a separate company, and Fortune Brands became the new corporate parent of the many disparate household, sports, and liquor brands. The company actually borrowed the name from its distilled spirits subsidiary in Australia because it liked the positive meanings of the word "fortune."

Then the hard work began to create name recognition from scratch with a new advertising campaign. CoreBrand's research showed an expected decline in familiarity with the Fortune Brands name but an immediate boost in favorability ratings and in the stock price.

Today, Fortune Brands executives don't like to talk much about their company's former identity. "Frankly," says spokesman Clarkson Hine, "no one we hear from considers us to be in any of the businesses we exited long ago."

YOU CAN RUN, BUT YOU CAN'T HIDE

A new name can certainly signal a fresh start—a chance to distance yourself from a tainted reputation. But make no mistake, you will never entirely escape your past. And despite Clarkson Hine's assertion, that includes Fortune Brands.

It's especially true if you're still tied to controversial businesses and past crises. At least Fortune Brands made a clean break from tobacco. But Philip Morris is well aware that its new name won't fool anyone because it still derives the bulk of its revenues and profits from tobacco. When it announced plans to adopt the name Altria Group, antismoking activists simply howled in amazement. The critics warned Philip Morris that whatever its name, the company could expect as much or more scrutiny of its tobacco-marketing activities.

"Our name change is not a PR thing," declares Steven Parrish, Altria's senior vice president for corporate affairs. "If people think we're trying to trick them and hide from our tobacco business, the result would be worse than not changing the name."

Philip Morris concluded that its corporate name and reputation were so tied to tobacco that it would never make much progress in showing people that it is also a major food manufacturer through its majority-owned Kraft Foods unit. When people thought of Philip Morris, images of Marlboro cowboys and lung cancer popped into their minds, not Oreo cookies and Kraft macaroni and cheese. In fact, Philip Morris was not only the corporate name, but also one of its cigarette brand names. The company still sells Philip Morris cigarettes in foreign countries, but no longer in the United States.

Still, it isn't an easy decision to forsake a corporate name that dates back 150 years. An Englishman named—you guessed it—Philip Morris opened a simple shop on London's Bond Street in 1854, selling tobacco and ready-made cigarettes. After Mr. Morris died, the business was taken over by his wife and brother and went public. Eventually, it was acquired by American stockholders and incorporated in Virginia. The American public became especially familiar with the corporate and brand names in the 1930s and 1940s, during radio's golden age. The company's memorable ad campaign featured a hotel bellhop who hollered out the page "Call for Philip Morrrrrisssssss."

Many people—both consumers and marketing experts—have long suggested that Philip Morris should get out of the tobacco business or at least change its name. But the company didn't give up its name lightly. Philip Morris executives seriously discussed and even considered replacement names in the early 1990s but abandoned the plan. The idea was revived in the late 1990s, when the company asked the corporate identity firm Landor Associates to create a logo to replace its outmoded coat of arms. After looking at some proposed logos, Philip Morris executives began asking themselves, "Why not a new name, too?"

The company became even more convinced that a new name was the right prescription for its ailing reputation after seeing the results of a lavish $250 million image campaign. Heartwarming ads showed employees of Philip Morris's various businesses performing good deeds—from providing food to refugees in war-torn regions to helping women who

DON'T LIKE ALTRIA?
HOW ABOUT ENCORDUS?

When Philip Morris announced that Altria Group would be its new name, many people scratched their heads. "What's an Altria?" they asked.

Like many new corporate names, Altria doesn't have a precise meaning. It's one of those words that's supposed to have strong connotations. In this case, Altria was derived from the Latin word *altus* meaning "high." The rationale: Altria will aim high to reach its peak performance. Corporate executives also wanted a made-up name that was vague enough to allow them to diversify into new businesses down the road. That's an important point because companies certainly don't want to undergo frequent name changes.

Altria also makes some people think of altruism. But the company denies that it intended to make that connection, despite its extensive corporate philanthropy programs.

"People would say we were trying to manipulate them by looking altruistic," says Steven Parrish, senior vice president for corporate affairs.

Still don't like Altria? Well, when you consider the other finalists to replace the Philip Morris name, Altria looks much more appealing. The company first eliminated hundreds of names from a list of more than a thousand candidates, mostly because of conflicts with other trademarks or linguistic problems.

Finally, four names came in for serious consideration. In addition to Altria, they included Marcade, which calls to mind the company's many trademark brands; Consumarc, which refers to both consumers and trademarks; and Encordus, which was meant to suggest "bringing people together, listening and engaging with one another."

Altria won hands down. "It was a much broader word than the others, and it doesn't put more emphasis on one corporate attribute over another," says Janine Rosen, director of internal communications. "Altria stands for financial strength, diversity of employees, corporate responsibility, integrity, and compliance."

Did you read all those meanings into that little six-letter word? Philip Morris—oops, Altria Group—certainly hopes you will now.

are victims of domestic violence. The campaign tried to drive home the point that Philip Morris is both benevolent and much more than a tobacco company.

The company watched its reputation scores gradually rise as more commercials aired, but then the ratings hit a plateau after the campaign had been running a while. Research showed that some people are fundamentally opposed to tobacco and are not going to change their views of Philip Morris easily.

"We realized that if we kept the same name, there are many people who won't be open to our messages," says Parrish. "The question became whether we could ever break through and make them understand the company is more than tobacco without a name change." The company concluded that it couldn't. Finally on January 27, 2003, Philip Morris was renamed Altria Group in the hope that its stock price and image might finally improve. The Philip Morris name remains, however, on its two tobacco subsidiaries.

In ads introducing its new name, Altria goes on about how "its roots are firmly planted in success" and its "branches are blue-chip operating companies." In addition to the name, Landor Associates developed a multicolored mosaic as the new corporate logo. The design is meant to suggest Altria's diversity of products and employees and represents a definite improvement over the staid Philip Morris coat of arms.

But reputations change slowly because people's memories and perceptions tend to be quite durable. And when all is said and done, companies should realize that the media are still likely to refer to them as "the company formerly known as . . ." A *New York Times* headline, for example, referred to the "ex–Philip Morris" rather than "Altria." And Altria should expect similar treatment for years to come. Even more than five years after ValuJet's name change to AirTran, media stories still routinely point out that the airline used to be ValuJet and then go on to describe the fiery Everglades crash.

GETTING THE TIMING RIGHT

Talk about fortuitous timing. Accenture couldn't have planned it better had it known what fate had in store for its former parent company.

But back in 2000, the consulting arm of Andersen Worldwide wasn't exactly thrilled at the prospect of changing its name. After an acrimonious fight with the Arthur Andersen accounting side of the house, Andersen Consulting was granted the divorce it had requested. But as part of the breakup, an arbitrator ordered Andersen Consulting to come up with a new name in 147 days. Not only was Andersen Consulting giving up what was then a highly respected name, dating back to 1913, but it also faced the stress of making the change in near-record time. Little did the consulting firm realize that the Andersen name would be worse than worthless just two years later.

"At the time, I felt that this is really tough to have to sit here and shoot our baby after ten years in business as Andersen Consulting," recalls Jim Murphy, global managing director for marketing and communications. "But thank God we had to do it when we did. The perceptual separation from Arthur Andersen would have been much harder" after the Enron scandal. By the time Enron and Arthur Andersen collapsed under the weight of accounting fraud, Accenture had succeeded in establishing both a high awareness of its name and a positive reputation with both existing and potential clients.

Accenture, of course, is a one-in-a-million case. More often than not, companies don't enjoy such perfect timing in changing their names. One of the biggest risks is making the switch prematurely. A company should wait until a reputation problem has been resolved and the negative publicity has subsided. Otherwise, the stigma will attach to the new corporate name.

WorldCom changed its battered corporate name to MCI, its long-distance telephone service provider, much too early. It understandably wanted to make a fresh start. But the company's financial and legal troubles continued to reverberate long after the name change, sullying the MCI moniker as well. In fact, in almost no time at all, a WorldCom critic changed his attack Web site from www.boycottworldcom.com to www.boycottmci.com. The site calls the name change "a pathetic attempt by the company to distance itself from itself" and declares that "MCI can change its name, but not the facts."

American Home Products Corporation also moved too soon in changing its name to Wyeth in 2002, and now an ongoing litigation battle will harm Wyeth's reputation. American Home Products said it wanted to take part of the name of its Wyeth–Ayerst Laboratories pharmaceutical subsidiary as its corporate name to better reflect its health care focus. The change was certainly understandable. The American

Home Products name made the company sound like a maker of household cleaning products.

But the company still faces litigation over its once popular diet drug combination known as "fen-phen." American Home Products resolved some of the litigation in 1999 with a $3.75 billion settlement, but the lawsuits keep coming. The controversial drugs, which were recalled after being linked to heart valve disease and an often fatal lung condition, are sure to tarnish the otherwise pure Wyeth name.

Enron has wisely taken its time in adopting a new name. After its bankruptcy filing, Enron realized it was probably the most hated name in America. So it began to research possible names in the event that it survived in some form after selling off parts of the business. "We wanted to wait until we saw what, if anything emerged after the auction process," says Enron spokesman Mark Palmer. "We don't want to poison the well by changing the name too early. But it will definitely *not* be called Enron." By mid-2003, Enron had announced new names for two surviving parts of the company: CrossCountry Energy Corporation and Prisma Energy International.

On the other hand, some companies with long-lasting reputation damage may be overly cautious—or stubborn—and cling too long and too tightly to their names. The Firestone unit of Bridgestone Corporation is certainly a prime name-change candidate. It has been severely hurt by the serious automobile accidents, injuries, and deaths related to the failure of its tires. But so far, the company has kept the Firestone name alive rather than replacing it with Bridgestone. Only time will tell whether that was a wise strategy, but at this point, the Firestone name still conjures up images of suffering and death and remains far from ideal.

A merger is often the ideal time for scrapping a tainted name. A company is undergoing a major transformation, and a new name seems especially appropriate. After the merger with Mobil, Exxon probably would have been better off to drop its name and become simply Mobil. It was the perfect chance to distance itself from the catastrophic 1989 *Exxon Valdez* accident.

Instead of adopting just the Mobil name, it became Exxon Mobil Corporation and still suffers from people's animosity over the environmental damage caused by the *Exxon Valdez*. The company decided that Exxon was a powerful name even if some gasoline buyers still boycott it because of the spill.

Philip Morris would have been viewed with less skepticism had it changed its name when it acquired General Foods and Kraft Foods in the 1980s. On the other hand, a new name adopted back then would have been tarnished by the tumultuous events of the 1990s, such as accusations of marketing cigarettes to teenagers, the company's acknowledgment of the health hazards and addictiveness of cigarettes, and the tobacco industry's $200 billion–plus settlement with a group of state attorneys general. All of which just points up the complexity of when to make the switch.

THE NAME GAME IS NOT AN AMATEUR SPORT

Call in the experts if you're sure a new name is the answer to your reputation problem. You'll need identity consultants and advertising and PR agencies, plus attorneys with expertise in trademark law. Name changes often lead to legal tangles with companies that have claimed the same or a similar trademark. Companies are all too ready to sue over the slightest similarity in names. Finally, don't forget the linguists. They're essential to assess whether the new name conveys the intended meaning in other languages and cultures.

Occasionally, a new name is created within a company and not by the corporate identity specialists. That's what happened at Andersen Consulting, which sponsored a "brandstorming" competition. A senior manager in Norway coined Accenture, a blending of "accent" and "future," and won a week's vacation to Accenture's golf tournament in Australia. But Andersen also enlisted Landor Associates to develop other potential names and help ensure that its new name didn't face any trademark conflicts or linguistic complications in other countries. Of the more than 5,000 names suggested by Accenture's own consultants and Landor's staff, only a handful survived the legal and linguistic screening.

But even hiring a corporate identity specialist and conducting a thorough search of trademarks don't guarantee smooth sailing. Philip Morris and Landor worked closely together to prevent any legal challenges and ultimately felt confident that there were no companies in the tobacco and food industries with names similar to Altria. But they didn't bargain on two other companies making a fuss. First, Altria Healthcare Corporation surfaced, complaining that as a health care business, it didn't want to be associated with a tobacco company. Then came *Altira*

Group, a venture-capital firm in Denver whose name wasn't even identical. Nevertheless, Altira sued Philip Morris in federal court. Ultimately, both complaints were resolved. Altria Group declines to comment on any financial settlements, but acknowledges that the venture-capital firm's suit delayed its name change by several months.

Lawsuits and consultants are certainly costly, but one of the greatest expenses will come after the name is actually changed: communicating the new identity alone can run well over $100 million.

Partly because of the speed of its name change, Accenture spent $175 million advertising its new name. Its elaborate communications plan involved 178 offices and client sites in forty-seven countries and included everything from running Super Bowl commercials to painting the Accenture name on taxis in London and blimps in Australia.

Beyond advertising, companies must budget in the expense and labor to change everything from stationery to T-shirts. Accenture's effort included 7 million business cards, 440 internal servers, 75,000 computer desktops and applications, and 1.2 billion pieces of promotional material. Accenture was forced to destroy millions of items bearing the Andersen Consulting logo, but it did find thankful recipients at homeless shelters for $2 million worth of Andersen T-shirts and hats.

Altria catalogued more than one thousand items with the Philip Morris name that required changing, including the usual business cards and signs and some unexpected things such as gift wrapping paper and the grates around the trees outside its headquarters on New York's Park Avenue. "It was a major overhaul—we must be the most crest-happy company in the world," says Janine Rosen, director of internal communications, who worked on the renaming project for more than two years. Along the way, she unearthed fifty different versions of the corporate logo and the way "Philip Morris Companies, Inc.," was written. "We're just lucky," she adds, "that we don't have vehicles, airplanes, and uniforms to worry about changing like FedEx and UPS."

WHAT WERE THEY THINKING?

Remember Allegis Corporation? If so, you have a crackerjack memory. That was one of the shortest-lived corporate names of all time. Back in 1987, UAL, the parent of United Airlines and car rental and hotel companies, thought a new name would improve its reputation, especially on

Wall Street, and communicate more effectively its strategy of becoming a synergistic travel services behemoth.

But the name proved to be a major flop, as did the strategy. Allegis sounded more like a new disease than a new corporate dynamo. Just a year later, Allegis dumped the name, along with CEO Richard Ferris and its hotel and car rental businesses, and the UAL name got a new lease on life.

Here's another memory teaser: Venator. No, it's not the name of a new superhero. That bizarre name actually took the place of a veritable American icon—Woolworth Corporation—when the era of the five-and-dime came to an end in 1998. Derived from the Latin word for hunter, Venator Group was supposed to be a fitting name for a company that had evolved from dime stores into athletic apparel and equipment stores. But the Venator name, which some disgruntled shareholders actively opposed, never caught on and joined the graveyard of corporate names after only three years. With that costly mistake behind it, the company decided to play it simple and borrow one of its own brand names, from its Foot Locker sporting goods stores, for its corporate moniker.

A corporate name is the essence of the company. It isn't like naming your children, when personal preferences matter far more than what others think. With corporate names, it's critical that the name meet the approval of employees, investors, and the general public, not just the CEO and the board of directors.

The unfortunate reality is that it's slim pickings in the name game. That's why you'll rarely find a new corporate name in an English dictionary. Most of the appealing names that have inherent meaning and best describe a company already have been taken. Thus we end up with such made-up meaningless hybrids as Dynegy and Verizon.

For reputation enhancement, it certainly helps if the name is descriptive of the company or at least has a positive connotation. If nothing else, make it easy to pronounce. And avoid initial names, which aren't likely to improve your reputation—or even create a clear image of who you are. It's hard to gain the familiarity of an IBM or AT&T. Waste Management realized that soon after it changed its name in 1993 to WMX Technologies, which some people said sounded like a rock music radio station. The new name was at least partly an attempt to escape the waste disposal industry's stigma. But a recognizable name is better than a meaningless one. So in 1997, Waste Management was revived as the corporate name.

NAME THAT COMPANY

Test your corporate name recognition skills. Match the current names in the first column with their predecessors in the second list. Answers are at the bottom.

1. Navistar International	a.	Consolidated Foods
2. Unisys	b.	International Harvester
3. Nike	c.	NGC
4. Sara Lee	d.	Sandoz and Ciba-Geigy
5. Clarica	e.	Sperry and Burroughs
6. Target	f.	Blue Ribbon Sports
7. Diageo	g.	Bell Atlantic and GTE
8. Dynegy	h.	Dayton Hudson
9. Verizon	i.	Mutual Life of Canada
10. Novartis	j.	Guinness and GrandMet

ANSWERS: 1-b, 2-e, 3-f, 4-a, 5-i, 6-h, 7-j, 8-c, 9-g, 10-d

A bad name is the fastest road to oblivion, but misguided name changes aren't as rare as you might think. Companies frequently wind up with downright awful names that become fodder for comedians. In Britain, people were both bemused and aghast when the post office changed its name to Consignia in 2001 to reflect a more modern, service-oriented culture. Just sixteen months later, the name Royal Mail was restored.

The notorious Enron name was actually never meant to be, and the energy company narrowly escaped a name with a most unfortunate meaning. Enron was a last-ditch substitute for the original name that had been developed for the merged Houston Natural Gas Corporation and InterNorth. The plan was to call the new company Enteron Corporation, but just before it became final, the company learned that the dictionary definition of "enteron" is the human digestive tract. In retrospect, some disgusted former employees might think Enteron would have been a much more appropriate name for the disgraced energy trader.

The recent corporate scandals produced a wave of new names from accounting firms, as they made plans to spin off their management consulting arms to prevent any conflicts of interest. There was the transformation of KPMG Consulting to BearingPoint, which doesn't exactly trip off the tongue. Most jarring of all, however, was the choice of Monday by PwC Consulting. The company explained that Monday is a real word that's easy to remember and it represents "a fresh start, a positive attitude, a part of everyone's life." But Monday isn't exactly the most positive thing in everyone's life. After all, people often call the first day of the workweek "blue Monday."

In the end, Monday the company wasn't meant to be. IBM snapped up Monday, ditched the too-cute name, and absorbed the Monday business into IBM Business Consulting Services. Wise move! In this era of corporate distrust, who would have wanted people to associate a consulting firm with the golden oldie song—"Monday, Monday. Can't trust that day."

ACKNOWLEDGMENTS

Many people contributed to this book, particularly the corporate managers who generously shared with me their insights and experiences in the struggle to manage their reputations. Given the current level of distrust and even contempt for corporate executives, it isn't a comfortable time for companies to discuss their reputations. But I found most companies quite candid about their reputation shortcomings and challenges.

On the editorial side, Fred Hills at Simon & Schuster deserves a medal for his patience and dedication to this book. Fred is a superb editor, who offered sage advice throughout the project and helped me maintain my momentum.

I am very grateful to Doug Sease for his guidance during the early stages of the book. His suggestions about the book's focus and structure were especially valuable. My thanks also go to Steve Adler and Roe D'Angelo for their constant support and enthusiasm for the book.

My collaborative relationship with Harris Interactive's reputation practice and the Reputation Institute has proven to be extremely fruitful. In particular, I want to express my appreciation to Joy Marie Sever and Charles Fombrun, two of the leading lights in reputation research. Majken Schultz, Jim Gregory, and Leslie Gaines-Ross also provided some fascinating research insights.

As I traveled from company to company while reporting my book, many people helped line up key executives for me to interview and provided critical background materials. I would like to single out a few who were particularly diligent as I pestered them for more information or more time with their executives: Brian Doyle, Jeff Leebaw, Bill Margaritis, Laura Castellano, Karen Brosius, Clifton Webb, Paul Critchlow, and Lori Bruce.

My family, Marybeth and Matthew, deserve special thanks for keeping me inspired and motivated over the past two years. They were incredibly good-humored when I neglected them for my manuscript.

And finally I want to acknowledge my parents, who long ago taught me the value of integrity and an honorable reputation.

INDEX

ABOUT THE AUTHOR

Ronald J. Alsop, a news editor and senior writer at *The Wall Street Journal,* has many years of experience reporting on and supervising the coverage of corporate brands and reputations. He has served as the newspaper's marketing columnist and was editor of its Marketplace page. His previous books include *The Wall Street Journal on Marketing* and *The Wall Street Journal Guide to the Top Business Schools.* He also is a seasoned speaker at international conferences on corporate reputation and has worked closely with leading research firms that measure corporate reputation. He lives with his wife and son in Summit, New Jersey.